Acknowledgement
The publishers wish to thank Jones & Brother, who kindly provided
a Hi-Speed Cooker for recipe development, testing, and
preparation for photography. The advanced MF2100 combination
cooker proved invaluable in the compilation of this book.

Compiled and Edited by Judith Ferguson
Designed by Philip Clucas
Photography by Peter Barry
Produced by Ted Smart,
David Gibbon and Gerald Hughes

THE
MICROWAVE
COOKBOOK

JUDITH FERGUSON

CONTENTS

CONTENTS

6

INTRODUCTION

Microwave ovens, whatever the make or model, have certain things in common. The energy that makes fast cooking possible is comprised of electromagnetic waves converted from electricity. These waves are a type of high frequency radio wave and are of short length, hence the name microwave.

Inside the oven is a magnetron, which converts ordinary electricity into microwaves. A wave guide channels the microwaves into the oven cavity and a stirrer fan circulates them evenly. Microwaves are attracted to the particles of moisture that form part of any food. As the microwaves are absorbed, to a depth of about 1½-2 inches, they cause the water molecules in the food to vibrate about 2000 million times per second. This generates the heat that cooks the food. The heat reaches the center of the food by conduction, just as in ordinary cooking, but this is accomplished much faster than in conventional cooking because no heat is generated until the microwaves are absorbed by the food. All the energy is concentrated on cooking the food rather than being wasted on heating the baking dishes or the oven itself. Standing time is often necessary to allow the food to continue cooking after it has been removed from the oven.

Microwave ovens have safety features built into them and are rigorously tested by their manufacturers and by independent agencies. The majority of microwave ovens are lined with metal, through which microwaves cannot pass. The doors have special seals to prevent the escape of microwaves, and have cut-out devices to cut off microwave energy immediately the door is opened. There are no pans to upset and no open flames or hot elements, the interior of the oven staying cool enough to touch. Although microwave ovens don't heat baking dishes, the heat generated by the cooking food does, so it is a good idea to use oven gloves or potholders to remove dishes from the oven.

Microwave ovens are cleaner and more hygienic to cook with than conventional gas or electric ovens. Foods do not spatter as much, and spills do not burn, so cleaning up is faster. Faster cooking times and lower electricity consumption combine to make microwave ovens cheaper to run, especially for cooking one or two portions of food. They also take up less space and are certainly more portable than conventional ovens.

Combination ovens seem to be the answer to the problem of browning in a microwave oven. While the power settings go by different names in different oven models, there is generally a setting for microwave cooking alone, a convection setting with conventional electric heat and a setting which combines the two, giving almost the speed of microwave cooking with the browning ability of convection heat. However, the wattage is usually lower than in standard microwave ovens, so cooking times will be slightly longer. On combination settings, use recipes developed for microwave ovens, but follow the instuctions for your particular oven for times and settings.

Safe, clean and versatile, your microwave oven will do much to speed up the cooking process and widen the scope of cooking available to you within the busy schedule of a full life. Once you understand your oven and its potential, the fun of cooking begins.

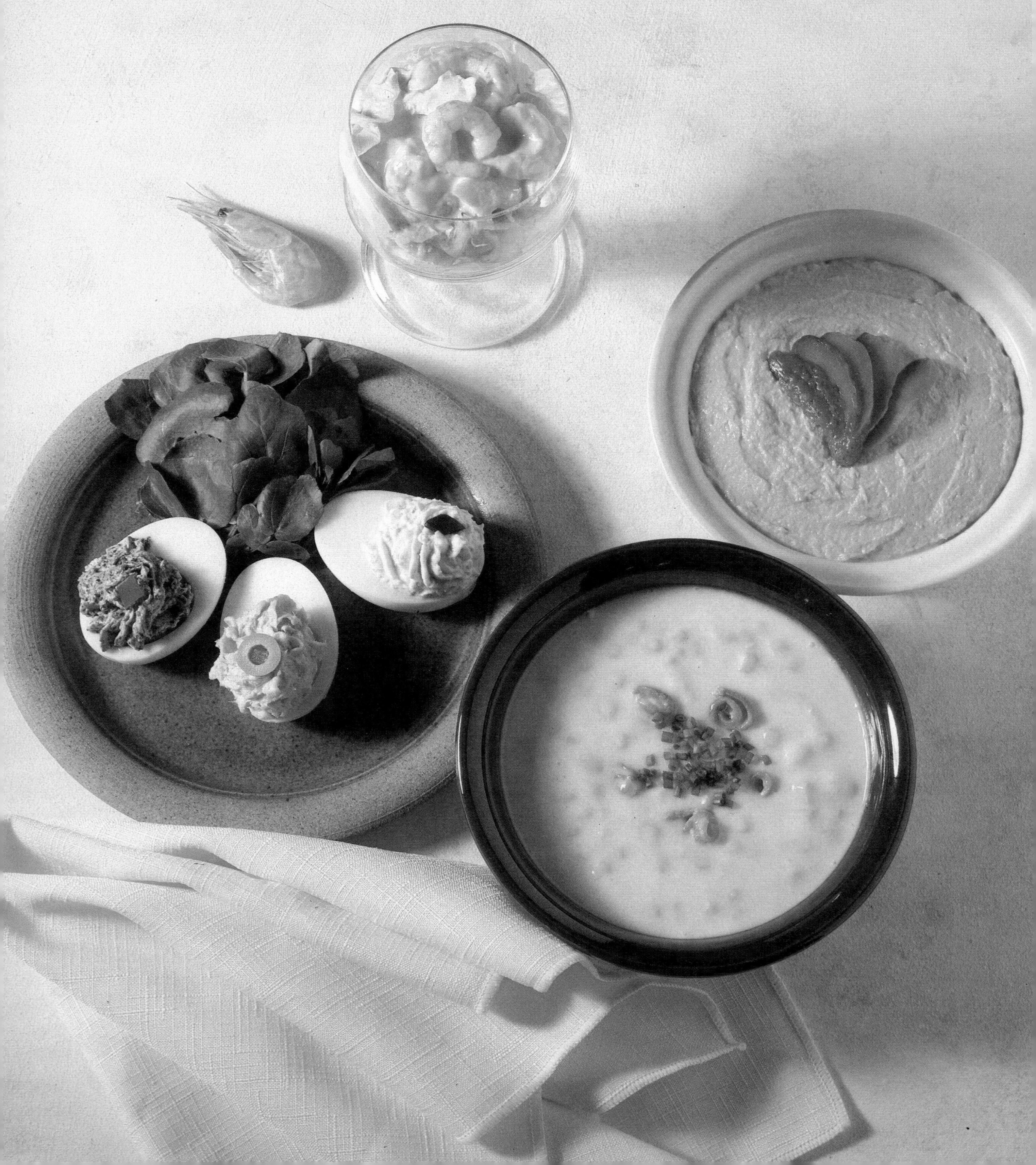

Microwave
SOUPS AND APPETIZERS

Microwave
SOUPS AND APPETIZERS

Soups and appetizers are the beginnings of a great meal. To make a memorable start, carefully consider how the soup or appetizer will co-ordinate with the rest of the meal. Consider color, texture and variety of ingredients.

Are soups and appetizers reserved only for the beginning of a meal? Absolutely not. They can be meals in themselves: soups, accompanied by salads and good bread, make wonderful cold weather lunches and dinners, while appetizers can double as light meals anytime. Microwave cooking makes light work of a light meal.

Soups can easily be made in small quantities in a microwave oven. Depending on your oven and your own preference, you may want to add 1½ times the flour quantity when adapting soup recipes for microwave cooking. Liquids do not evaporate as fast in microwave cooking as they do in conventional cooking and so more thickening may be required. The soup recipes in this book have been designed to include standing time, but always allow 1 to 2 minutes when adapting any soup recipe for your microwave oven.

Sauce recipes may need more flour, too, depending on your oven. These recipes were tested in a 700 watt maximum oven, but ovens with a lower maximum wattage may require a recipe with more flour.

Soufflés wait for no one, and those made in a microwave oven are no exception. I've included one, though, because they cook in a matter of minutes and are great fun to watch. Beware of over-cooking, though.

Pâtés are one food the microwave oven cooks excellently, and in a fraction of the time taken in a conventional oven. A custard cup of water in the oven with the pâté or terrine keeps the mixture moist.

A microwave oven can be a great boon when giving a dinner party. Preparations can be made ahead of time and then your first course can be reheated in a matter of minutes while you relax with your guests. Better still, soups and starters can be cooked and reheated in their serving dishes, providing they are safe for the microwave oven. Think of the advantage that will give when the time comes to washing the dishes!

Microwave
SOUPS AND APPETIZERS

CREAM AND PURÉE SOUPS

Crab Bisque

PREPARATION TIME: 15 minutes

MICROWAVE COOKING TIME: 17 minutes

SERVES: 4 people

SOUP
1lb crabmeat, fresh or frozen
3 tbsps butter or margarine
3 tbsps flour
1 shallot finely chopped
2 cups milk
½ cup cream
1 cup fish or chicken stock
1 bay leaf
Salt
Pepper
Tabasco
2 tbsps dry sherry

CROÛTONS
2 tbsps butter or margarine
2 slices bread, crusts removed
Salt
Pepper
Paprika

Put butter and shallot into a casserole. Cover and cook for 3 minutes on HIGH, stirring occasionally. Stir in the flour and cook for 2 minutes on HIGH. Stir in the milk, stock, seasonings, bay leaf and a few drops of tabasco and cover and cook on HIGH for 5 minutes, stirring frequently. Blend in the crabmeat and sherry. Cook on MEDIUM for 3-4 minutes. To prepare croûtons, place butter in a small bowl and cook on LOW for 15-20 seconds or until softened. Cut each slice of bread into 12-16 squares, depending on the size and thickness of the slices. Toss the cubes of bread in the melted butter with salt and pepper. Spread the bread out on a flat plate. Sprinkle the bread with paprika and cook on HIGH for 1½-2 minutes or until the croûtons are firm but not crisp. Stir and turn the croûtons several times during

This page: **Crab Bisque (top) and Cream of Chicken Soup (bottom).** Facing page: **Cream of Cucumber Soup (top) and Leek and Potato Soup (bottom).**

cooking. Let them stand for 5 minutes before serving. Re-heat the soup on HIGH for 1 minute. Stir in the cream just before serving, top with the croûtons and dust with more paprika.

Leek and Potato Soup

PREPARATION TIME: 10 minutes

MICROWAVE COOKING TIME: 20 minutes

SERVES: 4 people

3 leeks, washed and sliced thinly
3½ cups potatoes, diced
3 tbsps butter or margarine
2 cups milk
1½ cups chicken or vegetable stock
1 bay leaf
¼ tsp thyme
Salt
Pepper

GARNISH
1 bunch chives, chopped
½ cup sour cream

Put leeks, potatoes and butter into a large bowl. Cover with plastic wrap and pierce several times. Cook on HIGH for 10 minutes. Add milk, stock, thyme, bay leaf and seasoning, and cook for 7 minutes on HIGH. Leave standing, covered, for 1 minute. Uncover and allow to cool slightly. Remove bay leaf, pour soup into a food processor, and purée until smooth. Check seasoning and heat through for 3 minutes on HIGH. Serve with a spoonful of sour cream and chopped chives for each individual portion.

Cream of Chicken Soup

PREPARATION TIME: 15 minutes

MICROWAVE COOKING TIME: 31 minutes

SERVES: 4 people

1lb chicken breasts
1½ cups water
2 cups milk
1 chicken bouillon cube
2 tbsps butter
2 tbsps flour
¼ cup heavy cream
1 bay leaf
1 sprig thyme
¼ tsp sage, fresh or dried
Salt
Pepper

GARNISH
1 bunch chives, chopped

Put the chicken into a large bowl with the water. Cover with plastic wrap, pierce several times, and cook for 15 minutes on HIGH. Remove chicken from bowl and leave to cool. Strain the liquid from the chicken and set it aside. Put butter and flour into the bowl and cook for 1 minute on HIGH. Gradually stir in the liquid from the chicken and the milk. Add bay leaf, thyme and seasoning, and cook for 4 minutes on HIGH, stirring occasionally. Remove skin and bone from chicken, and cut into small pieces. Crumble the bouillon cube and add to the bowl along with the chicken and sage. Cook, uncovered, for 10 minutes on HIGH. Add cream and cook for 1 minute on HIGH. Serve garnished with chopped chives.

Lentil Soup with Smoked Sausage

PREPARATION TIME: 10 minutes

MICROWAVE COOKING TIME: 60-70 minutes

SERVES: 4 people

½lb smoked sausage
1½ cups brown lentils, washed
1 medium onion, chopped
1 bay leaf
¼ tsp thyme
1 tbsp Worcester sauce
Powdered cloves
4 cups chicken or vegetable stock

GARNISH
⅓ cup Parmesan cheese, grated

Put onion into a large bowl. Cover with plastic wrap and pierce in several places. Cook for 8 minutes on HIGH, or until onion is softened. Add lentils, herbs, Worcester sauce, pinch of powdered cloves and the stock. Re-cover bowl and cook on HIGH for about 20 minutes, stirring well. Reduce setting to MEDIUM and cook for about 20 minutes, stirring well. Remove skin from smoked sausage if desired. Add sausage to the bowl, and continue to cook for another 20-30 minutes, or until lentils are soft. Remove the bay leaf and the sausage. Purée the soup if desired. Slice the sausage into thin rounds and add to the soup. Stir soup well and adjust seasoning. Serve garnished with Parmesan cheese.

Creamy Spinach Soup

PREPARATION TIME: 15 minutes

MICROWAVE COOKING TIME: 16 minutes

SERVES: 4 people

2lbs fresh spinach, washed and stems removed
2 tbsps butter or margarine
2 tbsps flour
1 shallot, finely chopped
1½ cups milk
1½ cups chicken or vegetable stock
½ cup cream
¼ tsp marjoram
Squeeze of lemon juice
Grated nutmeg
Salt
Pepper

GARNISH
1 hard-boiled egg, chopped

Put washed spinach into a roasting bag and tie loosely. Stand the bag upright in the oven and cook for 2 minutes on HIGH, or until spinach has wilted. (It can also be cooked in a bowl covered with pierced plastic

Facing page: Creamy Spinach Soup (top) and Lentil Soup with Smoked Sausage (bottom).

wrap.) Put shallot and butter into a large bowl, cover and cook for 5 minutes on HIGH. Add flour, and cook for 2 minutes on HIGH. Stir in the milk and stock, and add marjoram, bay leaf and grated nutmeg. Cook for 2 minutes on HIGH, stirring occasionally. Add spinach, salt, pepper and lemon juice, and cook for 3 minutes on HIGH. Pour soup into a food processor and purée until smooth. Add cream, and adjust seasoning. Heat through for 2 minutes on HIGH. Serve garnished with egg.

Bouillabaisse

PREPARATION TIME: 15 minutes

MICROWAVE COOKING TIME:
10 minutes

SERVES: 4 people

1lb assorted fish (eg monkfish, red snapper,
    cod, white fish, rock salmon)
½lb assorted cooked shellfish (shrimp,
    lobster, crab)
2 leeks, cleaned and thinly sliced
1 small bulb Florentine fennel, sliced
2 tbsps olive oil
4 tomatoes, skinned, seeded and roughly
    chopped
1 tbsp tomato paste
3 cups water
⅔ cup white wine
1 clove garlic, crushed
1 strip orange rind
½ tsp saffron
1 bay leaf
1 tsp lemon juice
1 tbsp chopped parsley
Salt
Pepper

GARNISH
4 slices French bread, toasted
¼ cup prepared mayonnaise, mixed with
    1 clove garlic, crushed, and a pinch of
    Cayenne pepper

Cut fish into 2″ pieces. Remove shells from shellfish and cut crab and lobster into small pieces. Put leeks, fennel, garlic and olive oil into a large casserole. Cover and cook for 3 minutes on HIGH. Add orange

rind, saffron, bay leaf, lemon juice, water and wine. Stir in the tomato paste and seasoning, and mix well. Add fish and tomatoes and cook for 5 minutes, covered, on HIGH. Add shellfish and parsley, and cook for 2 minutes on HIGH. Mix the mayonnaise, garlic and Cayenne pepper and spread on the pieces of toasted French bread. Place bread in the bottom of the serving dish and spoon over the soup.

Cream of Celery Soup

PREPARATION TIME: 10 minutes

MICROWAVE COOKING TIME:
32 minutes

SERVES: 4 people

4 cups chopped celery, leaves reserved
1 shallot, finely chopped
2 tbsps butter
2 tbsps flour
1 cup chicken or vegetable stock
1½ cups milk
½ cup heavy cream
1 tbsp celery seeds (optional)
1 bay leaf
1 sprig thyme
Salt
Pepper

Put butter into a large casserole and heat for 1 minute on HIGH. Add celery and shallot, then cover and

**This page: Bouillabaisse.
Facing page: Cheddar Cheese Soup
(top) and Cream of Celery Soup
(bottom).**

cook for 10 minutes on HIGH, stirring frequently, or until celery and shallot are soft. Stir in the flour and cook for 1 minute on HIGH. Add stock, milk, bay leaf, thyme and seasoning. Cover and cook for 18 minutes on HIGH, stirring frequently. Allow the soup to cool slightly. Remove bay leaf and thyme, and pour soup into a food processor. Purée until smooth, and return the soup to the bowl. Add celery seeds and re-heat for 2 minutes on HIGH. Just before serving, stir in the cream, and garnish with reserved celery leaves.

Cheddar Cheese Soup

PREPARATION TIME: 10 minutes

MICROWAVE COOKING TIME: 22 minutes

SERVES: 4 people

2 cups mature Cheddar cheese and Colby cheese, grated and mixed
1 carrot, peeled and diced
2 sticks celery, diced
3 tbsps butter
¼ cup flour
2 cups milk
1½ cups chicken or vegetable stock
1 bay leaf
¼ tsp thyme

GARNISH
Chopped parsley

Put butter, celery and carrot into a bowl. Cover with plastic wrap and pierce several times. Cook for 5 minutes on HIGH. Stir in the flour, and add the stock gradually, mixing well. Add thyme and bay leaf, and cook for 10 minutes on HIGH, uncovered. Add milk and cook for 5 minutes on HIGH. Put cheese into a bowl and stir in ½ cup of the liquid from the soup. Return cheese mixture to soup and cook, uncovered, for 2 minutes on HIGH. Serve with a garnish of chopped parsley.

Cream of Cucumber Soup

PREPARATION TIME: 10 minutes

MICROWAVE COOKING TIME: 22 minutes

SERVES: 4 people

1 large cucumber
1 shallot, finely chopped
2 tbsps butter
2 tbsps flour
1 cup chicken or vegetable stock
2 cups milk
½ cup light cream
1 tbsp chopped parsley
1 small clove garlic, crushed
1 bunch dill, finely chopped
Grated nutmeg
Salt
Pepper

Put butter, shallot and garlic into a large bowl. Cover with plastic wrap and pierce several times. Cook for 3 minutes on HIGH. Add flour and blend thoroughly. Wash cucumber, reserve 4 slices for garnish, and grate the rest. Add it to the bowl and cook for 5 minutes on HIGH, until cucumber is slightly softened. Stir in the stock, parsley, nutmeg, chopped dill and seasoning. Re-cover bowl and cook for 7 minutes on HIGH. Stir in the milk and cream and pour into a food processor. Purée until smooth and return to the bowl. Heat through for 3 minutes on HIGH and serve garnished with the cucumber slices. Serve hot or cold.

Clam Chowder

PREPARATION TIME: 15 minutes

MICROWAVE COOKING TIME: 16 minutes

SERVES: 4 people

1 quart clams
1 cup water, mixed with 1 tsp lemon juice
1 shallot, roughly chopped
4 strips green streaky bacon (rindless and boneless)
2 cups diced potatoes
1 onion, finely sliced
3¼ cups milk
2 tbsps butter
2 tbsps flour
Light cream as necessary
1 bay leaf
¼ tsp thyme
2 tbsps chopped parsley
Salt and pepper

GARNISH
Paprika

Scrub clams well and discard any that are open or broken. Put into a large bowl with the water, shallot and bay leaf. Cover with pierced plastic wrap and cook for 2 minutes on HIGH. Drain through a fine strainer and reserve. Remove clams from shells and set aside. Put butter, sliced onion and diced bacon into the rinsed-out bowl, cover, and cook on HIGH for 3 minutes. Stir in flour and cook a further 2 minutes on HIGH, stirring frequently. Add potatoes, milk, reserved clam liquid, thyme and seasoning. Cook for 10 minutes on HIGH, stirring occasionally. Add parsley and clams and, if soup is very thick, some cream to thin it down. Cook for 1 minute on HIGH. Serve sprinkled lightly with paprika.

Vichyssoise

PREPARATION TIME: 10-12 minutes

MICROWAVE COOKING TIME: 25 minutes

SERVES: 4 people

3 tbsps butter or margarine
3 leeks
2-3 medium potatoes, peeled and sliced
3 cups chicken or vegetable stock
⅓ cup sour cream
½ cup milk
Salt and pepper

Facing page: Clam Chowder (top) and Vichyssoise (bottom).

Salt
Pepper

GARNISH
Parsley leaves

Put leeks, potatoes, carrots and butter into a large bowl. Cover with plastic wrap, and pierce several times. Cook for 10 minutes on HIGH. Add milk, stock, bay leaf, sprig of rosemary and seasoning. Re-cover and cook for 7 minutes on HIGH. Leave standing, covered, for 1 minute. Put parsley leaves and 1 tbsp water into a small dish. Cover with plastic wrap and pierce several times. Cook on HIGH for 1 minute. Uncover the soup and allow it to cool slightly. Remove bay leaf and rosemary, pour soup into a food processor, and purée until smooth. Check seasoning and heat through for 3 minutes on HIGH. Serve with a garnish of parsley leaves.

Pumpkin Soup

| **PREPARATION TIME:** 20 minutes |
| **MICROWAVE COOKING TIME:** 25 minutes |
| **SERVES:** 4-6 people |

1 whole pumpkin, weighing about 2lbs
2 medium potatoes, peeled and sliced
2 small onions, finely chopped
2 tbsps butter
3 cups chicken stock
1 cup milk
½ cup heavy cream
½ tsp tarragon
½ tsp chopped parsley
Nutmeg
Salt
Pepper

GARNISH
1 small bunch chives

Trim the white part of the leeks, slice thinly and wash well. Shred the green part finely, wash well and set aside. Put butter into a large bowl and cook, uncovered, for about 1½ minutes on HIGH. Add potatoes and white part of leeks to the butter. Cover with plastic wrap and pierce several times. Cook for 5 minutes on HIGH, stirring frequently. Add half the stock, re-cover and cook on HIGH for about 14 minutes or until the vegetables are very soft. Cool slightly, pour into a food processor, and purée until smooth. Add remaining stock and milk, and adjust the seasoning. Put reserved green part of the leeks into a small bowl with 2-3 tbsps of water. Cover the bowl with plastic wrap and pierce several times. Cook for about 2 minutes on HIGH. Re-heat soup on HIGH for 3 minutes.

Add more milk if the soup is too thick. To serve, top with the soured cream and the thinly shredded green part of leeks. Serve hot or cold.

French Country Soup

| **PREPARATION TIME:** 10 minutes |
| **MICROWAVE COOKING TIME:** 21 minutes |
| **SERVES:** 4 people |

3 leeks, washed and sliced thinly
1 cup chopped carrots
2 cups diced potatoes
2 cups milk
2 cups chicken or vegetable stock
3 tbsps butter or margarine
1 bay leaf
1 sprig fresh rosemary

This page: Pumpkin Soup.
Facing page: French Country Soup.

Cut top off pumpkin and scoop out pulp and discard seeds. Push as much of the pulp as possible through a strainer. Using a small, sharp knife or tablespoon, remove pumpkin flesh from inside shell, leaving a ½″ lining of flesh. Put flesh, pulp, potatoes and onions into a large bowl with the butter. Cover with plastic wrap and pierce several times. Cook on HIGH for 10 minutes. Add stock, milk, thyme, parsley, nutmeg, and salt and pepper. Re-cover the bowl and cook on HIGH for 10 minutes. Pour the soup into a food processor and purée until smooth. Add heavy cream and mix in well. Wash pumpkin shell and top, and dry well. Return soup to the bowl and re-heat for 5 minutes on HIGH. Pour soup into cleaned pumpkin shell to serve, and garnish with chopped chives.

Watercress and Potato Soup

PREPARATION TIME: 10 minutes

MICROWAVE COOKING TIME: 22 minutes

SERVES: 4 people

1 bunch (about 2 cups) watercress
3 cups diced potatoes
1½ cups chicken or vegetable stock
1½ cups light cream, or milk
1 shallot, finely chopped
3 tbsps butter or margarine
Nutmeg
Lemon juice
Salt and pepper

Put the butter, shallot and potatoes into a large bowl. Cover with plastic wrap and pierce several times. Cook for about 2 minutes on HIGH. Add stock, salt and pepper, and pinch of nutmeg. Re-cover the bowl and cook on HIGH for about 10 minutes or until the vegetables are soft. Chop the watercress leaves, reserving 4 sprigs for garnish. Add the chopped leaves to the other ingredients in the bowl, re-cover and cook for another 2 minutes on HIGH. Put into a food processor and purée until smooth.

Return to the bowl. Stir in the cream and cook for 3-4 minutes on LOW until heated through. Do not allow the soup to boil. Stir in the lemon juice to taste, and adjust the seasoning. Serve the soup garnished with sprigs of watercress. Serve hot or cold.

Bean and Bacon Soup

PREPARATION TIME: 10 minutes

MICROWAVE COOKING TIME: 1 hour 35 minutes and 10 minutes standing time

SERVES: 4 people

½lb navy beans, picked over and washed
½lb smoked bacon
1 large onion, finely chopped
1 stalk celery, finely chopped
1 bay leaf
¼ tsp thyme
Pinch of sage
½ clove garlic, crushed
1 tbsp chopped parsley
Salt
Pepper

This page: Watercress and Potato Soup.
Facing page: Bean and Bacon Soup (top) and Cream of Onion Soup (bottom).

Put beans into a large casserole and add 4 cups water. Cover and cook for 10 minutes on HIGH, or until boiling. Allow to boil for 2 minutes, then set aside, covered, for 1 hour. Heat a browning dish for 5 minutes on HIGH and brown the bacon for 2 minutes. Crumble and set aside, reserving the fat. Put onion, celery, garlic and bacon fat into a large casserole and cook on HIGH for 2 minutes. Drain beans, and add to the casserole along with the thyme, sage and bay leaf. Pour on 4 cups of fresh water, cover, and cook for 45-55 minutes on HIGH. Then stir in the bacon, reserving 4 tbsps for garnish. Re-cover dish and cook a further 25-35 minutes on HIGH, or until beans are soft but not breaking apart. Add water as necessary during cooking. Allow to stand, covered, for 10 minutes. Remove the bay leaf and serve garnished with the reserved bacon.

Mulligatawny Soup

PREPARATION TIME: 12 minutes

MICROWAVE COOKING TIME: 36-38 minutes

SERVES: 4 people

1 cup onions, thinly sliced
2 apples, peeled and grated
4 tbsps butter
4 tbsps flour
1 tbsp tomato paste
2 tsps curry powder
1 tbsp mango chutney
⅓ cup quick-cooking rice
4 cups beef or chicken stock
1 small bunch fresh coriander leaves
1 bay leaf
1 clove garlic, crushed
Salt
Pepper

GARNISH
⅓ cup plain yogurt

Reserve 4 sprigs of coriander for garnish and chop 1 tbsp of the remainder. Put butter, onion and garlic into a large casserole. Cover and cook for 5 minutes on HIGH.

Blend in the flour and curry powder, then cover and cook for 2 minutes on HIGH. Add tomato paste, stock and 1 tbsp coriander, and cook for 5 minutes on HIGH until boiling. Add apple, chutney, rice and seasoning, and cook for 10 minutes on MEDIUM, or until rice is tender. Cook an additional 2 minutes on HIGH if necessary. Serve topped with yogurt and reserved coriander leaves.

Cream of Mushroom Soup

PREPARATION TIME: 10 minutes

MICROWAVE COOKING TIME: 17 minutes

SERVES: 4 people

¾lb mushrooms
1 shallot, finely chopped
2 cups chicken or vegetable stock
1½ cups milk
2 tbsps butter or margarine
3 tbsps flour
¼ tsp thyme
2 tbsps dry sherry
⅓ cup heavy cream
Salt
Pepper

Reserve 4 mushrooms to use as garnish, and chop the rest finely. Put them with the butter and shallot into a large glass bowl. Cover with plastic wrap and pierce several times. Cook for 4 minutes on HIGH or until mushrooms are soft. Stir occasionally. Add flour and stir well. Gradually add the stock, re-cover, and cook for 5 minutes on HIGH. Stir the mixture several times while cooking. Add milk, thyme and sherry, and cook on HIGH for 6 minutes, or until boiling. Stir several times during cooking. Allow the soup to stand for 1-2 minutes, covered. Slice remaining mushrooms thinly. Put them in a small bowl with 1 tbsp of water and a squeeze of lemon juice. Cover bowl with plastic wrap and pierce several times, and cook for 1 minute on HIGH. Add cream to the soup and cook for 2 minutes on HIGH. Serve

the soup garnished with the slices of mushroom.

Cream of Broccoli Soup

PREPARATION TIME: 10 minutes

MICROWAVE COOKING TIME: 20 minutes

SERVES: 4 people

1lb broccoli spears, fresh or frozen
2 tbsps butter
2 tbsps flour
1½ cups chicken or vegetable stock
2 cups milk
1 bay leaf
¼ tsp thyme
1 tbsp chopped parsley
½ cup heavy cream
Salt
Pepper

Chop broccoli roughly, reserving 4-8 small flowerets for garnish. Put chopped broccoli into a loosely tied roasting bag with 2 tbsps water. Cook on HIGH for 5 minutes. (The broccoli may also be cooked in a bowl covered with pierced plastic wrap.) Put butter into a large bowl and cook for 1 minute on HIGH. Stir in the flour, and add the milk, stock, thyme, parsley, bay leaf and seasoning. Cook for 7 minutes on HIGH, stirring several times. Add broccoli and cook a further 3 minutes on HIGH. Pour the soup into a food processor and purée until smooth. Put reserved flowerets of broccoli into a small bowl with 1 tbsp of water. Cover with pierced plastic wrap and cook for 2 minutes on HIGH. Set aside. Add cream and re-heat the soup for 2 minutes on HIGH. Serve with a garnish of broccoli flowerets.

Facing page: Cream of Mushroom Soup (top) and Mulligatawny Soup (bottom).

3 cups beef stock
¼ cup white wine
1 bunch dill
1 bay leaf
Salt
Pepper

GARNISH
½ cup sour cream

Reserve 4 sprigs of dill for garnish and chop the rest. Put the dill, carrot, onion, potatoes, cabbage, garlic, bay leaf, seasoning, and half the stock into a large casserole. Cover and cook on HIGH for 15 minutes or until vegetables soften. Add the remaining stock, beets, wine and tomato paste, and cover and cook on HIGH for 10 minutes. Stir occasionally. Remove bay leaf. Pour soup into a food processor and purée until smooth. Add cream and blend thoroughly. Return soup to bowl and re-heat for 2 minutes on HIGH. Serve topped with sour cream and sprigs of dill.

Stilton Cheese and Walnut Soup

PREPARATION TIME: 10 minutes

MICROWAVE COOKING TIME: 18 minutes

SERVES: 4 people

2 cups Stilton cheese, crumbled (half Cheddar and half blue cheese may be substituted)
1 large onion, finely chopped
3 tbsps butter
2 tbsps flour
1½ cups chicken stock
1½ cups milk
¼ cup cream
½ cup walnuts, finely chopped
1 bay leaf
1 sprig thyme
Salt and pepper

Cream of Onion Soup

PREPARATION TIME: 10 minutes

MICROWAVE COOKING TIME: 18 minutes

SERVES: 4 people

1½lbs onions, finely chopped
2 tbsps butter
2 tbsps flour
2 cups beef or chicken stock
1½ cups milk
1 tbsp Madeira
½ cup cream

GARNISH
4 green onions, sliced

Put the butter into a large bowl and cook for 1 minute on HIGH. Add onions, and cook for 5 minutes on HIGH, stirring occasionally until light brown. Stir in the flour, stock, bay leaf, and salt and pepper. Cook for 10 minutes on HIGH. Pour the soup into a food processor and purée

until smooth. Pour milk into a small bowl and heat for 2 minutes on HIGH. Pour the soup back into a bowl, add the milk, and stir well. Re-heat on HIGH for 2 minutes and add the Madeira. Stir in the cream before serving and garnish with the sliced green onions.

Creamy Borscht

PREPARATION TIME: 15 minutes

MICROWAVE COOKING TIME: 27 minutes

SERVES: 4 people

3 beets, grated
1½ cups cabbage, shredded
1 medium carrot, thinly sliced
2 medium potatoes, peeled and thinly sliced
1 medium onion, finely chopped
1 small clove garlic, crushed
1 teaspoon tomato paste
½ cup cream

**This page: Creamy Borscht.
Facing page: Cream of Broccoli
Soup (top) and Stilton Cheese and
Walnut Soup (bottom).**

Jerusalem Artichoke and Almond Soup

PREPARATION TIME:	15 minutes
MICROWAVE COOKING TIME:	33-38 minutes
CONVENTIONAL OVEN TEMPERATURE:	350°F, 180°C
SERVES:	4 people

2½ lbs Jerusalem artichoke
2 shallots, finely chopped
¼ cup blanched almonds
2 tbsps butter or margarine
1 cup chicken stock
1½ cups milk
½ cup heavy cream
¼ cup white wine
1 bay leaf
Grated nutmeg
Lemon juice
Salt
Pepper

GARNISH
¼ cup sliced almonds, browned

Peel artichokes and keep in a bowl of cold water and lemon juice. Thinly slice them and put them into a bowl with shallots, butter and almonds. Cover with plastic wrap and pierce several times, and cook for 4 minutes on HIGH. Pour in the stock and wine, add the bay leaf, grated nutmeg and seasoning, and cook, uncovered, for 10 minutes on HIGH. Remove bay leaf, add cream and milk, and pour into a food processor. Purée until smooth and adjust seasoning. Meanwhile, brown almonds for garnish in a conventional oven for 15 minutes or in a microwave-convection oven on Combination for 7 minutes, stirring often. Re-heat soup for 2 minutes on HIGH, and serve garnished with the browned almonds and more grated nutmeg.

Put onion and butter into a large bowl. Cover with plastic wrap and pierce several times. Cook for 6 minutes on HIGH. Stir in flour, add the stock gradually and mix well. Add bay leaf, thyme, salt and pepper, and cook, uncovered, for 10 minutes on HIGH. Remove the herbs. Crumble the cheese into a bowl and add ½ cup of the soup to the cheese. Stir in well. Return cheese mixture to the rest of the soup and add cream. Cook 1 minute, uncovered, on HIGH. Add the walnuts to the bowl, reserving about 2 tbsps for garnish. Cook on HIGH for 1 minute. Serve garnished with the reserved walnuts.

This page: Jerusalem Artichoke and Almond Soup (top) and Cream of Carrot and Orange Soup (bottom). Facing page: Spiced Tomato Soup (top) and Green Pea Soup (bottom).

Green Pea Soup

PREPARATION TIME: 10 minutes

MICROWAVE COOKING TIME:
12 minutes

SERVES: 4 people

1lb frozen peas
2 tbsps butter
2 tbsps flour
1 cup chicken or vegetable stock
1½ cups milk
½ cup light cream
1 shallot, finely chopped
1 small bunch fresh mint
¼ tsp marjoram
1 tbsp chopped parsley
Salt
Pepper

Put butter and shallot into a large bowl and cover with pierced plastic wrap. Cook for 5 minutes on HIGH, then add the peas to the bowl, reserving ½ cup. Add the stock, milk, marjoram, parsley and seasoning. Cook for 5 minutes on HIGH. Pour into a food processor and purée until smooth. Chop the mint, reserving 4-8 leaves for garnish, if desired. Return soup to the bowl, and add chopped mint, cream and reserved peas. Re-heat soup for 2 minutes on HIGH. Garnish with the mint leaves.

Cream of Lettuce Soup

PREPARATION TIME: 10 minutes

MICROWAVE COOKING TIME:
18 minutes

SERVES: 4 people

2-3 potatoes, peeled and diced
1 onion, finely chopped
1 head romaine lettuce
1 cup chicken stock
2 cups milk
2 tbsps butter or margarine
½ cup cream
Ground nutmeg
¼ tsp thyme
1 tsp chopped parsley
Salt
Pepper

Put potatoes and onion into a large bowl with the butter and stock. Cover with plastic wrap and pierce several times. Cook on HIGH for 10 minutes. Wash lettuce well and shred leaves finely, reserving a small amount for garnish. Add to the bowl with the seasoning, thyme and ground nutmeg, and cook for 1 minute on HIGH. Add the milk and pour the soup into a food processor, and purée until smooth. Add the cream. Return to the bowl and re-heat for 7 minutes on HIGH. Serve soup garnished with reserved shredded lettuce. Serve hot or cold.

Spiced Tomato Soup

PREPARATION TIME: 10 minutes

MICROWAVE COOKING TIME:
22 minutes

SERVES: 4 people

28oz can tomatoes
2 onions, finely chopped
2 cups beef stock
1 tbsp cornstarch
1 tbsp tomato paste
¼ cup port or brandy
1 tsp thyme
½ stick cinnamon
2 whole cloves
3 black peppercorns
3 allspice berries
1 bay leaf
Salt
Sugar

GARNISH
2 tomatoes
4 tbsps heavy cream

Put tomatoes and their juice, stock, onion, herbs, spices and salt into a large bowl. Cook, uncovered, for 20 minutes on HIGH. Add a pinch of sugar if necessary, to bring out the tomato flavor. Sieve tomatoes, extracting as much pulp as possible. Blend cornstarch and port and stir into the soup. Put tomatoes for garnish into a bowl of water and cook on HIGH for 1 minute. Drain and put into cold water. Peel, remove seeds, cut into thin shreds and set aside. Return soup to oven and cook, uncovered, for 2 minutes on HIGH, stirring often. Adjust seasoning, and serve soup garnished with a swirl of heavy cream and the shreds of tomato.

Cream of Carrot and Orange Soup

PREPARATION TIME: 10 minutes

MICROWAVE COOKING TIME:
18 minutes

SERVES: 4 people

3 cups grated carrots
1 shallot, finely chopped
2 tbsps butter or margarine
1 cup chicken or vegetable stock
2 cups milk
⅓ cup heavy cream
Juice and rind of 1 orange
1 bay leaf
1 sprig of thyme
1 small bunch chives, chopped
Salt
Pepper

Pare the rind from the orange and squeeze the juice. Put butter into a large bowl and heat for 1 minute on HIGH. Add onion and cook for 5 minutes on HIGH. Add carrots, stock, bay leaf, thyme, and salt and pepper. Cover with pierced plastic wrap and cook for 10 minutes on HIGH. Add milk, orange juice and orange rind and cook for 1 minute on HIGH. Remove bay leaf, thyme, and orange rind, and pour into a food processor. Purée until smooth. Return soup to bowl, and heat through for 2 minutes on HIGH. Stir in the chives and the cream before serving. Serve hot or cold.

Facing page: Cream of Lettuce Soup.

Microwave
SOUPS AND APPETIZERS

VEGETABLE AND PASTA SOUPS

Chicken Vegetable Soup

PREPARATION TIME: 15 minutes

MICROWAVE COOKING TIME:
23 minutes

SERVES: 4 people

1lb chicken parts
4 cups water
1 chicken bouillon cube
1 small turnip, diced
1 onion, finely chopped
3 sticks celery, sliced
2 medium carrots, diced
¼ cup frozen peas
¼ cup fresh or frozen sliced green beans
½ cup mushrooms, quartered
¼ tsp thyme
1 bay leaf
1 tbsp chopped parsley

Put the chicken parts and the water into a large casserole with the thyme, bay leaf and seasoning. Cover and cook on HIGH for 15 minutes. Remove chicken and leave to cool. Remove the skin and bones and cut the chicken into small pieces. Set aside. Strain stock. Return stock to casserole and skim any fat from the surface. Taste and, if necessary, add the bouillon cube. Add the carrot, onion, celery and turnip; cover and cook for 10 minutes on HIGH. At this stage, if using fresh beans, cut into even sized lengths and add to the stock with the mushrooms. Cover and cook for 4 minutes on HIGH. Add frozen peas and parsley and cook a further 1 minute on HIGH. (If using frozen beans, add with the peas.) Add chicken. Adjust seasoning, and heat through for 3 minutes on HIGH. Serve.

Greek Lemon Soup

PREPARATION TIME: 8 minutes

MICROWAVE COOKING TIME:
17 minutes

SERVES: 4 people

3 lemons
1 onion, finely chopped
3 tbsps butter or margarine
2 tbsps flour
1 cup quick-cooking rice
4 cups chicken stock
¼ tsp powdered oregano
Nutmeg
Salt
Pepper

Put butter and onion into a bowl. Cover with plastic wrap and pierce several times. Cook on HIGH for about 3 minutes. Add flour to bowl and cook on HIGH for an additional 1½-2 minutes. Gradually stir in the stock. Grate rind and squeeze juice from 2 lemons, and add to the bowl with the bay leaf, pinch of nutmeg, oregano, salt and pepper. Cook on HIGH for 5 minutes. Add rice, re-cover the bowl, and cook for 5 minutes on HIGH, stirring frequently. Additional cooking time may be needed if the rice is not tender. Leave to stand, covered, about 2 minutes. Slice remaining lemon thinly and garnish each serving of soup with a slice of lemon.

Minestrone

PREPARATION TIME: 15 minutes

MICROWAVE COOKING TIME:
26 minutes

SERVES: 4 people

2 small leeks, washed and cut into thin strips
2 tbsps oil
1½ cups canned tomatoes
1 green pepper, sliced
7oz can canellini, or haricot, beans
1 carrot, cut into 1" strips
2 sticks celery, cut into 1" strips
1 zucchini, cut into 1" strips
1 clove garlic, crushed
¼ lb ham, cut into thin strips
4 cups stock (preferably ham)
⅓ cup macaroni
1 bay leaf
½ tsp basil
½ tsp oregano
½ tsp fennel seed
Salt and pepper
Sugar

GARNISH
½ cup Parmesan cheese, grated

Put oil, leeks, carrot, celery, garlic and herbs in a large casserole. Cover and cook 6 minutes on HIGH. Add macaroni, tomatoes and their juice, stock, ham, drained beans, salt, pepper and a pinch of sugar, and cook, covered, on HIGH for 6 minutes. Add zucchini, green pepper and parsley, and cook 5 minutes on HIGH, or until pasta is tender. Serve with grated Parmesan cheese.

Facing page: Minestrone.

Cream of Asparagus Soup

PREPARATION TIME: 10 minutes
MICROWAVE COOKING TIME:
32 minutes
SERVES: 4 people

1lb asparagus, fresh or frozen
3 tbsps butter or margarine
3 tbsps flour
1 shallot, finely chopped
3 cups chicken stock
½ cup cream
1 bay leaf
¼ tsp thyme
Salt
Pepper
Nutmeg

Place butter and shallot into a large casserole. Cover and cook on HIGH for 6 minutes. Stir in the flour and cook a further 1 minute on HIGH. Stir in the stock and cook for 15 minutes on HIGH, until boiling. Chop asparagus roughly and, if using fresh, reserve 4 tips for garnish. Add asparagus, bay leaf, seasoning, and a pinch of grated nutmeg, and cook for 10 minutes on MEDIUM. Remove the bay leaf, and pour the soup into a food processor and purée until smooth. Put reserved asparagus tips into a small bowl with 1 tbsp of water. Cover with plastic wrap and pierce several times. Cook for 1 minute on HIGH and set aside. Add the cream to the soup, cover, and re-heat for 2-3 minutes. Serve garnished with the reserved asparagus tips and more grated nutmeg.

French Onion Soup

PREPARATION TIME: 10 minutes
MICROWAVE COOKING TIME:
27 minutes
SERVES: 4 people

1½ lbs onions, thinly sliced
4 tbsps butter or margarine
2 tbsps flour
½ cup dry cider or white wine
2 tbsps Calvados or brandy
4 cups beef stock
¼ tbsp thyme
1 bay leaf
4 slices French bread, toasted and
*   buttered*
½ cup Gruyère or Swiss cheese
Salt
Pepper

Place onions, butter, salt and pepper into a large bowl and cook on HIGH for 8 minutes. Stir occasionally. Stir in the flour, add the stock, cider, Calvados, thyme and bay leaf. Cover bowl with plastic wrap and pierce several times. Cook on HIGH for 10 minutes. Uncover and stir occasionally. Reduce the setting to LOW and cook a further 8 minutes.

Leave the bowl to stand covered for 1-2 minutes. Put slices of toast on a plate, and sprinkle over the grated cheese thickly. Cook on LOW until cheese starts to melt, and then broil conventionally until lightly browned. Spoon the soup into individual micro-proof bowls. Top each with the cheese toast and heat through for 1 minute on HIGH. Serve immediately.

This page: Chicken Vegetable Soup.
Facing page: Cream of Asparagus Soup (top) and French Onion Soup (bottom).

Chinese Chicken and Mushroom Soup

PREPARATION TIME: 8 minutes

MICROWAVE COOKING TIME:
36 minutes

SERVES: 4 people

6 dried Chinese mushrooms
2 chicken breasts
1 cup water
1 small can water chestnuts, sliced
1 small can bamboo shoots, sliced
1 bunch green onions, sliced diagonally
¼lb fine Chinese egg noodles
¼lb pea pods
1 tbsp light soy sauce
2 tbsps dry sherry
1 tsp sesame seed oil
1 tbsp cornstarch
3 cups chicken stock
Salt and pepper

Put mushrooms into a small bowl and cover with cold water. Cover bowl with plastic wrap and pierce several times. Heat on HIGH for 2 minutes and leave to stand. Put chicken breasts into a bowl with 1 cup water. Cover with pierced plastic wrap and cook for 15 minutes on HIGH. Put noodles into a bowl with 2 pints water. Cover with pierced plastic wrap and cook for 3 minutes on HIGH. Leave standing, covered, for 5 minutes. Drain and slice mushrooms, and put into a large bowl with the stock. Cover with pierced plastic wrap and cook for 1 minute on HIGH. Skin, bone and shred chicken and add to bowl with green onions, pea pods, water chestnuts and bamboo shoots and cook for 1 minute on HIGH. Mix cornstarch, soy sauce and sherry with a tbsp of the hot liquid. Pour into the bowl with the rest of the soup and cook, stirring several times, for 5 minutes on HIGH. Drain noodles and add them to the bowl with the sesame seed oil. Heat soup through for 2 minutes on HIGH. Serve garnished with more chopped green onion if desired.

Potato Soup

PREPARATION TIME: 10 minutes

MICROWAVE COOKING TIME:
21 minutes

SERVES: 4 people

4 cups diced potatoes
3 tbsps butter or margarine
1 onion, thinly sliced
1 cup water
3 cups milk
1 bay leaf
1 sprig of thyme
Salt
Pepper
Nutmeg

GARNISH
½ cup Colby cheese, grated

Put potatoes, onions and butter into a large bowl. Cover with plastic wrap and pierce several times. Cook for 10 minutes on HIGH. Add milk, water, thyme, bay leaf, seasoning and grated nutmeg, and cook for 7 minutes on HIGH. Leave standing, covered, for 1 minute. Uncover and allow to cool slightly. Remove bay leaf and thyme, pour soup into a food processor, and purée until smooth. Check seasoning and consistency. If too thick, add more milk. Cover and heat through for 3 minutes on HIGH. Serve garnished with the grated cheese.

**This page: Potato Soup (top) and
Greek Lemon Soup (bottom).
Facing page: Chinese Chicken and
Mushroom Soup.**

Chili Corn Chowder

PREPARATION TIME: 15 minutes

MICROWAVE COOKING TIME:
24 minutes

SERVES: 4 people

3 tbsps butter or margarine
1 shallot, finely chopped
4 strips smoked bacon (rindless and
    boneless)
3 tbsps flour
2 cups chicken stock
1½ cups milk
2 medium potatoes, peeled and cut into
    ½" dice
1 red pepper, diced
1 green chili pepper, finely chopped
1½ cups corn, frozen
½ cup light cream
1 tbsp chopped parsley
¼ tsp ground cumin
1 bay leaf

GARNISH
4 green onions

Put butter into a bowl and cook for
1 minute on HIGH. Dice bacon and
add it with the shallot to the butter.
Cover with pierced plastic wrap and
cook for 5 minutes on HIGH until
onions are softened. Stir in the flour
and cumin, and cook for 1 minute on
HIGH. Gradually stir in the stock
and milk, and add potatoes and bay
leaf. Cook for 6 minutes on HIGH or
until boiling. Add red pepper and as
much of the chili pepper as desired.
Cook for 10 minutes or until potatoes
soften. Remove bay leaf, add corn,
cream, parsley and seasoning, and
cook for 3 minutes on HIGH. Serve
garnished with chopped green onion.

Italian Onion Soup

PREPARATION TIME: 10 minutes

MICROWAVE COOKING TIME:
16-23 minutes and 1-2 minutes
standing time

SERVES: 4 people

1½lbs onions, thinly sliced
16oz can plum tomatoes

3 tbsps butter or margarine
2 tbsps flour
½ cup red wine
1½ cups beef stock
¼ tsp basil
¼ tsp oregano
1 bay leaf
Salt
Pepper
Tomato paste
4 slices French bread, toasted and
    buttered
2 tbsps Parmesan cheese, grated
2 tbsps Cheddar cheese, grated

Place onions, butter, salt and pepper
into a large bowl and cook on HIGH
for 6 minutes. Stir occasionally. Stir
in flour, add the stock, tomatoes, red
wine, basil, oregano and bay leaf.
Cover the bowl with plastic wrap
and pierce several times. Cook on
HIGH for 8 minutes. Uncover and
stir occasionally. Reduce setting to
LOW and cook for a further 4

minutes. Leave the bowl to stand
covered for 1-2 minutes. Adjust
seasoning and add tomato paste, if
necessary, for color and flavor. Mix
the cheeses together, put the slices of
toast on a plate, and sprinkle over
the grated cheese. Cook on LOW
until cheese starts to melt, and then
broil conventionally until lightly
browned. Use the Combination
setting on convection microwave
oven for 7 minutes. Spoon the soup
into individual micro-proof bowls.
Top each with the cheese toast and
heat through for 1 minute on HIGH.

**This page: Chili Corn Chowder.
Facing page: Curried Cauliflower
Soup (top) and Italian Onion Soup
(bottom).**

Curried Cauliflower Soup

PREPARATION TIME: 10 minutes

MICROWAVE COOKING TIME:
15 minutes

SERVES: 4 people

4 cups cauliflowerets, or 1 small
  cauliflower cut into flowerets
2 shallots finely chopped
2 tbsps butter or margarine
2 tbsps flour
2 tsps curry powder
1½ cups chicken or vegetable stock
2 cups milk
Salt
Pepper

GARNISH
⅓ cup sliced almonds, browned

Put cauliflowerets into a roasting bag
with the shallot and bay leaf. Tie bag
loosely and cook for 8 minutes on
HIGH. (Cauliflower may also be
cooked in a bowl covered with
pierced plastic wrap.) Put butter into
a large bowl and cook for 1 minute
on HIGH until melted. Stir in the
curry powder and flour, and cook for
1 minute on HIGH. Add milk and
cook for 3 minutes on HIGH, stirring
occasionally. Pour the soup into a
food processor, add the cauliflower,
and purée until smooth. Return the
soup to the oven to heat through for
2 minutes on HIGH. Serve garnished
with the browned sliced almonds.

Vegetable Soup

PREPARATION TIME: 10 minutes

MICROWAVE COOKING TIME:
21 minutes

SERVES: 4 people

1 large carrot, peeled and diced
1 large turnip, peeled and diced
2 leeks, washed and sliced thinly
2 potatoes, peeled and diced
¼ cup frozen peas
¼ cup frozen corn
½ cup fresh or frozen sliced green beans
¼lb okra (optional)
16oz can plum tomatoes

2 cups chicken or vegetable stock
⅓ cup soup pasta
1 bay leaf
¼ tsp marjoram or savory
1 tbsp chopped parsley
Pepper

Put butter into a large bowl and cook
for 45 seconds on HIGH until it
melts. Add carrots, turnips, leeks and
potatoes and mix together. Cover
with plastic wrap and pierce several
times. Cook on HIGH for 10 minutes
or until vegetables begin to soften.
Stir occasionally. Add stock,
tomatoes, bay leaf, marjoram, pasta,
salt and pepper. Cover and cook for
7 minutes on HIGH. Slice beans (if

fresh), trim okra, and slice into
rounds, and add to bowl. Re-cover
bowl and cook for 2 minutes on
HIGH. Add corn, peas and parsley.
Cook for 1 minute on HIGH or until
pasta is tender. Sprinkle with more
chopped parsley, if desired, before
serving.

This page: Vegetable Soup.
Facing page: Jellied Vegetable
Terrine with Tomato Dressing.

TARTS, TERRINES AND PÂTÉS

Jellied Vegetable Terrine with Tomato Dressing

PREPARATION TIME: 15 minutes

MICROWAVE COOKING TIME: 11 minutes

SERVES: 4 people

TERRINE
1 tbsp gelatine
1 chicken bouillon cube
2 cups boiling water (less 2 tbsps)
2 tbsps dry sherry
8oz green beans, ends trimmed
1 large carrot, peeled
1-2 Jerusalem artichokes, peeled
4oz mushrooms, cleaned
½ cup frozen peas

DRESSING
14oz can tomato sauce
1 tsp tomato paste
Juice and grate rind of half a lemon
¼ tsp chives, snipped
¼ tsp parsley, chopped
¼ tsp thyme, chopped
¼ tsp basil, chopped
3-4 tbsps olive oil
2 tbsps red wine vinegar
¼ tsp Dijon mustard
1 bay leaf
Sugar
Salt
Pepper

GARNISH
1 bunch watercress

Heat water in a glass measuring cup for 3-4 minutes on HIGH until boiling. Add sherry and stir in the gelatine and bouillon cube. Leave to cool at room temperature, then put into a bowl of cold water. The aspic must be cold but liquid. If it sets too quickly in the cup, melt again for 1-2 minutes on HIGH. Then chill again in the cold water, and repeat the process again when necessary. Leave green beans whole and cook for 8 minutes on HIGH with 2 tbsps water in a small, shallow dish covered with pierced plastic wrap. Cut carrots lengthwise into ¼″ sticks and cook for 10 minutes in the same way as the beans. Cut artichokes into thin rounds and cook for 8 minutes.

Chicken and Asparagus Terrine with Lemon Mousseline Sauce

PREPARATION TIME: 15 minutes

MICROWAVE COOKING TIME: 33 minutes

SERVES: 4-6 people

TERRINE
1lb chicken breasts
1½ cups cream
12oz low-fat cheese
2 tbsps white wine
½ cup water
3 eggs
1lb asparagus spears, fresh or frozen
Salt
Pepper
Nutmeg
1 bay leaf

SAUCE
½ cup butter
3 egg yolks
Rind and juice of 1 lemon
¼ cup whipping cream
1 bay leaf
1 blade mace
Salt
Pepper

Cut tips off asparagus spears, trim stalk ends, and cook on HIGH for 6 minutes with 2 tbsps water in a shallow dish covered with pierced plastic wrap. Leave to cool. Put chicken breasts into a bowl with the white wine, water and bay leaf. Cover with pierced plastic wrap and cook for 15 minutes on HIGH. Cool and remove skin and bones. Put chicken, cheese, seasoning, nutmeg and 2 eggs into a food processor, and purée until smooth. In a clean bowl, purée the asparagus spears with 1 egg, salt and pepper. Put half the chicken mixture into a loaf pan and smooth evenly. Cover with half the asparagus mixture and layer on the reserved asparagus tips. Cover with remaining

This page: Chicken and Asparagus Terrine with Lemon Mousseline Sauce.
Facing page: Tomato Tarts Niçoise (top) and Cheese and Mushroom Tarts (bottom).

Remove stalks from mushrooms and slice caps thinly. Cook them for 3 minutes on HIGH, then the frozen peas for 1 minute on HIGH. Dampen a 1lb loaf pan with water and pour in a ¼" layer of cool aspic. Chill until set. Arrange a layer of peas on top and pour over a thin layer of aspic to set the peas in place. Chill until set, then add more aspic to just cover the peas. Chill again until set. Repeat the process with a layer of artichokes, green beans, carrots and mushrooms. Fill the pan to the top with aspic and chill for 1-2 hours until firm. Meanwhile, put tomato sauce, paste,

garlic, bay leaf, seasoning and sugar into a bowl. Cover with pierced plastic wrap and cook for 10 minutes on HIGH, stirring frequently. Allow sauce to cool completely. Whisk oil, vinegar and mustard together until thick. Whisk in the tomato sauce, add chopped herbs, and adjust seasoning. Unmold the terrine and cut into ½" slices. Serve with tomato dressing and small bouquets of watercress or parsley.

asparagus mixture, then the remaining chicken mixture. Cover the dish with plastic wrap and cook for 10 minutes on HIGH. Cover and weight down the top, leaving to stand for 5 minutes. Serve hot with the lemon mousseline sauce.

To make sauce: Put the butter into a glass measuring cup or a small, deep bowl and cook for 1 minute on HIGH to melt. Put lemon juice, bay leaf and mace into another bowl and heat for 1 minute on HIGH. Beat egg yolks, lemon rind and seasoning, and strain on the juice. Pour egg yolk mixture into the butter and stir well. Have a bowl of ice water ready. Put the sauce mixture into the oven and cook for 15 seconds on HIGH. Remove and stir, repeating the process until sauce has thickened – approximately 2 minutes. Put the jug immediately into the ice water to stop the cooking. Whip cream, fold into the sauce and serve at once with the terrine.

Country Pâté

PREPARATION TIME: 10 minutes

MICROWAVE COOKING TIME: 15 minutes

SERVES: 6-8 people

½ lb ground pork
½ lb ground veal
¼ lb ham, ground
¼ lb pork liver
3oz ground pork fat
1 clove garlic, crushed
4 tbsps brandy
Ground allspice
Thyme
1 bay leaf
2 tsps green peppercorns in brine, rinsed
8 slices bacon, bones and rind removed
Salt
Pepper

Line a 1lb glass loaf dish with the bacon. Remove skin and ducts from liver, grind in a food processor, and mix with the ground meats, garlic, herbs, spices, brandy, peppercorns and seasoning. Press meat mixture into the dish on top of bacon. Place

bay leaf on top. Fold edges of bacon over the top and cover with plastic wrap. Put a custard cup of water into the oven with the pâté, and cook on MEDIUM for 6 minutes. Leave to stand for 5 minutes and cook for a further 10 minutes on MEDIUM. Cover with foil, press down and weight. Leave to chill 2-4 hours. Remove the bay leaf, and cut mixture into thin slices (about 18) to serve.

Asparagus with Orange Hollandaise

PREPARATION TIME: 10 minutes

MICROWAVE COOKING TIME: 11 minutes

SERVES: 4 people

2lbs asparagus spears
½ cup butter
3 egg yolks
Juice of half a lemon
Grated rind and juice of ½ an orange
1 small bay leaf
1 blade mace
Salt
Pepper

Trim any thick ends from the asparagus spears and rinse them well. Put into a shallow casserole with 3-4 tbsps water. Cover and cook for 7 minutes until just tender. Leave covered while preparing sauce. Put the butter in a glass measuring cup or jug, or small, deep bowl and cook for 1 minute on HIGH to melt. Put orange juice, lemon juice, bay leaf and mace into another bowl and heat for 1 minute on HIGH. Beat egg yolks, orange rind and seasoning together, and strain on the juice. Pour egg yolk mixture into the butter and stir well to mix. Have a bowl of ice water on hand. Put the sauce mixture into the oven and cook for 15 seconds on HIGH. Remove and stir well, and repeat the process until sauce is thickened. It should take about 2 minutes. Put the jug immediately into the ice water to prevent sauce from cooking further. Serve at once with the asparagus.

Cheese and Mushroom Tarts

PREPARATION TIME: 10 minutes

MICROWAVE COOKING TIME: 11 minutes

SERVES: 4 people

1½ cups wholewheat crackers
½ cup butter or margarine
½ cup Cheddar cheese, grated
½ lb mushrooms, roughly chopped
4 tbsps chopped chives
1 tbsp flour
1 tbsp butter
⅓ cup chicken or vegetable stock
1 egg, beaten
2 tbsps light cream
½ cup Colby cheese, grated
Cayenne pepper
Salt
Pepper

Crush the crackers into a food processor and grate in the cheese. Melt ⅓ cup of the butter on HIGH for 1 minute and pour into the crumbs and cheese. Process to mix. Press the mixture firmly into 8 individual tart pans or a muffin pan. Cook for 2 minutes on HIGH, and cool. Melt the remaining butter on HIGH. Mix in flour, chives, seasoning and stock, and cook for 2 minutes on HIGH, or until sauce has thickened. Fill the tart shells with the mushrooms. Beat egg, cream, Cayenne pepper and seasonings together until frothy. Fold in the Colby cheese. Pour on top of the mushroom filling and cook for 2 minutes on HIGH until the cheese sets. Tops may be browned under a broiler if desired, or cooked for 5 minutes on the Combination setting in a microwave-convection oven. Serve immediately.

Facing page: Country Pâté (top) and Asparagus with Orange Hollandaise (bottom).

Press mixture firmly onto the ham. Cover with plastic wrap and cook for 6 minutes on MEDIUM. Leave to stand for 5 minutes, then cook for a further 7 minutes on MEDIUM. Cover with foil and weight down the top. Leave to chill for 4-5 hours, and serve with tarragon sauce.

To make sauce: Have ready a bowl of ice water. Beat egg and sugar in a small glass bowl until creamy. Add vinegar and cook on HIGH for 30 seconds. Remove and stir. Repeat the process until sauce thickens (approximately 2 minutes). Put immediately into ice water to stop the cooking, and leave to go cold, stirring occasionally. Whip the cream and fold into the sauce with the chopped tarragon.

Tomato Tarts Niçoise

PREPARATION TIME: 20 minutes

MICROWAVE COOKING TIME: 10 minutes

SERVES: 4 people

PASTRY
1 cup flour
1½ tbsps butter or margarine
1½ tbsps baking powder
⅓ cup milk
Pinch salt
1 tbsp chopped parsley, basil and thyme, mixed

FILLING
1 onion, finely sliced
½ lb tomatoes, skinned and thickly sliced
1 tbsp olive oil
16 black olives, stoned
1 tbsp capers
8 anchovies
¼ tsp oregano or basil
½ cup Gruyère cheese, grated

To make pastry: Sift flour with salt and cut in the butter until mixture resembles fine breadcrumbs. Add herbs and milk, and mix to a soft dough. It may not be necessary to add all the milk. Turn out and knead lightly. Divide dough into 4 pieces and roll each out to line a muffin pan or 8 tart pans.

Terrine of Duck and Cherries with Tarragon Sauce

PREPARATION TIME: 15 minutes

MICROWAVE COOKING TIME: 15 minutes

SERVES: 6-8 people

TERRINE
1 5lb duck, skinned and boned
6 slices boiled ham
⅓ cup ground pork
⅓ cup ground veal
½ clove garlic, crushed
8oz can cherries, drained and pitted
4 tbsps white wine
Allspice
2 tsps tarragon, chopped
1 tbsp kirsch
Salt
Pepper

SAUCE
1 egg
3 tbsps tarragon vinegar
¼ tsp chopped fresh tarragon
2 tbsps sugar
½ cup whipping cream

To prepare terrine: Grind duck meat in a food processor and mix with pork and veal. Add garlic, kirsch, wine, tarragon, allspice and seasoning. Fold in the cherries. Line a 1lb glass loaf dish with the ham slices.

Facing page: Terrine of Duck and Cherries with Tarragon Sauce. This page: Ham and Mushroom Pâté (left) and Stuffed Tomatoes Provençal (right).

To make filling and assemble tarts: Bring 2 cups water to the boil for 3 minutes on HIGH. Put in the tomatoes for 5 seconds, remove and plunge them into cold water. Peel, drain and slice them. Put olive oil in a bowl, add onion, and cook for 3 minutes on HIGH or until softened. Season, mix with half the cheese. Put into the bottom of each pastry shell. Layer tomatoes, seasoning and sprinkling the herbs between each layer. Decorate with anchovies,

capers and olives, and sprinkle with remaining cheese. Bake for 4 minutes on HIGH, turning pans once. Brown under a broiler if desired. Do not overbake or pastry will become hard.

Ham and Mushroom Pâté

PREPARATION TIME: 10 minutes
MICROWAVE COOKING TIME: 20 minutes
SERVES: 6-8 people

1lb cooked ham, minced
1 cup fresh white breadcrumbs
3 eggs
3 tbsps butter
4oz mushrooms, finely chopped

1 shallot, finely chopped
1 clove garlic, crushed
2 tbsps dry sherry
¼ tsp thyme
¼ tsp parsley
Nutmeg
Salt and pepper

Melt the butter in a small bowl and add the shallot. Cover with pierced plastic wrap and cook for 2 minutes on HIGH. Add the thyme, parsley and mushrooms, and cook for a further 4 minutes, uncovered, on HIGH. Add the seasoning and ¼ cup of the breadcrumbs. Leave to cool. Add 1 beaten egg only if necessary to bind together. Mix ham, remaining breadcrumbs, garlic, sherry, nutmeg and seasonings. Beat in up to 2 of the eggs, 1 at a time, until mixture holds together. Put half the ham mixture into a 1lb glass loaf dish and pack down firmly. Make a channel down the center and mound the mushroom mixture into it. Cover with remaining ham mixture, packing it carefully around the mushroom mixture to cover it completely. Cover dish with plastic wrap and put into the microwave oven with a custard cup of water. Cook for 10 minutes on MEDIUM, leave to stand for 2 minutes, then cook for another 2 minutes on MEDIUM until firm. Cover with foil and weight the top of the dish. Chill for 4-5 hours and cut into slices to serve with toast or French bread.

Stuffed Tomatoes Provençal

PREPARATION TIME: 10 minutes

MICROWAVE COOKING TIME: 6 minutes

SERVES: 4 people

4 large ripe tomatoes
8oz mushrooms, finely chopped
1 shallot, finely chopped
2 tbsps butter or margarine
1 cup fresh white breadcrumbs
1 tbsp white wine
1 clove garlic, crushed
1 tsp Dijon mustard
1 tsp chopped parsley
1 tsp chopped basil
¼ tsp thyme

GARNISH
Parsley sprigs

Cut the rounded ends of the tomatoes off to form caps, and remove the green cores from the bottoms. Scoop out the pulp and seeds, and strain the juice. Put the butter into a small bowl with the garlic and shallot and cook for 2 minutes on HIGH. Stir in the mushrooms and wine and cook for 2 minutes on HIGH. Add bread-crumbs, herbs, seasoning, mustard and tomato pulp, and mix well. Stuff the tomatoes and put into a shallow

dish. Place the tops on at a slight angle and cook, uncovered, for 2 minutes on HIGH. Garnish with the parsley sprigs.

Langoustine Parisienne

PREPARATION TIME: 10 minutes

MICROWAVE COOKING TIME: 14 minutes

SERVES: 4 people

1lb langoustines, shelled and uncooked
  (Gulf shrimp may be substituted)
8oz mushrooms
⅔ cup butter or margarine
3 tbsps flour
1 shallot, finely chopped
1½ cups milk
1 tbsp chopped parsley
2 tbsps dry sherry
⅓ cup dry breadcrumbs
Lemon juice
Paprika
Salt
Pepper

Cut mushroom stalks level with the caps and cut mushrooms into quarters. Put 3 tbsps of the butter into a large bowl, then add shallot and cook for 1 minute on HIGH. Stir in the mushrooms and cook, uncovered, for 6 minutes on HIGH. Add flour and seasoning, and stir in the milk and sherry. Cook for 3 minutes on HIGH, stirring frequently. Add parsley, and set aside. Put langoustines into a small bowl with 2 tbsps water, cover with pierced plastic wrap and cook for 2 minutes on HIGH. Cut each langoustine into 2 or 3 pieces if large, then stir them into the mushroom sauce. Heat a browning tray and melt the remaining butter. Stir in the breadcrumbs and cook until golden brown and crisp. Put the shellfish-mushroom mixture into 4 custard cups and scatter over the crumbs. Sprinkle over the paprika and heat for 2 minutes on HIGH. If using a microwave convection oven, melt the butter for 1 minute on HIGH microwave setting, mix in the crumbs, fill the custard cups with the

shellfish-mushroom mixture and scatter the crumbs over. Sprinkle with paprika and cook for 3 minutes on the Combination setting to brown.

Chicken Liver Pâté

PREPARATION TIME: 8 minutes

MICROWAVE COOKING TIME: 9 minutes

SERVES: 4 people

1lb chicken livers
1 shallot, finely chopped
1 clove garlic, crushed
1 large sprig rosemary
1 tsp parsley
1 tbsp Madeira
1 tbsp cream
⅓ cup butter
Nutmeg
Salt
Pepper

GARNISH
Juniper berries
Small sprigs of rosemary

Pick over the livers, removing any discolored parts. Put livers, shallot, garlic, 1 sprig rosemary, half the butter, seasonings and a pinch of nutmeg into a bowl. Cover with pierced plastic wrap and cook for 6 minutes on HIGH, stirring once. Remove rosemary and put the mixture into a food processor with the Madeira, cream and parsley, and purée until smooth. Divide between 4 custard cups. Put remaining butter in a bowl and cook for 3 minutes on HIGH until boiling. Leave to stand and skim off salt rising to surface. Spoon the butter oil over each pâté to seal. Chill until firm, decorate with small sprigs of rosemary and juniper berries, and serve with hot toast or French bread.

Facing page: Chicken Liver Pâté (top) and Langoustine Parisienne (bottom).

Microwave
SOUPS AND APPETIZERS

MEAT AND SEAFOOD APPETIZERS

Sparkling Shrimp

PREPARATION TIME: 5 minutes

MICROWAVE COOKING TIME:
2½ minutes

SERVES: 4 people

1½ lbs peeled shrimp
1 tbsp peppercorns packed in brine, rinsed
½ cup dry sparkling white wine
½ cup heavy cream
Juice and grated rind of half an orange
Salt
Pepper

GARNISH
12 thin orange slices

Put orange rind and juice, peppercorns, seasoning and wine into a
bowl. Heat for 30 seconds on HIGH.
Stir in the shrimp and heat for
1 minute on HIGH. Lightly whip the
cream, fold in, and heat for a further
1 minute on HIGH. Adjust seasoning
before putting into serving dishes.
Garnish with the orange slices.

Moûles Marinière à la Moutarde

PREPARATION TIME: 5 minutes

MICROWAVE COOKING TIME:
9 minutes

SERVES: 4 people

2 pints mussels
1½ tbsps butter or margarine
2 shallots, finely chopped
1 clove garlic, crushed
4 tbsps Dijon mustard
1 cup white wine

½ cup heavy cream
1 tbsp flour
1 tbsp parsley, chopped
1 tbsp dill, chopped
Salt
Pepper

Scrub mussels well and discard any
that are open or broken. Put butter

**This page: Moûles Marinière à la
Moutarde.
Facing page: Sparkling Shrimp.**

into a large bowl and cook for
1 minute on HIGH. Add shallot,
garlic, wine and seasoning. Cover

with pierced plastic wrap and cook for 2 minutes on HIGH. Add mussels, and cover and cook for 3 minutes or until the shells are open. Stir half-way through the cooking time. Remove mussels from the bowl, put into a serving dish and keep them warm. Strain the liquid from them and set it aside. Put flour into a clean bowl and gradually pour on the mussel liquid, stirring well to mix. Cook, uncovered, for 2 minutes on HIGH or until thick, stirring occasionally. Stir in the mustard, cream and chopped herbs and heat through for 1 minute on HIGH. Pour over the mussels and serve with French bread.

Pork Satay with Peanut Sauce

PREPARATION TIME: 10 minutes and 1 hour to marinate pork

MICROWAVE COOKING TIME: 13 minutes

SERVES: 4 people

1½ lbs pork tenderloin, cut into 1" cubes
1 large red pepper, cut into 1" slices
2 tbsps oil
Lime juice
1 clove garlic, crushed
1 small green chili pepper, finely chopped
½ cup crunchy peanut butter
½ cup chicken or vegetable stock
1 tsp ground cumin
1 tsp ground coriander
1 shallot, finely chopped
Salt
Pepper

GARNISH
1 bunch fresh coriander leaves (optional)
Lemon wedges

Mix lime juice, salt and pepper together and mix in the pork. Leave in a cool place for 1 hour. Heat 1 tbsp oil in a small bowl and add shallot. Cook for 2 minutes on HIGH, add chili pepper and cook for 1 minute more on HIGH. Stir in stock, peanut butter, spices and seasoning. Cook for 1 minute on HIGH. Set aside.

Thread meat and red pepper onto 12 small, wooden skewers. Heat a browning tray for 5 minutes on HIGH. Add oil and brown the satay for 3 minutes on HIGH, turning frequently. Transfer onto a roasting rack, and cook for 6 minutes on MEDIUM. Arrange sprigs of coriander leaves on serving plates and put the satay on top. Spoon over some of the peanut sauce and serve the rest separately.

Spicy Chicken Kebabs with Avocado Sauce

PREPARATION TIME: 10 minutes

MICROWAVE COOKING TIME: 6 minutes

SERVES: 4 people

CHICKEN AND MARINADE
3 chicken breasts, skinned and boned
2 tbsps vegetable oil
1 clove garlic, crushed
1 tbsp curry powder

This page: Pork Satay with Peanut Sauce (top) and Spicy Chicken Kebabs with Avocado Sauce (bottom).
Facing page: Stuffed Zucchini.

¼ tsp Cayenne pepper
1 tbsp chopped coriander leaves
Juice and grated rind of 1 lime
Salt
Pepper

SAUCE
1 large avocado, peeled and stone removed
½ cup plain yogurt
1 tbsp vegetable oil
½ tsp finely chopped onion
1 tsp mango chutney
Lime juice

Cut chicken into strips 1" wide. Combine ingredients for the marinade and mix in the chicken to coat each piece. Leave to marinate for 1 hour. Thread the meat onto wooden skewers and put onto a roasting rack. Cook for 5 minutes on

HIGH. Turn kebabs while cooking. Leave to stand, covered in plastic wrap, for 1 minute. Put oil and onion for the sauce into a small bowl. Cook for 1 minute on HIGH, and stir in chutney. Put avocado flesh into a food processor with seasoning, yogurt and lime juice. Add onion and chutney, and process until smooth. Serve with the chicken kebabs.

Stuffed Zucchini

PREPARATION TIME: 10 minutes

MICROWAVE COOKING TIME: 18 minutes

SERVES: 4 people

4 small, even-sized zucchini
¼lb crabmeat, fresh or frozen
1 shallot, finely chopped
½ cup cream cheese
½ cup mushrooms, chopped
¼ tsp tomato paste
¼ cup grated Parmesan cheese
4 tbsps dry breadcrumbs
2 tbsps milk
1 tbsp chopped parsley
4 tbsps butter, melted
Tabasco
Salt and pepper

Top and tail the zucchini and put into a large dish with 1 cup of water. Cover with pierced plastic wrap and cook for 4-5 minutes on HIGH. Rinse in cold water until completely cooled. Cut in half lengthwise, and carefully scoop out the flesh with a teaspoon, leaving a thin lining of flesh inside the skin. Leave to drain. Chop flesh roughly and set aside. Melt 2 tbsps of butter in a bowl for 1 minute on HIGH. Add the shallot and mushrooms, and cook, covered, for 2 minutes on HIGH. Add zucchini flesh, cover and cook for 1 minute on HIGH. Beat the cream cheese, tomato paste and milk together. Add crabmeat, parsley, seasoning, and a few drops of tabasco. Stir into the zucchini mixture and pile the filling into each zucchini shell. Mix breadcrumbs and Parmesan cheese together, and top each filled zucchini. Melt the remain-

ing butter and sprinkle over the zucchini. Heat through, uncovered, for 5 minutes on HIGH and brown under a broiler or on the Combination setting of a microwave convection oven for 10 minutes. Serve immediately.

Potted Smoked Fish

PREPARATION TIME: 15 minutes

MICROWAVE COOKING TIME: 8 minutes

SERVES: 4 people

2 smoked fish fillets
1 tbsp butter or margarine
1 tbsp flour
⅓ cup cream cheese
⅓ cup milk
6-8 pimento-stuffed olives, sliced
2 tsps Dijon mustard
Salt and pepper

GARNISH
½ cup butter for clarifying
Pimento-stuffed olives
Black peppercorns

Skin the fish fillets and break up into small pieces. Melt butter for 1 minute on HIGH. Stir in the flour and cook for 2 minutes on HIGH. Blend in the cheese, milk, half the olives, mustard and seasoning. Add fish and mix until well blended. Put into 4 custard cups and smooth the top. Cover each with plastic wrap and cook for 1 minute on HIGH to set the mixture. Put butter into a medium bowl and heat for 3-4 minutes on HIGH, or until boiling. Leave to stand for 10-15 minutes. Skim the salt off the top and spoon the butter oil carefully over each pot of fish. Fill nearly to the top, and leave until almost set. Then place the remaining olives and peppercorns on top of the butter. Chill and when set, cover the decoration with another thin layer of clarified butter and refrigerate again until set. Serve with hot toast.

Artichokes with Mustard Butter

PREPARATION TIME: 8 minutes

MICROWAVE COOKING TIME: 21 minutes

SERVES: 4 people

4 globe artichokes
1 tbsp lemon juice
Pinch salt
2 cups water
1 tbsp oil
1 bay leaf
1 slice onion

SAUCE
½ cup butter
3 tbsps Dijon mustard
Salt and pepper
Squeeze of lemon juice

Break stems from the base of each artichoke and twist to remove any stringy fibers. Trim the base of each so the artichokes sit level. Trim tips of artichoke leaves using kitchen scissors. Wash artichokes under cold running water. Put lemon juice, salt, water, oil, bay leaf and onion slice into a large bowl and cook 3-4 minutes on HIGH, or until the water boils. Put artichokes upright in the bowl, cover with plastic wrap and pierce several times. Cook for 15 minutes on HIGH, or until lower leaves can be pulled away easily. Leave to stand covered while preparing the sauce. Put butter, seasoning and lemon juice into a glass measuring cup or jug and cook for 2 minutes on HIGH, or until butter has melted. Beat in the mustard until sauce holds together. Put artichokes onto special artichoke serving plates, or onto small serving plates each on top of a larger plate, to give room for the discarded leaves. Serve the sauce separately, or remove the "choke" and serve the sauce in the center of the artichoke.

Facing page: Potted Smoked Fish (top) and Artichokes with Mustard Butter (bottom).

CHEESE AND EGG APPETIZERS

Eggs Florentine

PREPARATION TIME: 15 minutes

MICROWAVE COOKING TIME: 18 minutes

SERVES: 4 people

2¼ lbs fresh spinach, washed and stems removed
2 tbsps butter or margarine
4 eggs
2 tomatoes, skinned and seeded
Nutmeg
Salt
Pepper

MORNAY SAUCE
3 tbsps butter or margarine
3 tbsps flour
1½ cups milk
⅓ cup Cheddar cheese, grated
Dry mustard
Cayenne pepper
Salt
Pepper

To prepare spinach and tomatoes: Put spinach into a roasting bag and tie loosely. Stand upright and cook for 5 minutes on HIGH. (Spinach may also be cooked in a bowl covered with pierced plastic wrap.) Drain spinach well, and chop roughly. Boil 2 cups of water in a large bowl on HIGH and put in the tomatoes for 5 seconds. Put the tomatoes immediately into cold water. Peel, squeeze out the seeds and juice, and chop roughly.
To poach the eggs: Pour water into each of 4 custard cups to a depth of 1". Put the dishes in a circle and heat on HIGH until the water boils. Break 1 egg into each cup and pierce the yoke with a sharp knife. Cook on DEFROST or LOW for 3 minutes, or until whites have set. Turn the dishes at 1 minute intervals.
To prepare Mornay sauce: Melt butter in a medium bowl for 1 minute on HIGH. Stir in the flour, mustard and a pinch of Cayenne pepper, and add the milk gradually. Cook for 4-5 minutes on HIGH, stirring frequently. Add the cheese, reserving some for the top. Add seasoning and stir until blended. Melt 2 tbsps of butter for 1 minute on HIGH. Stir in the spinach, seasoning and grated nutmeg to taste. Heat for 1 minute on HIGH, then add tomatoes. Put some of the spinach mixture into each individual serving dish and top with a poached egg. Coat each with Mornay sauce and sprinkle on grated cheese. Brown under a broiler, or on the Combination setting in a microwave convection oven for 2 minutes.

Baked Eggs with Mushrooms and Mustard Cream

PREPARATION TIME: 10 minutes

MICROWAVE COOKING TIME: 9 minutes

SERVES: 4 people

8oz mushrooms, finely chopped
4 eggs
½ cup cream, whipped
1oz chopped chives
1 tsp sherry
2 tsps Dijon mustard
Paprika
Salt
Pepper

Melt butter in a small bowl for 1 minute on HIGH. Add mushrooms and cook for 4 minutes on HIGH. Add chives, sherry and seasoning and divide into 4 custard cups. Make a slight well in the center of each portion and break an egg into it. Pierce the yoke with a small, sharp knife. Fold the mustard, cream and seasonings together and spoon over the eggs. Sprinkle with paprika and cook for 4 minutes on HIGH. Leave to stand for 1 minute before serving.

Cheese Custards

PREPARATION TIME: 10 minutes

MICROWAVE COOKING TIME: 30 minutes

SERVES: 4 people

¼ cup butter or margarine
¼ cup flour
½ tsp dry mustard
1 cup light cream
½ cup heavy cream
¾ cup Cheddar cheese, grated
4 eggs, separated
¼ tsp cream of tartar
Cayenne pepper
Salt
Pepper
Paprika

Melt the butter for 1 minute on HIGH. Add the flour, mustard, Cayenne pepper and seasoning to the bowl and stir in the cream gradually.

Facing page: Eggs Florentine (top) and Cheese Custards (bottom).

Cook for 6 minutes on HIGH, stirring frequently until thickened. Add ½ cup of the cheese and stir to melt. Beat in the egg yolks and beat egg whites with the cream of tartar until stiff but not dry. Fold whites into cheese mixture and pour into 8 small custard cups. Arrange in a larger dish filled with hot water. Cook for 3 minutes on HIGH. Turn the cups and cook for 1½ minutes more on HIGH. If the mixture appears set and begins to pull away from the sides of the cups, turn the custards out. If not, cook for 30 seconds longer on HIGH. Put the custards into individual baking dishes, allowing 2 per person. Pour over the heavy cream and sprinkle on the remaining cheese and paprika. Bake for 2 minutes on HIGH and serve immediately.

Sour Cream and Caviar Cheesecake

PREPARATION TIME: 10 minutes

MICROWAVE COOKING TIME: 15 minutes

SERVES: 4 people

1 cup Cheddar cheese crackers
¼ cup butter
2 tbsps Parmesan cheese
8oz package cream cheese
1 cup Gruyère cheese, grated
¼ cup milk
2 eggs
½ cup sour cream
⅓ cup chives, chopped
1 jar red salmon caviar
1 jar black lumpfish caviar

Crush the crackers in a food processor and melt the butter for 1 minute on HIGH. Add half the Parmesan cheese and all the butter to the crumbs in the processor and work until well mixed. Mix cream cheese, Gruyère and remaining Parmesan together. Beat in eggs and sour cream, reserving 2 tbsps for the top, and stir in the chives. Add seasoning. Line the base of a 6" microwave cake pan with wax paper

and pour in the cheesecake mixture. Bake for 5 minutes on HIGH until lightly set. Sprinkle on the crumbs and press down gently. Bake for another 10 minutes on MEDIUM. Leave to cool at room temperature, then chill for 1 hour. Invert onto a serving dish, spread with remaining sour cream and decorate the top with caviar. Cut into wedges to serve.

Eggplant Caviar

PREPARATION TIME: 30 minutes

MICROWAVE COOKING TIME: 13 minutes

SERVES: 4 people

This page: Sour Cream and Caviar Cheesecake.
Facing page: Baked Eggs with Mushrooms and Mustard Cream (top) and Eggplant Caviar (bottom).

1 large or 2 small eggplants
1 clove garlic, crushed
4 tbsps olive oil
Juice of half a lemon
2 tsps chopped fresh coriander
1 tbsp chopped parsley
1 tsp cumin seeds
1 cap pimento, finely chopped
Cayenne pepper
Salt
Pepper
Pitta bread

Dice the eggplant, then spread out on paper towels, sprinkle with salt

and leave for 30 minutes to draw out any bitterness. Rinse and dry well. Put into a large bowl with 4 tbsps water, cover with pierced plastic wrap and cook for 10 minutes on HIGH, stirring 2-3 times. Drain and leave to cool. Put cumin seeds on a plate and roast, uncovered, for 3 minutes on HIGH, stirring occasionally. Put the eggplant into a food processor with the garlic, and blend until smooth, adding olive oil slowly through the feed tube. Add lemon juice, seasoning, Cayenne pepper and cumin seeds, and process once. Add herbs and pimento and process again once. Adjust seasoning and chill. Wrap pitta bread in paper towels and warm for 30 seconds on HIGH. Cut into triangles and serve with the eggplant caviar.

Pasta Shells Stuffed with Garlic Cheese

PREPARATION TIME: 10 minutes

MICROWAVE COOKING TIME: 20 minutes

SERVES: 4 people

8 large pasta shells (conchiglie)
2 pkts garlic and herb soft cheese
4 tomatoes, skinned and seeded
3 tbsps butter or margarine
3 tbsps flour
2 cups milk
½ cup Gruyère cheese, grated
1 tbsp chopped parsley
Nutmeg
Salt and pepper

Heat 4 cups water on HIGH for 5 minutes, until boiling. Put in the tomatoes for 5 seconds, then remove them and put immediately into cold water. Peel, seed and shred them thinly, then set aside. Put the pasta into the water with 1 tbsp oil and cook for 9 minutes, or until just tender. Leave to stand for 5 minutes. Drain and dry. Beat cheese to soften. Put into a pastry bag fitted with a wide, plain tube. Fill each shell with the garlic cheese and put into 4 baking dishes. Melt butter in a

small bowl for 1 minute on HIGH and stir in the flour. Stir in the milk and seasoning, and blend well. Heat for 2-3 minutes on HIGH, stirring frequently. Add half of the cheese, stirring to melt. Stir in the tomato strips and coat over the pasta shells in the baking dishes. Sprinkle on the remaining cheese. Heat for 2 minutes on HIGH. Serve immediately.

This page: Pasta Shells Stuffed with Garlic Cheese.
Facing page: Stuffed Vine Leaves Bordelaise.

VEGETABLE APPETIZERS

Stuffed Vine Leaves Bordelaise

PREPARATION TIME: 15 minutes

MICROWAVE COOKING TIME:
53 minutes and 5 minutes standing time

SERVES: 4 people

12 packaged vine leaves
¼ cup butter
1 shallot, finely chopped
1 cup mushrooms, finely chopped
½ cup rice
4 strips bacon (rind and bones removed)
2 tbsps dried blackcurrants
1 tbsp parsley
Salt and pepper

SAUCE
1 shallot, finely chopped
1½ tbsps flour
1½ tbsps butter or margarine
¾ cup red wine
¾ cup beef stock
1 clove garlic, crushed
1 tsp tomato paste

To make stuffed vine leaves: Put
3 cups water and the rice into a large,
deep bowl. Cover with pierced
plastic wrap and cook for 14 minutes
on HIGH. Add the blackcurrants and
leave to stand for 5 minutes. Drain
and cool. Put the butter and shallot
for the filling into a bowl, cover and
cook for 1 minute on HIGH. Add
mushrooms and cook for 6 minutes
on HIGH, stirring occasionally. Heat
a browning dish for 3-4 minutes on
HIGH and cook the bacon for
1 minute each side until crisp.
Crumble the bacon and add to the
mushrooms with the rice, parsley and
seasoning. Mix well and put a mound

of filling on each leaf. Roll up, tucking in the sides to enclose the filling completely.

To make the sauce: Heat a browning dish for 3-4 minutes on HIGH. Melt the butter and add shallot and flour. Cook until golden brown, or about 4 minutes on HIGH. Put into a bowl and stir in the stock, wine, garlic, tomato paste and seasoning. Cook, covered with pierced plastic wrap, for 4 minutes on HIGH. Put vine leaves into a casserole, seamed side down, and pour over the sauce. Cover and cook for 5 minutes on HIGH. Serve immediately.

Celeriac Moutarde

PREPARATION TIME: 10 minutes

MICROWAVE COOKING TIME:
15 minutes

SERVES: 4 people

1 large root celeriac, peeled
2 tbsps white wine

MUSTARD CREAM SAUCE
3 tbsps butter
3 tbsps flour
2 cups milk
4 tbsps Dijon mustard
1 tbsp celery seed
Salt and pepper
4 tbsps dry breadcrumbs
2 tbsps butter or margarine

Cut celeriac into ¼″ slices, then into sticks about 1″ long. Put into a bowl with the wine, and toss to mix. Cover with pierced plastic wrap and cook for 4 minutes on HIGH. Melt butter in a small deep bowl for 1 minute on HIGH. Add flour and cook for 1 minute more on HIGH. Stir in milk, mustard, celery seed and strained cooking liquid from the celeriac. Season and cook for 3 minutes on HIGH, stirring occasionally, until sauce has thickened. Put celeriac into 4 baking dishes and coat with the sauce. Heat a browning tray for 3-4 minutes on HIGH. Put in 2 tbsps butter and dry breadcrumbs, and cook until golden brown. Sprinkle the breadcrumbs on

top of the celeriac and heat through for 2 minutes on HIGH. If using a microwave convection oven, melt the butter for 1 minute, then stir in the breadcrumbs. Sprinkle on top of the celeriac and cook on the Combination setting for 5 minutes. Serve immediately.

Vinaigrette de Jardin

PREPARATION TIME: 15 minutes

MICROWAVE COOKING TIME:
7 minutes

SERVES: 4 people

SALAD AND DRESSING
4oz pea pods
2 zucchini, sliced in rounds
4 green onions, sliced
4oz broccoli flowerets
1 small head cauliflower, cut into
*   flowerets*
2 carrots, sliced in rounds
4 tomatoes, seeded and sliced into strips
1 banana pepper, sliced into strips
6 tbsps olive oil
2 tbsps white wine vinegar
1 tbsp Dijon mustard
1 tbsp herbs (eg chives, chervil, parsley,
*   basil), chopped*
Salt and pepper

GARLIC BREAD
1 small loaf French bread
⅓ cup butter
1 clove garlic, crushed
2 tbsps poppy seeds

Cook each of the vegetables on HIGH in 2 tbsps water, in a shallow, covered dish: pea pods, 2 minutes; zucchini, 3 minutes; broccoli, 3 minutes; cauliflower, 5 minutes; carrots, 5 minutes. When cooked, rinse immediately in cold water to stop the cooking. Drain and leave to dry. Boil 2 cups water for 3-4 minutes on HIGH and put tomatoes in for 5 seconds. Then put them immediately into cold water, peel and quarter them, remove the seeds, and cut them into thin shreds. Cut pepper into thin slices and add, with the tomato, to the drained vegetables. Mix oil, vinegar, Dijon

mustard, herbs and seasoning, and pour over the mixed vegetables. Toss lightly and leave to marinate. Serve with the garlic bread.

To make garlic bread: Cut the loaf into thick slices without cutting through the base. Mix the butter, garlic and poppy seed, and spread between each slice. Wrap loosely in paper towels and heat for 1½ minutes on HIGH or until butter has melted. Serve with the vegetable salad.

Cheese and Herb Soufflés

PREPARATION TIME: 8 minutes

MICROWAVE COOKING TIME:
8-10 minutes

SERVES: 4 people

1 cup Colby and Parmesan cheese, grated
*   and mixed*
¼ cup butter or margarine
¼ cup flour
1½ cups milk
6 eggs, separated
1 tsp cream of tartar
¼ tsp parsley, chopped
¼ tsp chives, chopped
¼ tsp thyme, chopped
¼ tsp sage, chopped
Dry mustard
Paprika
Salt
Pepper

Put the butter in a bowl and heat for 1 minute on HIGH. Stir in the flour, Cayenne pepper and mustard, and blend in the milk. Cook for 4 minutes on HIGH, stirring frequently until thickened. Add cheese, herbs and seasoning. Beat egg yolks into the cheese mixture one at a time. Beat egg whites until stiff but not dry with the cream of tartar, and fold in carefully. Divide the mixture between 4 small soufflé dishes. Cook on MEDIUM for 4-6 minutes. The

Facing page: Cheese and Herb Soufflés (top) and Celeriac Moutarde (bottom).

inside the shell. Sprinkle the scooped-out flesh and shell with lemon juice. Heat a browning tray for 3 minutes on HIGH, brown bacon for 1 minute each side, crumble it and set aside. Brown shallot, pepper and mushrooms lightly for 1 minute in the bacon fat and combine with avocado flesh. Melt 1 tbsp butter for 1 minute on HIGH. Stir in flour and milk. Heat for 2 minutes until thickened, stirring frequently. Add all ingredients save cheese and breadcrumbs. Stir in seasoning and a few drops of tabasco. Pile into the shells. Sprinkle on the cheese and breadcrumbs. Melt remaining butter for 1 minute. Sprinkle over the avocado and cook for 3 minutes in a microwave-convection oven on Combination setting, or brown under a broiler. Serve immediately.

Stuffed Mushrooms

PREPARATION TIME: 8 minutes

MICROWAVE COOKING TIME: 6-8 minutes

SERVES: 4 people

12-16 large mushrooms
4oz ham, finely chopped
½ cup fresh white breadcrumbs
⅓ cup finely chopped walnuts
1 egg, beaten
1 bunch snipped chives
1 tbsp chopped parsley
1 tbsp Dijon mustard
Dry breadcrumbs
3 tbsps butter, melted
Salt
Pepper

Clean the mushrooms, trimming stalks, and chop them finely. Mix with the ham, breadcrumbs, walnuts, herbs, mustard and seasoning. Beat in the egg gradually to bind. Pile on top of the mushrooms, then put on a

COMBINATION setting of a microwave convection oven may be used for 6 minutes. Sprinkle with paprika and serve immediately.

Stuffed Avocados

PREPARATION TIME: 10 minutes

MICROWAVE COOKING TIME: 10 minutes

SERVES: 4 people

2 large avocados
4 slices smoked bacon

1 cup peeled cooked shrimp, shelled
1 shallot, finely chopped
½ cup mushrooms, roughly chopped
1 green pepper, roughly chopped
1½ tbsps butter or margarine
2 tbsps flour
½ cup milk
2 tomatoes, skinned, seeded and chopped
⅓ cup Parmesan cheese
4 tbsps dry breadcrumbs
1 tbsp parsley
1 tsp marjoram
Tabasco
Salt and pepper
Lemon juice

Halve avocados and remove stones. Scoop out flesh, leaving ¼″ lining

**This page: Vinaigrette de Jardin.
Facing page: Stuffed Avocados (top)
and Stuffed Mushrooms (bottom).**

plate and cook for 5 minutes on HIGH. Sprinkle over the dry crumbs and melted butter. Cook for a further 1 minute on HIGH. Brown under a broiler, or cook for 2 minutes in a microwave-convection oven on the Combination setting.

Spinach Gnocchi in Ricotta Sauce

PREPARATION TIME: 10 minutes

MICROWAVE COOKING TIME: 8 minutes

SERVES: 4 people

GNOCCHI
*1lb fresh spinach, washed and stems
   removed
1 cup Gruyère cheese, grated
4 slices white bread, crusts removed
2 tbsps finely chopped walnuts
1 tbsp finely chopped shallot
1 clove garlic, crushed
1 egg, beaten
Nutmeg
Salt
Pepper*

RICOTTA SAUCE
*8oz Ricotta cheese
3 tbsps grated Parmesan cheese
½ tsp basil, fresh or dried
¼ tsp chopped parsley
⅔ cup cream or milk
Salt
Pepper
Paprika*

To prepare gnocchi: Put spinach into a roasting bag and tie loosely. Stand upright and cook for 3 minutes on HIGH. (Spinach may also be cooked in a bowl covered with pierced plastic wrap.) Drain the spinach well, and chop finely. Make crumbs from the bread slices using a food processor or liquidizer. Add to the spinach along with the Gruyère, walnuts, nutmeg, seasoning and egg. Beat well and shape into 2″ balls or ovals. Put gnocchi onto a plate, cover loosely with plastic wrap, and cook for 2 minutes on HIGH. Set aside and keep warm.
To make sauce: Mix Ricotta cheese with the other ingredients except the

paprika and heat for 1 minute on HIGH.
Divide the gnocchi between 4 gratin dishes and coat with the sauce. Sprinkle with paprika and heat for 2 minutes on HIGH. Serve at once.

Salade Alsacienne

PREPARATION TIME: 10 minutes

MICROWAVE COOKING TIME: 13-15 minutes

SERVES: 4 people

*¾ lb new potatoes, scrubbed but not
   peeled (or regular potatoes, peeled)
Half head (white) cabbage, shredded
2 tbsps white wine
8oz smoked sausage or kielbasa*

*2 tsps caraway seeds
½ cup blue cheese, crumbled
½ cup sour cream
1 tbsp white wine vinegar
3 tbsps vegetable oil
¼ tsp French mustard
Salt
Pepper*

GARNISH
4 green onions, chopped

Prick potato skins with a fork, if using new potatoes. Put potatoes into a casserole dish with 2 tbsps water, cover, and cook for 10-12 minutes on HIGH until tender. Drain and cut into large pieces. Mix vinegar, oil, mustard and seasoning together and pour over the potatoes. Stir and leave to stand. Prick sausage skin and cook, covered, for 1 minute on

HIGH. Slice thinly and add to the potatoes. Put cabbage into a casserole dish with the wine, caraway seeds and seasoning. Cover and cook for 2 minutes on HIGH. Add to the potatoes and sausages. Add blue cheese and sour cream, and mix carefully, so that the potatoes do not break up. Garnish with chopped green onions.

Fondue Pots

PREPARATION TIME: 10 minutes

MICROWAVE COOKING TIME:
10-13 minutes

SERVES: 4 people

FONDUE
2 cups Gruyère cheese, grated

Facing page: Spinach Gnocchi in Ricotta Sauce.
This page: Salade Alsacienne (left) and Fondue Pots (right).

2 cups Swiss cheese, grated
1½ cups dry white wine
1½ tbsps cornstarch
1½ tbsps kirsch
1 clove garlic, crushed
Dry mustard
Nutmeg
Salt and Pepper

BREADSTICKS
12 slices white bread, crusts removed
1 stick butter
4 tbsps herbs (eg thyme, parsley, sage)
  chopped

To make breadsticks: Roll out each slice of bread to flatten. Mix herbs and half the butter together and spread over the bread. Roll up from each end to the middle and cut in half to form 2 breadsticks. Melt remaining butter for 1 minute on HIGH and brush over breadsticks. Put bread onto a plate and cook for 5 minutes in a microwave convection oven on the Combination setting until pale brown. Keep warm. (Breadsticks may also be baked in a conventional oven for 20 minutes at 400°F, 200°C.
To make fondue: Put garlic, wine, mustard, nutmeg and seasoning into a bowl and cook for 5 minutes on HIGH. Mix cornstarch, kirsch and cheese, and blend well into the wine. Cook for 5-8 minutes on MEDIUM, stirring frequently until thick and

creamy. Heat individual custard cups and pour fondue mixture into each. Serve immediately with the warm breadsticks or raw vegetables.

Garlic Mushrooms

PREPARATION TIME: 5 minutes

MICROWAVE COOKING TIME: 6 minutes

SERVES: 4 people

1½ lbs mushrooms, cleaned and quartered
2 cloves garlic, crushed
¼ cup butter
3 tbsps white wine
8 slices French bread, ½" thick
¼ tsp fresh thyme, chopped
¼ tsp fresh sage, chopped
¼ tsp parsley, chopped
Salt
Pepper

GARNISH
2 tbsps chopped chives

Heat butter for 1 minute on HIGH or until melted in a large bowl. Add garlic and cook for 2 minutes on HIGH. Mix in the herbs, wine, seasoning and mushrooms. Pour into a shallow casserole, and cook, uncovered, for 3 minutes on HIGH. Heat the bread for 1 minute on HIGH. Garnish with snipped chives and serve on French bread.

Leek and Ham Tarts Bernaise

PREPARATION TIME: 10 minutes

MICROWAVE COOKING TIME: 19½ minutes

SERVES: 4 people

TART SHELLS AND FILLING
8-12 slices wholewheat bread, crusts removed
1-2 leeks, washed and sliced
¼ cup butter or margarine
4oz ham, chopped
2½ tbsps flour
3 tbsps white wine
2 tbsps milk or chicken stock

BERNAISE SAUCE
½ cup butter
3 egg yolks
1 tbsp white wine or tarragon vinegar
1 bay leaf

This page: Leek and Ham Tarts Bernaise (top) and Garlic Mushrooms (bottom). Facing page: Pumpkin Creams with Dill Sauce.

1 blade mace
1 tsp chopped tarragon
1 tsp chopped parsley
Salt
Pepper
Lemon juice

To prepare shells and filling: Roll out the slices of bread to flatten slightly. Cut out large rounds with a pastry cutter. Melt half the butter for 1 minute on HIGH and brush over both sides of the bread rounds. Mold into custard cups or a muffin pan and cook for 3 minutes on HIGH until crisp. Melt the remaining butter in a bowl for 1 minute on HIGH and add the leek slices. Cover with pierced plastic wrap and cook for 8 minutes on HIGH, stirring occasionally. Add ham and flour, and cook for 1 minute on HIGH. Stir in the wine, milk or stock, and seasoning. Cook, uncovered, for 2 minutes or until sauce thickens. Set aside.

To make Bernaise sauce: Have a bowl of ice water ready. Melt the butter in a deep bowl on HIGH for 1 minute. Put vinegar, bay leaf and mace in a small dish and heat through for 30 seconds on HIGH. Beat egg yolks and seasoning together and strain on the vinegar. Pour into the bowl with the butter and stir well. Cook for 15 seconds on HIGH, remove bowl and stir sauce. Repeat until sauce has thickened – which takes about 2 minutes. Put bowl immediately into ice water to stop the cooking. Remove the prepared shells from the custard cups and put onto a plate. Fill with the ham and leek mixture and coat each with a spoonful of the Bernaise sauce. Broil until lightly browned. Serve immediately.

Pumpkin Creams with Dill Sauce

PREPARATION TIME: 15 minutes

MICROWAVE COOKING TIME: 27 minutes

SERVES: 4 people

2½ cups mashed pumpkin
1 shallot, finely chopped
½ cup Ricotta cheese
½ cup Parmesan cheese, grated
2 eggs
¼ cup sour cream
¼ pint/½ cup heavy cream
1 tbsp parsley
2 bunches dill
Crushed garlic (optional)
Nutmeg
Salt
Pepper

GARNISH
Whole sprigs of dill

Put the mashed pumpkin into a food processor and add eggs, shallot, cheeses, parsley, nutmeg and seasoning. Process until well blended. Divide between 4 custard cups and cook for 6 minutes on HIGH until set. Leave to stand for 5 minutes before turning out. Heat the cream for 2 minutes on HIGH in a small bowl with the crushed garlic, if desired. Chop the dill finely, reserving 4 whole sprigs. Stir the chopped dill into the hot cream with the sour cream. Turn out the pumpkin creams and serve immediately with the dill sauce. Garnish with whole sprigs of dill.

Microwave
FISH AND SEAFOOD

Microwave
FISH AND SEAFOOD

A microwave oven is a fish kettle par excellence. In fact, many people prefer microwaved fish and shellfish to that cooked by conventional methods. Microwave cooking retains the natural moisture of food, something that is important in well-prepared fish. Fish and shellfish both require quick cooking, so the microwave oven really comes into its own.

Poaching is the fish cooking method that the microwave oven performs best. Use a shallow dish or a cooking bag and add white wine or water and lemon juice with peppercorns, onion slices and aromatic herbs, spices and vegetables. In a microwave oven all the flavor cooks into the fish, and low evaporation means plenty of liquid to make a good sauce.

A whole fish, such as a salmon or sea bass, can easily be poached providing the fish is not too large to allow it to turn freely. It is best to choose a fish no heavier than 2lbs in weight. Use a large cooking bag, securely tied, or a large, shallow dish covered with plastic wrap. Wrap the head and tail with foil to keep them from over-cooking and falling off. Cook 7-10 minutes on HIGH, or slightly longer on MEDIUM. The fish will continue to cook as it stands, so keep it covered while preparing sauces to accompany the fish. If you are not sure whether the fish is cooked, check close to the bone in an inconspicuous place. The flesh should be firm and opaque.

Even frying is possible, after a fashion, in a microwave oven. Dredge fish fillets or small whole fish with seasoned flour and preheat a browning dish. Fry in butter briefly on both sides to get a light brown, slightly crisp coating; a surprising result from a microwave oven.

Shellfish need careful cooking in a microwave oven or they toughen. Cook them no longer than 3 minutes on the highest setting or add them to a hot sauce at the last minute.

In the classification of fish there are four main categories: Flat fish, such as sole; Round fish, such as trout; Shellfish and Smoked fish, more popular in England and Europe than in the United States. Flat fish and round fish can be subdivided into oily fish, such as trout or salmon, and whitefish, such as sole or cod. But whatever fish you choose, your microwave oven will help you cook it to perfection.

Microwave
FISH AND SEAFOOD

FISH SOUPS

Spicy Clam Chowder

PREPARATION TIME: 15 minutes

MICROWAVE COOKING TIME:
12 minutes

SERVES: 4 people

2 tbsps butter or margarine
1 green pepper, diced
1 onion, finely sliced
1½ cups potatoes, diced
1lb can plum tomatoes
1lb can clams, liquid reserved
1 small chili pepper, finely chopped
Pinch cinnamon
Pinch nutmeg
Salt and pepper

Melt the butter in a large bowl for **30 seconds** on HIGH. Add the green **pepper**, onion, potatoes and the **liquid** from the clams. Cover the **bowl** loosely and cook for 10 minutes **on** HIGH or until the potatoes are **tender.** Add the plum tomatoes, **clams,** chili pepper, cinnamon, **nutmeg,** and salt and pepper. Cook, **uncovered,** for 2 minutes more on HIGH. Serve immediately.

Mariners' Chowder

PREPARATION TIME: 15 minutes

MICROWAVE COOKING TIME:
12 minutes

SERVES: 4 people

8oz whitefish
½ pint clams
½ pint mussels
8oz raw shrimp, peeled
3 tbsps butter
3 tbsps flour
1 onion, finely chopped

4 cups milk
¼ cup white wine
½ cup cream
1 bay leaf
2 tbsps chopped parsley
Salt and pepper

This page: Mariners' Chowder (top) and Spicy Clam Chowder (bottom). Facing page: Cheese and Clam Chowder (top) and Curried Prawn Soup (bottom).

Scrub the clams and mussels well. Discard any with broken or open shells. Put into a bowl with 2 tbsps water and cover loosely. Cook for 4 minutes on HIGH until the shells open. Discard any shellfish that do not open, remove the others from their opened shells, and set them aside. Combine the fish, shrimp and wine in a casserole and cook for 4 minutes, covered, on HIGH. Melt the butter for 30 seconds on HIGH in a large bowl. Add the onion and cook for 2 minutes on HIGH. Add the flour, milk, wine from the fish, salt and pepper. Cook for 5 minutes on HIGH, stirring frequently. Add the fish, shellfish, cream and parsley. Heat through for 1 minute on HIGH. Remove the bay leaf and serve.

Cheese and Clam Chowder

PREPARATION TIME: 15 minutes

MICROWAVE COOKING TIME: 13 minutes

SERVES: 4 people

2 1lb cans clams, liquid reserved
2 cups diced potatoes
1 onion, finely chopped
2 sticks celery, chopped
1 green pepper, chopped
3¼ cups milk
2 tbsps butter or margarine
2 tbsps flour
½ tsp dry mustard
Light cream as necessary
1 bay leaf
¼ tsp thyme
Dash Worcestershire sauce
2 tbsps chopped parsley
1 cup grated Colby cheese
Salt and pepper

Put the butter, onion, celery and pepper into a large bowl. Cover loosely and cook on HIGH for 2 minutes. Stir in the flour, mustard, milk and clam liquid. Blend well and add potatoes, thyme, salt and pepper. Put in the bay leaf, and cook on HIGH for 10 minutes, stirring occasionally. Remove the bay leaf and add the clams, cheese and

Worcestershire sauce. Heat for 2 minutes on MEDIUM to melt the cheese. Add light cream to thin the soup if it is too thick. Add the parsley to the soup and serve immediately.

Curried Prawn Soup

PREPARATION TIME: 10 minutes

MICROWAVE COOKING TIME: 8 minutes

SERVES: 4 people

3 tbsps butter or margarine
3 tbsps flour
2 tbsps curry powder
1 shallot, finely chopped
1 tsp mango chutney
1 tbsp lime juice
3 cups milk
1 cup fish or chicken stock
8oz cooked shrimp
Salt and pepper

GARNISH
Fresh coriander leaves or parsley
Plain yogurt

Melt the butter for 30 seconds on HIGH in a large bowl. Add the curry powder and the shallot and cook for 1 minute on HIGH. Stir in the flour, milk, stock, chutney, lime juice, salt and pepper. Cook for 5-6 minutes on HIGH until thickened. Add the shrimp and cook for 30 seconds on HIGH. Serve garnished with coriander and yogurt.

Lobster Bisque

PREPARATION TIME: 15 minutes

MICROWAVE COOKING TIME: 9 minutes

SERVES: 4 people

1 large lobster tail, uncooked
4 tbsps butter or margarine
4 tbsps flour
1 shallot, finely chopped
2 cups milk
1 cup cream
1 cup fish or chicken stock
1 bay leaf
Celery salt

Pepper
Cayenne pepper
4 tbsps dry sherry

Remove the lobster tail meat from the shell. Break the shell into small pieces. Melt the butter in a small bowl for 30 seconds on HIGH. Put in the shell pieces and the shallot and cook for 1 minute on HIGH or until the shell turns red. Strain the butter into a large, clean bowl. Cut the lobster meat into small pieces and add to the butter. Cook for 1-2 minutes on HIGH. Remove the meat and set it aside. Stir the flour, celery salt and Cayenne pepper into the butter. Add the bay leaf, milk and stock. Cook for 5-6 minutes on HIGH to thicken. Add the sherry and the lobster meat and heat through for 1 minute on HIGH. Remove the bay leaf and swirl the cream through the soup. Serve immediately.

Smoked Salmon Cream Soup

PREPARATION TIME: 15 minutes

MICROWAVE COOKING TIME: 7-8 minutes

SERVES: 4 people

8oz whitefish, cut into 1" chunks
8oz smoked salmon, cut into 1" pieces
3 tbsps butter or margarine
2 tbsps flour
½ cup white wine
3 cups milk
½ cup light cream
Pepper

GARNISH
Sour cream
Chopped chives

Cook the whitefish and wine for 2 minutes on HIGH. Melt the butter for 30 seconds on HIGH. Stir in the flour and milk, the whitefish and its

Facing page: Smoked Salmon Cream Soup (top) and Lobster Bisque (bottom).

cooking liquid. Cook for 5-6 minutes, stirring frequently, until thick. Add pepper, smoked salmon and cream. Work in a food processor until smooth. Re-heat for 1 minute on HIGH and add salt to taste. Garnish each serving with a spoonful of sour cream and a sprinkling of chopped chives.

Creamy Crab Soup

PREPARATION TIME: 15 minutes

MICROWAVE COOKING TIME: 9 minutes

SERVES: 4 people

1lb crabmeat, fresh or frozen
4 tbsps butter or margarine
4 tbsps flour
1 shallot, finely chopped
3 cups milk
½ cup cream
½ cup stock
2 tbsps white wine
Cayenne pepper
Salt and pepper

GARNISH
Chopped chives

Put the butter and shallot into a casserole. Cover and cook for 3 minutes on HIGH, stirring occasionally. Stir in the flour, milk, stock, Cayenne pepper, salt and pepper. Cook for 5 minutes on HIGH, stirring frequently until thickened. Add the crabmeat, cream and wine, and cook for a further 1 minute on HIGH. Serve garnished with chopped chives.

Shrimp and Chinese Mushroom Soup

PREPARATION TIME: 15 minutes

MICROWAVE COOKING TIME: 9 minutes

SERVES: 4 people

4oz fine Chinese egg noodles
8 dried Chinese mushrooms
¾ cup shrimp, cooked and peeled

1 small can water chestnuts, sliced
1 small can bamboo shoots, sliced
Bunch green onions, sliced diagonally
¼ lb peapods, trimmed
1 tbsp light soy sauce
2 tbsps dry sherry
1 tsp sesame seed oil
1 tbsp cornstarch
4 cups chicken or fish stock
Salt and pepper

Put the mushrooms into a small bowl with enough water to cover. Cook on HIGH for 2 minutes and leave to stand. Mix the cornstarch with 2 tbsps stock, and set aside. Combine the remaining stock, peapods and noodles. Cook for 2 minutes on HIGH. Add the cornstarch mixture and all the remaining ingredients, and cook for a further 5 minutes on HIGH. Serve immediately.

Oyster and Watercress Soup

PREPARATION TIME: 15 minutes

MICROWAVE COOKING TIME: 13 minutes

SERVES: 4 people

1lb can oysters
Bunch watercress

3 cups diced potatoes
1½ cups liquid reserved from oysters
1½ cups light cream
1 cup milk
1 shallot, finely chopped
3 tbsps butter or margarine
Nutmeg
Lemon juice
Salt and pepper

Drain the oysters and add water to the liquid, if necessary, to measure 1½ cups. Melt the butter in a large bowl for 30 seconds on HIGH. Add the potatoes, shallot, stock, nutmeg, salt and pepper. Cover loosely and cook on HIGH for 10 minutes, or until the potatoes are tender. Add the milk and half the oysters. Chop the watercress, reserving 4 sprigs for garnish, and add to the bowl. Cook, uncovered, for 2 minutes on HIGH. Put into a food processor and purée until smooth. Return to the bowl and add the remaining oysters, cream and lemon juice. Heat through for 1 minute on HIGH. Serve garnished with the reserved watercress.

This page: Shrimp and Chinese Mushroom Soup. Facing page: Creamy Crab Soup (top) and Oyster and Watercress Soup (bottom).

Microwave
FISH AND SEAFOOD

APPETIZERS AND FIRST COURSES

Florentine Shrimp Tarts

PREPARATION TIME: 20 minutes

MICROWAVE COOKING TIME:
9-10 minutes

SERVES: 4 people

4 slices wholewheat bread
¼ cup butter, melted
1½ lbs fresh spinach, washed (or ¾ lb
    frozen spinach, thawed)
2 tbsps heavy cream
Nutmeg, grated
8 large, unpeeled shrimp, cooked

SAUCE
½ cup butter
3 egg yolks
1 tbsp white wine vinegar
Cayenne pepper
Salt and pepper

GARNISH
Fresh chives or chervil

Cut the crusts off the bread and roll
out each slice very thinly. Cut out a
4″ round from each slice and brush
both sides with melted butter. Mold
into 4 individual pie or flan pans,
preferably false-bottomed. Cook on
HIGH for 2-3 minutes until crisp.
Cook the fresh spinach in a large
bowl, loosely covered, for 2 minutes
on HIGH with 2 tbsps water. Drain
the spinach well, squeezing out all
the moisture whether using fresh or
frozen spinach. Heat 1 tbsp of the
remaining butter in a large bowl for
1 minute on HIGH. Toss in the
spinach, salt, pepper and nutmeg.
Stir in the cream and set aside. Peel
the shrimp carefully and set aside.
Prepare the sauce by melting the
butter in a small, deep bowl for
1 minute on HIGH. Mix the egg
yolks, salt, pepper, Cayenne pepper
and vinegar together, and pour into
the hot butter, beating constantly.
Have a bowl of ice water ready. Cook
the sauce for 30 seconds on HIGH,
then beat well. Repeat until the sauce
thickens, which takes about
2 minutes. Put the sauce bowl
immediately into ice water to stop
the cooking. Remove and set aside.
Put the spinach into the bread shells
and top with the shrimp. Heat
through for 30 seconds on HIGH.
Pour over the sauce and heat for
20 seconds on MEDIUM. Serve
garnished with chives or chervil.

**This page: Florentine Shrimp
Tarts. Facing page: Shrimp Kebabs
Vera Cruz.**

Shrimp Kebabs Vera Cruz

PREPARATION TIME: 15 minutes

MICROWAVE COOKING TIME:
4 minutes

SERVES: 4 people

2 dozen large shrimp, peeled and
    uncooked
4oz chorizo or pepperoni, cut into
    ¼" slices.
1 large green pepper
2 tbsps olive oil
1 ripe avocado
2 tomatoes, peeled, seeded and finely
    chopped
1 clove garlic, crushed
Cayenne pepper
Lemon juice
Salt and pepper

Alternate the shrimp, sausage and
green pepper on wooden skewers.
Brush with oil. Peel and mash the
avocado with the garlic, lemon juice,
Cayenne pepper, and salt and pepper.
Stir in the tomatoes. Cook the
kebabs on a roasting rack for
3 minutes on HIGH, and heat the
sauce for 30 seconds on HIGH.
Serve immediately.

Layered Seafood Terrine

PREPARATION TIME: 20 minutes

MICROWAVE COOKING TIME:
12 minutes, plus 5 minutes standing
time

SERVES: 4 people

12oz whitefish, skinned and cut into
    chunks
3oz crabmeat
3oz lobster
¼ cup cream cheese
2 eggs
1 cup fresh white breadcrumbs
2 tbsps heavy cream
2 tbsps white wine
Chopped parsley
Cayenne pepper
Salt and pepper

BERNAISE SAUCE
3 egg yolks
½ cup butter
1 tbsp chopped mixed herbs
1 tbsp white wine vinegar
Salt and pepper

Combine the eggs, whitefish, cheese,
cream, crumbs, wine, salt and pepper
in a food processor and work until
smooth. Divide the mixture into
thirds. Mix the crab and parsley into
one third, the lobster and Cayenne
pepper into another third, and leave
the remaining third plain. Line a 1lb
glass loaf dish with wax paper, and
layer in the crabmeat, whitefish and
lobster mixtures. Cover well with
plastic wrap and cook for 10 minutes
on MEDIUM. Put a small dish of
water into the oven with the terrine
to keep it moist. Allow to stand for
5 minutes while preparing the sauce.
Beat the egg yolks, vinegar, herbs and
salt and pepper together. Melt the
butter for 1 minute on HIGH in a
small, deep bowl. Beat the egg yolks
into the butter. Have a bowl of ice
water ready. Cook the sauce
ingredients for 15 seconds on HIGH
and then stir well. Repeat the process
until the sauce thickens, which takes
about 2 minutes. Put the sauce
immediately into the bowl of ice
water to stop the cooking. Slice the
terrine and serve with the Bernaise
Sauce.

Crab-Stuffed Pea Pods

PREPARATION TIME: 20 minutes

MICROWAVE COOKING TIME:
2 minutes

SERVES: 4 people

1lb pea pods

FILLING
½ cup crabmeat
1 package garlic-and-herb soft cheese
2 tbsps white wine
1 tbsp milk or light cream

Mix the filling ingredients together,
breaking up the crabmeat well. Wash
the pea pods and carefully split down
one side of each to form pockets.
Blanch for 1 minute on HIGH with 4
tbsps water in a loosely-covered
bowl. Rinse under cold water and dry
well. Carefully open each pocket. Put
the filling into a pastry bag fitted with
a ½" plain tube and pipe the filling
into the pea pods. Arrange on
individual dishes and heat for
30 seconds on HIGH. Serve with
lemon slices or wedges.

Herbed Fish Pâté with Lemon-Orange Hollandaise Sauce

PREPARATION TIME: 20 minutes

MICROWAVE COOKING TIME:
12 minutes, plus 5 minutes standing
time

SERVES: 4 people

1lb whitefish (sole, flounder or cod)
4oz Parma ham, thinly sliced
4 tbsps chopped mixed herbs
1 cup fresh white breadcrumbs
2 eggs
¼ cup low-fat soft cheese, or Ricotta
    cheese
2 tbsps heavy cream
Salt and pepper

HOLLANDAISE SAUCE
3 egg yolks
½ cup butter
1 tbsp lemon juice
1 tbsp orange juice and rind
Salt and pepper

Line a 1lb glass loaf dish with the
slices of Parma ham. Skin and cut the
fish into chunks. Combine all the
remaining pâté ingredients in a food
processor and work until smooth.
Spoon onto the ham and smooth
out. Fold the ends of the ham over
the pâté mixture. Cover well with
plastic wrap and cook on MEDIUM
for 10 minutes, or until just firm. Put
a small dish of water into the
microwave oven with the pâté to
keep it moist. Leave to stand for 5
minutes before turning out and
slicing for serving. To prepare the

**Facing page: Layered Seafood
Terrine (top) and Herbed Fish
Pâté with Lemon-Orange
Hollandaise Sauce.**

½ tsp grated horseradish
1 tbsp snipped chives or chopped green
   onion
1 tbsp sesame seeds
1 tbsp poppy seeds
2 tbsps butter, melted
Salt and pepper

Scrub, but do not peel, the potatoes,
Pierce them several times with a fork.
Mix the cheese, crab, horseradish,
chives and salt and pepper together.
Cook the potatoes with enough
water to barely cover for 4 minutes
on HIGH. When cooked, slice ½" off
the top of each potato and reserve.
Spoon 1 tsp of the crab filling into
the bottom portion of the potatoes.
Top with the lids and put the filled
potatoes onto a plate. Pour some of
the melted butter over each potato
and sprinkle on a mixture of the
sesame and poppy seeds. Heat for 30
seconds on HIGH.

Scallops with Red and Gold Sauces

PREPARATION TIME: 15 minutes

MICROWAVE COOKING TIME:
12 minutes

SERVES: 4 people

2lb fresh scallops
½ lb fresh bean sprouts
1 large, ripe avocado
4 tbsps lime juice
2 sweet red peppers
2 yellow peppers
1 tbsp grated ginger
1 cup water
2 tbsps desiccated coconut
1 tbsp ground almonds
Pinch Cayenne pepper
Salt and pepper

Put scallops in a casserole with 4
tbsps water and 1½ tsps lime juice.
Cover loosely and cook on HIGH

sauce, melt the butter in a small glass
bowl for 1 minute on HIGH. Beat the
egg yolks with the salt, pepper, lemon
juice, orange juice and rind. Mix the
egg yolks with the butter, stirring
constantly. Have a bowl of ice water
ready. Cook the sauce for 15 seconds
on HIGH. Stir well, and repeat the
process until the sauce thickens,
which takes about 2 minutes. Put the
sauce immediately into the bowl of
ice water to stop the cooking. Serve
with the pâté.

Crab-Stuffed New Potatoes

PREPARATION TIME: 15 minutes

MICROWAVE COOKING TIME:
5 minutes

SERVES: 4 people with
3 potatoes each

12 small new potatoes, uniform in size
½ cup cream or low-fat soft cheese
½ cup crabmeat

**This page: Scallops with Red and
Gold Sauces. Facing page: Crab-
Stuffed Pea Pods (top) and Crab-
Stuffed New Potatoes (bottom).**

for 1 minute. Turn the scallops over after 30 seconds. Slice the scallops in half through the middle if they are large. Slice the red and yellow peppers, and put them into separate bowls with half the remaining lime juice and water in each. Cover with pierced plastic wrap and cook each for 5 minutes on HIGH, or until the peppers are very soft. Put the yellow peppers and liquid into a food processor with the ginger and salt and pepper, and work to a smooth purée. Strain if necessary. Work the red peppers in the same way but with the almonds, coconut, Cayenne pepper, and salt and pepper. Peel and slice the avocado thinly. Divide the red sauce evenly on 4 salad plates, covering one side, and put the equivalent gold sauce on the other side of each plate. Arrange the scallops, bean sprouts and avocado slices on top of the sauce to serve.

Oysters Florentine

PREPARATION TIME: 15 minutes

MICROWAVE COOKING TIME:
5 minutes

SERVES: 4 people

2 dozen oysters on the half shell
1lb spinach, washed, or ½ lb frozen
    spinach, thawed
¼ cup heavy cream
Nutmeg
Salt and pepper

SAUCE
3 egg yolks
½ cup butter
1 shallot, finely chopped
2 tbsps lemon juice mixed with Tabasco

GARNISH
Lemon slices

Cook the spinach with 1 tbsp water for 1 minute on HIGH in a large bowl loosely covered. Drain well and season with salt and pepper. Add the nutmeg and cream. Put a spoonful of spinach on top of each oyster. Melt the butter on HIGH for 1 minute with the shallot. Mix the egg yolks with lemon juice and Tabasco, and

pour into the hot butter, beating constantly. Have a bowl of ice water ready. Cook for 30 seconds on HIGH and stir. Repeat the process until the sauce thickens (about 2 minutes). Put the sauce bowl immediately into ice water to stop the cooking. Remove and set aside. Top each oyster with a spoonful of the sauce and heat through for 30 seconds on MEDIUM. Garnish with lemon slices.

NOTE: Oysters can be opened easily in microwave ovens. Clean the shells well, and leave to soak in clean water for 2 hours. Cook for 45 seconds on

HIGH, insert a knife near the hinge and pry open.

Crab-Stuffed Avocados

PREPARATION TIME: 15 minutes

MICROWAVE COOKING TIME:
3 minutes

SERVES: 4 people

This page: Crab-Stuffed Artichoke (top) and Crab-Stuffed Avocados (bottom). Facing page: Oysters Florentine.

2 ripe avocados, cut in half and stones
  removed
½ lb crabmeat
1 green pepper, diced
2 sticks celery, diced
2 green onions, chopped
1 cup prepared mayonnaise
2 tbsps heavy cream
1 tbsp chili sauce
Lemon juice
Salt and pepper
Paprika

Scoop out some of the avocado and chop the flesh roughly. Sprinkle the shell and the chopped flesh with lemon juice. Put the pepper, celery and onion into a small bowl with 2 tbsps water. Cover loosely and cook for 2 minutes on HIGH to soften. Drain away the water and mix in the crab, mayonnaise, cream, chili sauce and salt and pepper. Carefully fold in the reserved avocado flesh. Pile into the avocado shells and sprinkle with paprika. Cook for 1 minute on HIGH, with the narrow end of the avocados pointing to the middle of the dish. Serve immediately.

Stuffed Artichokes

PREPARATION TIME: 20 minutes
MICROWAVE COOKING TIME:
17-19 minutes
SERVES: 4 people

4 globe artichokes
1 bay leaf
1 slice lemon

FILLING
1 cup crabmeat, flaked
3 tbsps butter
3 tbsps flour
2 tbsps Dijon mustard
2 tbsps snipped chives
1 cup milk
½ cup white wine
Salt and pepper

Trim the points of the artichoke leaves and cut the stems so that the artichokes will sit upright. Put them into a large, deep bowl with enough water to barely cover. Add the bay

leaf and lemon slice. Cook for 15 minutes on HIGH. Drain upside-down. Melt the butter in a small, deep bowl for 30 seconds on HIGH. Stir in the flour, milk, wine, salt and pepper. Cook for 2-3 minutes on HIGH. Stir every 30 seconds. Add the mustard and chives. Add the crabmeat and keep warm. Remove the center leaves of the artichoke and carefully lift away the thistle-like choke with a teaspoon. Pour in the crabmeat filling and serve hot.

Lobster Julienne

PREPARATION TIME: 20 minutes
MICROWAVE COOKING TIME:
9-10 minutes
SERVES: 4 people

1 large lobster tail, uncooked
2 tbsps butter or margarine
2 carrots, cut in thin, 2″ strips
1 leek, cut in thin, 2″ strips
2 zucchini, cut into 2″ strips
2 sticks celery, cut in 2″ strips
8 mushrooms, thinly sliced
½ cup white wine
2 tbsps cornstarch
1 tbsp lemon juice
½ cup whole milk yogurt
2 tsps crushed tarragon
Salt and pepper

GARNISH
Chopped parsley

Melt half the butter for 30 seconds on HIGH in a small casserole. Add the carrot and celery and 1 tbsp white wine. Cover and cook for 1 minute on HIGH. Add the zucchini, leek and mushrooms. Cover the casserole and cook for 2 minutes on HIGH and set aside. Heat a browning dish for 3 minutes on HIGH. Remove the lobster tail meat from the shell and cut into ½″ slices. Drop the remaining butter into the browning dish and add the lobster meat. Cook for 1 minute on HIGH. Remove the lobster and mix with the vegetables. Mix the cornstarch with the lemon juice, remaining wine, tarragon, salt and pepper. Cook for 1-2 minutes on

HIGH until thickened. Stir in the yogurt and heat through for 30 seconds on HIGH. Toss the lobster and vegetables with the sauce and serve immediately, garnished with chopped parsley.

Chinese Shrimp Parcels

PREPARATION TIME: 20 minutes
MICROWAVE COOKING TIME:
6-7 minutes
SERVES: 4 people

1 head Chinese cabbage

FILLING
½ cup cashew nuts
4 green onions, chopped
8oz cooked shrimp
½ cup chopped water chestnuts
2 cups bean sprouts
8 dried Chinese mushrooms, soaked
1 red pepper, chopped
1 tbsp cornstarch
2 tbsps white wine

**SWEET AND SOUR MUSTARD
SAUCE**
2 tbsps honey
2 tbsps white wine vinegar
4 tbsps Dijon mustard
1 tbsp cornstarch
½ cup white wine
½ cup water
2 tbsps soy sauce

Separate 8 of the largest and best-looking leaves of the Chinese cabbage. Trim down their spines to make them easier to roll up. Put them into a large bowl with 2 tbsps water. Cover the bowl loosely and cook the leaves for 30 seconds on HIGH to soften slightly. Slice the mushrooms and roughly chop the cashews, then mix with the remaining filling ingredients. Put 2 leaves together, slightly overlapping, and

**Facing page: Lobster Julienne
(top) and South Seas Tidbits
(bottom).**

1lb can pineapple chunks, juice reserved
1 papaya, peeled and cut into 1" chunks
8oz raw shrimp, peeled
8oz scallops

SAUCE
2 tbsps brown sugar
1 tbsp cornstarch
1 tbsp soy sauce
1 tbsp cider vinegar
Large pinch ground ginger
2 tbsps desiccated coconut
2 green onions, chopped

Mix all the sauce ingredients, except the coconut, together with ¾ cup reserved pineapple juice. Cook for 2-3 minutes on HIGH, stirring until thickened. Add the shrimp and scallops and cook for a further 2 minutes on HIGH. Add the pineapple, papaya and coconut and cook for a further 30 seconds on HIGH. Serve as an appetizer.

Steamed Crabmeat Wontons

PREPARATION TIME: 20 minutes

MICROWAVE COOKING TIME: 5 minutes for wontons; 2-3 minutes per sauce

SERVES: 4 people

30 fresh wonton skins

FILLING
12oz cooked crabmeat, fresh or frozen
2 green onions, chopped
6 water chestnuts, chopped
1 tbsp grated fresh ginger root
1 tbsp sherry or white wine
1 tbsp sesame seed oil
1 egg
Salt and pepper

SWEET AND SOUR SAUCE
¾ cup orange juice
2 tbsps soy sauce
1½ tbsps brown sugar
1½ tbsps cider vinegar
2 tsps cornstarch
1½ tbsps ketchup

divide the filling equally among all the leaves. Tuck the sides of the leaves around the filling and roll up. Repeat with the remaining leaves and filling. Put folded edge down in a large casserole with 2 tbsps water. Cover loosely and cook for 3 minutes on HIGH. Set aside while preparing the sauce. Mix all the sauce ingredients together and cook for 2-3 minutes on HIGH. Stir every 30 seconds until the sauce thickens. Set aside.

Above: Chinese Shrimp Parcels (top) and Steamed Crabmeat Wontons (bottom).

South Seas Tidbits

PREPARATION TIME: 15 minutes

MICROWAVE COOKING TIME: 5-6 minutes

SERVES: 4 people

HOT MUSTARD SAUCE
4 tbsps dry mustard
1½ tsps cornstarch
4 tbsps white wine vinegar
½ cup water
¼ cup honey
Salt

Mix all the filling ingredients together. Just before filling each skin, brush both sides with water. Put a rounded tsp of the filling in the center of each skin and pinch the edges together, leaving some of the filling showing. Lightly grease a plate or microwave baking sheet and place the wontons on it. Pour 2 tbsps water over the wontons. Cover them loosely with plastic wrap and cook for 1 minute on HIGH. Lower the setting to LOW and cook for 4 further minutes. Cook in two batches. Brush the wontons several times with water while cooking. Serve with one or both of the sauces. For the sweet and sour sauce, mix the sauce ingredients and cook in a small, deep bowl, uncovered, for 2-3 minutes on HIGH. Stir every 30 seconds until the sauce has thickened. For the hot mustard sauce, mix the mustard and corn-starch together. Beat in the water, vinegar and honey gradually until the sauce is smooth. Add salt and cook, uncovered, in a small, deep bowl for 2-3 minutes on HIGH. Stir every 30 seconds until thickened.

Coriander Mussels

PREPARATION TIME: 15 minutes
MICROWAVE COOKING TIME: 4-6 minutes
SERVES: 4 people

1 quart mussels
2 shallots, finely chopped
1 cup white wine
1 tbsp coriander seeds, crushed
1 tbsp butter
1 tbsp flour
½ cup cream
1 tbsp chopped coriander
1 tbsp chopped parsley
Salt and pepper

Scrub the mussels well and discard

any with broken or open shells. Put the mussels into a large bowl with the shallots, wine and coriander seeds. Cook for 1-2 minutes on HIGH, stirring every 30 seconds, until shells open. Discard any mussels that do not open. Strain the cooking liquid. Melt the butter in a small, deep bowl for 30 seconds on HIGH. Stir in the flour, cream, strained liquid, and salt and pepper. Cook for 2-3 minutes on HIGH until thickened, stirring every 30 seconds. Add the chopped coriander and parsley. Divide the mussels into

Above: Coriander Mussels.

individual bowls and pour over the sauce to serve.

Brandied Shrimp

PREPARATION TIME: 10 minutes
MICROWAVE COOKING TIME: 4 minutes
SERVES: 4 people

2¼ lbs uncooked shrimp, peeled
1½ cups dry breadcrumbs
4 tbsps brandy

½ cup butter
2 shallots, chopped
4 tbsps chopped parsley
Paprika
Salt and pepper

GARNISH
4 lemon wedges

Mix the shallot, salt, pepper, parsley and shrimp together and divide between 4 small baking dishes. Pour brandy over each dish and cook for 30 seconds on HIGH. Heat a browning dish for 5 minutes on HIGH. Drop in the butter and cook for a further 30 seconds on HIGH. Stir in the breadcrumbs and cook for 1-2 minutes to brown. Spoon the breadcrumbs over the shrimp and sprinkle on the paprika. Cook for 1 minute on HIGH or until the shrimp are cooked. Serve with lemon wedges.

Marinated Herring with Tomatoes

PREPARATION TIME: 20 minutes

MICROWAVE COOKING TIME:
5-7 minutes

SERVES: 4 people

8 herring fillets

MARINADE
2 onions, finely chopped
¾ cup red wine vinegar
¼ cup water
¼ cup sugar
6 black peppercorns
2 whole allspice berries

SAUCE
4 tomatoes, peeled, seeded and cut into
    thin strips
2 tbsps tomato paste
2 tbsps snipped chives
⅓ cup vegetable oil
¼ cup reserved marinade
Salt and pepper

Combine the marinade ingredients and cook, uncovered, for 5-7 minutes on HIGH until rapidly boiling. Allow to cool slightly, and pour over the fish fillets. Leave the fish to cool

completely in the marinade. Mix the oil and strained reserved marinade together with the tomato paste, chives, salt and pepper. Pour over the herring and top with the tomato strips to serve.

Smoky Cheese and Shrimp Dip

PREPARATION TIME: 15 minutes

MICROWAVE COOKING TIME:
5 minutes

SERVES: 4 people

1½ cups shredded Cheddar cheese

This page: Smoky Cheese and Shrimp Dip. Facing page: Brandied Shrimp (top) and Marinated Herring with Tomatoes (bottom).

1 cup shredded smoked or smoky cheese
1 tbsp butter
1 shallot, finely chopped
½ cup shrimp, chopped
¾ cup light cream
½ oz flour
Salt and pepper
Raw vegetables

Melt the butter in a small, deep bowl for 30 seconds on HIGH. Add the shallot and cook for 1 minute on HIGH to soften. Toss the cheese and

flour together and add to the bowl with the shallot. Stir in the cream, salt and pepper. Cook for 4 minutes on MEDIUM or until the cheese has melted. Stir the mixture twice while cooking. Serve hot with vegetable crudités for dipping.

Herring in Mustard Dill Sauce

PREPARATION TIME: 20 minutes

MICROWAVE COOKING TIME: 7-9 minutes

SERVES: 4 people

4 herring fillets, cut in chunks

MARINADE
2 onions, finely chopped
¾ cup white wine vinegar
¼ cup water
¼ cup sugar
4 sprigs fresh dill
1 tbsp dried dill
6 black peppercorns
2 whole allspice berries

SAUCE
1 tbsp flour
2 tbsps mustard
1 tbsp chopped dill
¼ cup sour cream

Combine the marinade ingredients and cook, uncovered, for 5-7 minutes until rapidly boiling. Allow to cool slightly, and pour over the fish. Leave the fish to cool in the marinade. Strain the marinade and beat gradually into the flour. Add the mustard and cook for 2 minutes on HIGH, stirring every 30 seconds until thickened. Mix with the chopped dill, and chill. Mix in the sour cream and herring. Serve as an appetizer, or on a bed of lettuce as a first course.

Oysters Romanoff

PREPARATION TIME: 10 minutes

MICROWAVE COOKING TIME: 1 minute

SERVES: 4 people

2 dozen oysters on the half shell
1½ tbsps snipped chives
1 cup sour cream
1 jar red lumpfish or salmon caviar
Lemon juice
Salt and pepper

Put a drop of lemon juice on each oyster. Mix the chives and cream together with salt and pepper. Put a spoonful of the mixture on top of each oyster. Heat through for 1 minute on HIGH on a large plate. Heat in 2 batches if necessary. Put a spoonful of the caviar on each oyster before serving. Serve with lemon wedges and watercress.

This page: **Pickled Mussels (top)** and **Herring in Mustard Dill Sauce (bottom)**. Facing page: **Oysters Romanoff**.

Pickled Mussels

PREPARATION TIME: 15 minutes

MICROWAVE COOKING TIME: 6 minutes

SERVES: 4 people

1 quart mussels
½ cup white wine
½ cup white wine vinegar

2 tbsps sugar
1 tbsp mustard seed
1 cinnamon stick
4 whole allspice berries
4 black peppercorns
4 whole cloves
2 shallots, finely chopped
Salt and pepper

Scrub the mussels well and discard any with broken or open shells. Put the mussels into a large bowl with 2 tbsps water. Cook on HIGH for 45-50 seconds, until the shells open, stirring twice. Discard any mussels that do not open. Combine the remaining ingredients, and cook for 5 minutes on HIGH or until boiling. Allow to cool slightly. Remove the mussels from their shells and combine with the pickling mixture. Leave to cool and then refrigerate. Keep no longer than 2 days.

Salmon Terrine

PREPARATION TIME: 15 minutes

MICROWAVE COOKING TIME:
10 minutes

SERVES: 4 people

1lb salmon
2 eggs
1 cup fresh white breadcrumbs
¼ cup cream cheese
2 tbsps heavy cream
Salt and pepper

DRESSING
1 cucumber, grated
1 cup sour cream
½ cup prepared mayonnaise
2 tbsps chopped dill
Salt and pepper

GARNISH
Red lumpfish caviar

Skin the salmon and cut into chunks. Combine with the remaining terrine ingredients in a food processor and work until smooth. Line the bottom of a 1lb glass loaf dish with waxed paper. Fill with the salmon mixture and smooth out. Cover well with plastic wrap and cook for 10 minutes

on MEDIUM, with a small dish of water to keep it moist. Allow to cool and then chill well. Turn out and cut into slices. Mix all the dressing ingredients together and serve with the terrine. Garnish with the lumpfish caviar.

Smoked Oyster Pâté

PREPARATION TIME: 15 minutes

MICROWAVE COOKING TIME:
10 minutes, plus 5 minutes standing time

SERVES: 4 people

1 can smoked oysters
1lb whitefish
1 cup fresh white breadcrumbs
Butter
2 eggs
¼ cup cream cheese
2 tbsps cream
1 tbsp chopped parsley
2 tsps Worcestershire sauce
1 tbsp lemon juice
Salt and pepper

Roughly chop the smoked oysters. Combine the remaining ingredients in a food processor and work until smooth. Fold in the oysters. Line the bottom of a 1lb glass loaf dish with waxed paper. Spoon in the pâté mixture and smooth out. Cover well with plastic wrap and cook for 10 minutes on MEDIUM. Put a small dish of water into the oven with the pâté to keep it moist. Leave to stand for 5 minutes, then chill before serving. Serve with buttered toast.

Paprika Shrimp

PREPARATION TIME: 15 minutes

MICROWAVE COOKING TIME:
10 minutes

SERVES: 4 people

2lbs raw shrimp, peeled
¼ cup butter or margarine
1 tbsp paprika
2 chopped shallots
1 red pepper, thinly sliced

2 tbsps chopped parsley
1½ cups sour cream
1 tbsp lemon juice
Salt and pepper

TOPPING
¼ cup butter or margarine
½ cup breadcrumbs

Heat a browning dish for 5 minutes on HIGH. Melt the butter for the topping and stir in the breadcrumbs. Cook on HIGH for 2 minutes, stirring every 30 seconds. Set aside. Melt the remaining butter in a large casserole for 30 seconds on HIGH. Add the paprika, shallot and sliced pepper. Cook for 2 minutes on HIGH, stirring frequently. Add the shrimp, lemon juice, salt and pepper, and continue cooking for 2 minutes more on HIGH. Stir in the sour cream. Put into individual serving dishes and sprinkle over the browned crumbs. Cook for 30 seconds on MEDIUM to heat through, and serve with hot rolls or French bread.

Calamares España

PREPARATION TIME: 20 minutes

MICROWAVE COOKING TIME:
8 minutes

SERVES: 4 people

2 medium-sized squid
2 tbsps olive oil
2 tbsps flour flour
1 clove garlic, finely chopped
2 cups canned plum tomatoes
1 chili pepper, finely chopped
Grated rind and juice of 1 orange
½ cup white wine
1 tbsp tomato paste
1 tsp oregano
1 tsp basil
1 bay leaf
Salt and pepper

GARNISH
Fresh coriander leaves

Facing page: Smoked Oyster Pâté (top) and Salmon Terrine (bottom).

This page: Garlic Shrimp and Mushrooms. Facing page: Paprika Shrimp (top) and Calamares España (bottom).

Separate heads of the squid from the tails. Remove the ink-sac and reserve for the sauce if desired. Remove the quill and discard. Cut the tentacles above the eyes, and reserve. Discard the eyes and head. Peel the purplish membrane off the tail portion of the squid. Split the tail in half, lengthwise, and wash it well. Cut the tail into pieces about 2″ wide. Score each section in a lattice pattern at ¼″ intervals. Separate the tentacles. Put the squid, bay leaf and onion into a casserole with hot water. Cover loosely and cook for 1 minute on HIGH. Heat the olive oil for 30 seconds on HIGH in a medium-sized bowl. Add the garlic and onion, and cook for a further 1 minute on HIGH. Stir in the flour. Mix the cooking liquid from the squid with the tomatoes and the other sauce ingredients. If using the ink, break the ink-sac into the sauce ingredients. Cook the sauce, uncovered, for 5 minutes on HIGH. Mix with the squid and serve garnished with fresh coriander leaves.

Garlic Shrimp and Mushrooms

PREPARATION TIME: 10 minutes

MICROWAVE COOKING TIME: 3-4 minutes

SERVES: 4 people

4-8 (depending on size) oyster or wild
*　mushrooms*
½ cup butter
1½ lbs raw shrimp, peeled
1 large clove garlic, chopped
2 tbsps chopped parsley
Salt and pepper
Lemon juice

Leave the mushrooms whole, but remove the stalks. Melt the butter in a shallow casserole for 30 seconds on HIGH. Add the mushrooms, garlic, salt, pepper and lemon juice. Cook for 2 minutes on HIGH. Remove and set aside. Add the shrimp to the casserole and cook on HIGH for 1 minute, stirring several times. Cook for 30 seconds more on HIGH, if required, to cook the shrimp thoroughly. Mix in the parsley and add more seasoning if necessary. Arrange the mushrooms in individual dishes and spoon over the shrimp and any remaining butter in the dish. Serve with French bread.

Microwave FISH AND SEAFOOD

LIGHT DISHES

Codfish Pie

PREPARATION TIME: 15 minutes

MICROWAVE COOKING TIME:
11-12 minutes

SERVES: 4 people

4 cod fillets
2 tbsps lemon juice
2 tbsps water
1 bay leaf

SAUCE
3 tbsps butter
1 shallot, finely chopped
3 tbsps flour
1½ cups milk
2 tbsps chopped parsley
Salt and pepper

TOPPING
2 large potatoes, peeled and very thinly
  sliced
¼ cup grated Colby cheese
Paprika

Put the fillets in a casserole with the
water, lemon juice and bay leaf.
Cover loosely and cook for 2
minutes on HIGH. Melt the butter in
a deep bowl for 30 seconds on
HIGH. Add the shallot and cook for
a further 1 minute on HIGH. Stir in
the flour, milk, liquid from the fish,
salt, pepper and parsley. Cook for
2-3 minutes on HIGH or until thick,
stirring frequently. Pour over the cod.
Slice the potatoes on a mandolin or
with the fine blade of a food
processor. Layer on top of the cod

**This page: Codfish Pie (top) and
Tuna, Pea and Fennel Casserole
(bottom). Facing page: Sea Lion.**

and season with salt and pepper. Cover the dish tightly and cook for 3 minutes on HIGH. Sprinkle on the cheese and paprika and cook, uncovered, for a further 2 minutes on MEDIUM to melt the cheese. Serve immediately.

Crab Lasagne

PREPARATION TIME: 15 minutes

MICROWAVE COOKING TIME: 10 minutes

SERVES: 4 people

8 quick-cooking green lasagne noodles
4 tomatoes, peeled and sliced
8oz crabmeat, flaked
12oz Ricotta cheese
¼ cup grated Parmesan cheese
½ cup milk
1 small clove garlic, minced
Pinch marjoram
Pinch nutmeg
Pinch dry mustard
Salt and pepper

TOPPING
¼ cup seasoned dry breadcrumbs
1 tbsp butter
Paprika

Boil 3½ cups water on HIGH with a pinch of salt. Put in the lasagne and leave for 1 minute. Remove the noodles and rinse under hot water. Dry on paper towels. Mix the remaining ingredients, except the tomatoes, together. If the mixture is very thick, add more milk. Layer up the noodles, tomatoes and crabmeat filling, ending with filling. Melt the butter on HIGH for 30 seconds and stir in the breadcrumbs. Scatter over the top of the lasagne and sprinkle on some paprika. Cook for 3 minutes on HIGH and serve immediately.

Sea Lion

PREPARATION TIME: 20 minutes

MICROWAVE COOKING TIME: 5 minutes

SERVES: 4 people

CRABMEAT BALLS
1lb crabmeat, flaked
3 tbsps sherry
1 tbsp soy sauce
4 water chestnuts, finely chopped
2 green onions, finely chopped
2 tbsps cornstarch
1 egg white, lightly beaten
Pinch ginger
Salt and pepper

ACCOMPANIMENT
1 head Chinese cabbage, shredded
1 tbsp cornstarch
2 tbsps soy sauce
1 tsp sugar
½ cup chicken stock

GARNISH
Sesame seeds

Mix all the ingredients for the crabmeat balls together and shape into 2" balls. Place them in a large casserole with 2 tbsps water. Cover loosely and cook for 2 minutes on MEDIUM. Remove from the casserole and keep warm. Combine the ingredients for the accompaniment and cook in the casserole for 2 minutes on HIGH, or until the cornstarch thickens. Put the crabmeat balls on top of the cabbage and heat through for 1 minute on HIGH. Sprinkle over the sesame seeds to serve.

Monkfish Provençale

PREPARATION TIME: 20 minutes

MICROWAVE COOKING TIME: 19 minutes

SERVES: 4 people

1½ lbs monkfish tails
1 eggplant, cut in ½" chunks
2 zucchini, cut in ½" chunks
1 large red pepper, cut in thin strips
¾ cup sliced mushrooms
1 large onion, thinly sliced
2 tbsps olive oil
1 clove garlic, crushed
½ cup white wine
7oz can plum tomatoes
2 tbsps tomato paste
Pinch dried thyme
1 bay leaf
Salt and pepper
½ cup grated cheese

Cut the eggplant in half lengthwise and lightly score the surface. Sprinkle with salt and leave to stand for 30 minutes. Wash and pat dry before cutting in cubes. Heat the olive oil in a browning dish for 3 minutes on HIGH. Add the vegetables and garlic. Cook for 2 minutes on HIGH. Add the canned tomatoes, tomato paste, thyme, bay leaf, half the wine, salt and pepper. Pour the contents into a casserole dish, cover, and cook for 10 minutes on HIGH. Stir 3 or 4 times during cooking. Cook the fish separately in the remaining wine for 2 minutes on HIGH. Transfer the fish to a baking dish and cover with the Provençale vegetables. Sprinkle on the cheese and cook for 2 minutes on MEDIUM to melt.

Tuna, Pea and Fennel Casserole

PREPARATION TIME: 15 minutes

MICROWAVE COOKING TIME: 10 minutes, plus 10 minutes standing time

SERVES: 4 people

8oz green and whole-wheat noodles
1 cup frozen peas
1 small bulb Florentine fennel chopped
8oz can tuna, drained
3 tbsps butter or margarine
3 tbsps flour
¼ cup white wine
1¼ cups milk
Pinch oregano
1 small clove garlic, minced
Salt and pepper

TOPPING
Paprika
Parmesan cheese

Facing page: Monkfish Provençale (top) and Crab Lasagne (bottom).

Put the noodles in a large bowl with 3½ cups water. Cook for 6 minutes on HIGH and then leave to stand for 10 minutes. Drain, rinse under hot water, then leave to dry. Put the fennel into a casserole with 2 tbsps water. Cover and cook for 1 minute on HIGH. Drain and combine with the noodles, tuna and peas. Melt the butter for 30 seconds on HIGH with the garlic. Stir in the flour, wine, milk, oregano, salt and pepper. Pour over the noodles and mix well. Sprinkle on grated Parmesan cheese and paprika. Heat for 2 minutes on HIGH before serving.

Shrimp Curry

PREPARATION TIME: 10 minutes

MICROWAVE COOKING TIME: 5-7 minutes

SERVES: 4 people

3 tbsps butter or margarine
3 tbsps flour
1 small onion, finely chopped
1 tbsp curry powder
1½ cups milk
¼ cup plain yogurt
1 cap pimento, chopped
8oz shrimp, cooked and peeled

This page: Seafood Stir-fry. Facing page: Shrimp Curry (top) and Pasta alla Vongole (bottom).

Desiccated coconut or chopped green onion

Melt the butter for 30 seconds on HIGH. Add the onion and cook for 30 seconds on HIGH to soften. Stir in the curry powder and cook for 1 minute on HIGH. Add the flour, salt, pepper and milk. Cook for 3-4 minutes, stirring often until thickened. Add the yogurt, pimento and shrimp. Heat for 30 seconds on HIGH and serve on a bed of rice. Sprinkle on the coconut or onion.

Seafood Stir-fry

PREPARATION TIME: 20 minutes

MICROWAVE COOKING TIME: 16 minutes

SERVES: 4 people

4oz thin Chinese egg noodles
2 tbsps vegetable oil
2 large or 4 small scallops
½ cup crabmeat, flaked
½ cup shrimp, cooked and peeled
4 water chestnuts, sliced
4 ears baby corn
2oz peapods
1 small red pepper, sliced
8oz bean sprouts
½ cup chicken or fish stock
2 tbsps soy sauce
1 tbsp cornstarch
1 tbsp sherry
Dash sesame seed oil
Salt and pepper

Boil 3½ cups water with a pinch of salt for 5 minutes on HIGH. Put in the noodles and leave them to stand for 6 minutes. Drain and rinse under hot water and leave to dry. Heat the oil for 5 minutes on HIGH in a browning dish. Cook the scallops for 3 minutes on HIGH, turning several times. Add the pepper, peapods and baby corn. Cook for 1 minute on HIGH. Add the bean sprouts and noodles. Mix the remaining ingredients together and add to the dish with the shrimp and crab. Toss the ingredients together and heat for 2 minutes on HIGH or until the sauce thickens. Serve immediately.

Pasta alla Vongole

PREPARATION TIME: 15 minutes

MICROWAVE COOKING TIME: 9 minutes, plus 10 minutes standing time

SERVES: 4 people

2 cups red, green and plain pasta shells (or other shapes)

3 tomatoes, peeled, seeded and sliced in strips
3 tbsps butter or margarine
½ clove garlic, crushed
2 shallots, finely chopped
3 tbsps flour
½ cup white wine
1 cup milk, or light cream
1 tbsp chopped parsley
Pinch oregano or basil
1½ cups small clams, shelled
Salt and pepper
Grated Parmesan cheese

Put the pasta into 3½ cups hot water with a pinch of salt. Cook for 6 minutes on HIGH. Leave to stand for 10 minutes, then drain and rinse in hot water. Melt the butter in a small, deep bowl for 30 seconds on HIGH. Add the garlic and shallot and cook for 30 seconds on HIGH to soften. Stir in the flour, wine and milk or cream, and add the herbs, salt and pepper. Cook for 2-3 minutes on HIGH, stirring every 30 seconds. Cut the tomatoes into thin strips and add to the hot sauce with the clams. Heat through for a further 30 seconds on HIGH. Toss the sauce and pasta together and serve with grated Parmesan cheese if desired.

Microwave

FISH AND SEAFOOD

MAIN DISHES

Turbot with Almonds and Emerald Sauce

PREPARATION TIME: 20 minutes

**MICROWAVE COOKING TIME:
11 minutes**

SERVES: 4 people

4 turbot fillets
1 slice onion
1 bay leaf
2 black peppercorns
½ cup water

SAUCE
1lb fresh spinach, well washed
1 tbsp fresh chives, chopped
1 tbsp white wine vinegar
Nutmeg
Cayenne pepper
1 tbsp butter
½ cup cream

GARNISH
½ cup sliced almonds

Heat a browning dish for 5 minutes on HIGH and toast the almonds for 1-2 minutes on HIGH, stirring frequently until browned. Put the fish into a casserole with the slice of onion, bay leaf, peppercorn, lemon juice and water. Cover loosely and cook on HIGH for 2 minutes. Set aside. Put the spinach, nutmeg, Cayenne pepper and butter into a large bowl with 1 tbsp water. Cover loosely and cook on HIGH for 2 minutes. Purée in a food processor.

This page: Salmon and Broccoli Fricassée. Facing page: Turbot with Almonds and Emerald Sauce.

Add the cream, chives and some of the fish cooking liquid if the sauce is too thick. Sprinkle the toasted almonds on the fish and serve with the emerald sauce.

Garlic-Braised Tuna Steaks

PREPARATION TIME: 20 minutes

MICROWAVE COOKING TIME: 11-12 minutes

SERVES: 4 people

4 tuna steaks, cut 1" thick
1 clove garlic, peeled and cut in thin slivers
8oz button or pickling onions, peeled
1 tbsp butter
½ cup red wine
½ cup water
1 bay leaf

SAUCE
Cooking liquid from the fish
1 tbsp butter or margarine
1 tbsp flour
1 tbsp tomato paste
½ tsp thyme
1 tbsp chopped parsley
Squeeze lemon juice
Salt and pepper

GARNISH
1lb fresh spinach, washed and thinly shredded
1 tbsp butter

Make small slits in the tuna steaks with a knife and insert a sliver of garlic into each slit. Heat a browning dish for 3 minutes on HIGH. Drop in 1 tbsp butter and the peeled onions. Heat for 1-2 minutes on HIGH, stirring occasionally, until the onions begin to brown. Pour in the water and wine. Transfer the contents of the browning dish to a large casserole. Add the bay leaf and fish to the casserole, cover loosely and cook for 5 minutes on HIGH. Remove the fish and onions from the casserole and keep them warm. Melt 1 tbsp butter in a small, deep bowl for 30 seconds on HIGH. Stir in the flour and cook for 1-2 minutes on HIGH or until the flour is lightly browned. Pour in the cooking liquid from the fish, and add the tomato paste and thyme. Cook for 2-3 minutes on HIGH, stirring occasionally until thickened. Add the parsley, lemon juice, salt and pepper, and set aside with the fish. Melt the remaining butter in a small casserole on HIGH for 30 seconds. Put in the spinach, cover loosely and cook for 1-2 minutes on HIGH. Spread the spinach onto a serving plate and combine the fish and sauce to re-heat for 30 seconds on HIGH. Arrange the fish and onions on top of the bed of spinach and pour over the sauce to serve.

Salmon and Broccoli Fricassee

PREPARATION TIME: 20 minutes

MICROWAVE COOKING TIME: 10-12 minutes

SERVES: 4 people

2lbs salmon fillets or tail pieces
½ cup sliced almonds, toasted
1lb broccoli
½ cup white wine
1 cup sliced mushrooms
1 tbsp butter
1 tbsp flour
1 cup chow mein noodles
1 tsp chopped dill
1 tsp chopped parsley
¾ cup cream
Salt and pepper

Put the fillets into a casserole with enough water to barely cover. Cover the dish loosely and cook for 2 minutes on HIGH. Reserve the cooking liquid, flake the fish and set aside. Put the broccoli into a bowl with 2 tbsps water. Cover loosely and cook for 4 minutes on HIGH. Drain and arrange the broccoli in a casserole with the flaked salmon. Melt the butter in a small bowl for 30 seconds on HIGH. Stir in the flour, cream, fish liquid and sliced mushrooms. Cook for 2-3 minutes on HIGH. Season with salt and pepper. Add dill and parsley and pour over the fish and broccoli. Sprinkle over the almonds and noodles. Heat through for 2 minutes on HIGH before serving.

Halibut à la Normande

PREPARATION TIME: 15 minutes

MICROWAVE COOKING TIME: 5-7 minutes

SERVES: 4 people

4 halibut fillets or steaks
½ cup white wine, dry cider or unsweetened apple juice
¼ cup water
1 tbsp flour
2 tbsps butter or margarine
1 shallot, finely chopped
2 medium-sized apples
¼ cup light cream
1 bay leaf
Salt and pepper
Lemon juice

GARNISH
Chopped parsley

Put the halibut into a casserole with the wine, cider or juice, water and bay leaf. Cover loosely and cook for 2 minutes on HIGH. Set aside and keep warm. In a small bowl melt half the butter. Add the shallot and cook, uncovered, for 1 minute on HIGH, stirring once. Peel and chop one of the apples. Add the shallot, cover the bowl loosely and cook for 2 minutes on HIGH, or until the apple is soft. Stir in the flour, add the cooking liquid from the fish and heat for 2 minutes on HIGH. Stir the sauce twice until thickened. Add the cream and heat for 30 seconds on HIGH. Season with salt, pepper and lemon juice to taste. Heat a browning dish for 5 minutes on HIGH and drop in the remaining butter. Core and slice the second apple, but do not peel it. Brown the slices for 1-2 minutes on HIGH in the butter. Coat the fish with the sauce and garnish with the parsley. Serve surrounded with the apple slices.

Facing page: Garlic-Braised Tuna Steaks.

Monkfish Medallions Piperade

PREPARATION TIME: 15 minutes

MICROWAVE COOKING TIME:
7 minutes, plus 1 minute standing time

SERVES: 4 people

2lbs monkfish tails
½ cup white wine
1½ cups tomato sauce
1 shallot, finely chopped
1 red pepper, sliced
1 green pepper, sliced
1 yellow pepper, sliced
1 clove garlic, finely minced
½ tsp thyme
1 bay leaf
Salt and pepper

GARNISH
Chopped parsley

Cut the monkfish tails into round slices ½″ thick. Put into a casserole with the wine and bay leaf. Cover loosely and cook for 2 minutes on HIGH. Set aside. Combine the shallot, garlic and thyme in a small, deep bowl. Pour on the fish cooking liquid and cook, uncovered, for 3 minutes on HIGH to reduce by half. Add the tomato sauce, peppers, salt and pepper. Cover loosely and cook for 2 minutes on HIGH. Leave to stand for 1 minute and pour over the fish to serve.

Salmon in Chive Sauce

PREPARATION TIME: 15 minutes

MICROWAVE COOKING TIME:
5 minutes

SERVES: 4 people

1 side of salmon (about 1½-2lbs)
2 tbsps butter or margarine
1 cup sour cream
½ cup light cream
1 tsp cornstarch
3 tbsps snipped chives
1 tsp coarsely ground black pepper
Salt

Slice the salmon horizontally into very thin slices. Heat a browning dish for 3 minutes on HIGH. Drop in the butter and heat for 30 seconds on HIGH. Lay in the salmon slices and cook for 30 seconds each side. Cook the fish in several batches. Remove the fish from the dish. Cover and keep warm. Mix the cream, sour cream, and cornstarch together. Pour into the dish and cook for 30 seconds on HIGH. Stir well and repeat the process until the cornstarch has cooked and thickened

This page: Monkfish Medallions Piperade. Facing page: Halibut à la Normande (top) and Salmon in Chive Sauce (bottom).

the sauce. The sauce should not bubble too rapidly, but the cornstarch will help prevent the sour cream from curdling. Stir in the chives, pepper and salt, and pour over the salmon slices. Serve with fine green noodles.

Sole in Lettuce Leaf Parcels

PREPARATION TIME: 20 minutes

MICROWAVE COOKING TIME:
5 minutes

SERVES: 4 people

4 double fillets of sole or flounder
8 large leaves of romaine lettuce
8oz small shrimp
1 finely chopped shallot
½ cup chopped mushrooms
2 tbsps chopped parsley
4 large caps canned pimento
1 cap pimento, chopped
½ cup white wine
½ cup heavy cream
1 cup low-fat soft cheese
Salt and pepper

Combine the shrimp, mushrooms, half the parsley, salt and pepper, and stuff the pimento caps with the mixture. Roll the fish fillets around the pimento and set aside. Put the lettuce leaves into a large casserole with 2 tbsps water. Cover tightly and cook for 30 seconds on HIGH to

This page: Sole in Lettuce Leaf Parcels. Facing page: Mackerel and Mustard (top) and Trout with Hazelnuts (bottom).

soften. Roll the leaves carefully around the stuffed fillets. Put seam-side down into a casserole with the wine and shallot. Cover loosely and cook for 3 minutes on HIGH. Remove the parcels and keep them warm. Cook the wine for a further 2-3 minutes on HIGH to reduce. Stir

in the cream and bring to the boil for 2 minutes on HIGH. Add the cheese, salt, pepper, the remaining parsley and chopped pimento. Serve the sauce with the sole parcels.

Trout with Hazelnuts

PREPARATION TIME: 15 minutes

MICROWAVE COOKING TIME: 12-13 minutes

SERVES: 4 people

4 small rainbow trout, cleaned
4 tbsps butter
¾ cup crushed hazelnuts
4 green onions, shredded
Juice of 1 lemon
Salt and pepper

Heat a browning dish for 5 minutes on HIGH. Put in the hazelnuts and cook for 2-3 minutes on HIGH, stirring often until browned. Set aside. Melt half the butter in the browning dish. Add the trout and cook for 5 minutes per side. If the butter has browned too much, wipe out the dish. Melt the remaining butter and allow to brown lightly. Add the nuts, lemon juice and green onion, and season with salt and pepper. Pour over the fish to serve.

Hangchow Fish

PREPARATION TIME: 15 minutes

MICROWAVE COOKING TIME: 19 minutes

SERVES: 4 people

1 sea or freshwater bass, 2-2¼ lbs in weight, cleaned
½ cup white wine
½ cup water
1 small ginger root, sliced
¼ cup sugar
⅓ cup rice vinegar
2 tbsps soy sauce
1 tbsp cornstarch
1 clove garlic, minced
1 carrot, thinly sliced in rounds
4 water chestnuts, thinly sliced

4 green onions, diagonally sliced
Salt and pepper

Combine the wine, water and a few slices of ginger in a large casserole. Cut 2 or 3 slashes on each side of the fish to help it cook faster, and put it into the casserole. Cover and cook for 25 minutes on MEDIUM. Set the fish aside and keep it warm. Combine the cornstarch, sugar, vinegar, soy sauce, salt, pepper and ½ cup of the fish cooking liquid. Add the garlic and cook on HIGH for 2 minutes, stirring frequently. Add the water chestnuts, carrots and remaining slices of ginger. Cook the sauce for a further 1-2 minutes on HIGH. Add the green onions and pour over the fish to serve.

Mackerel and Mustard

PREPARATION TIME: 15 minutes

MICROWAVE COOKING TIME: 14-16 minutes

SERVES: 4 people

4 small mackerel, cleaned
1 cup white wine
1 tsp whole mustard seed
3 whole peppercorns
1 bay leaf
1 slice onion

SAUCE
1½ tbsps flour
1½ tbsps butter
2 tbsps Dijon or spicy brown mustard
2 tbsps chopped herbs (eg chives, parsley, thyme, dill)
½ cup milk
Salt and pepper

Put the mackerel into one or two casseroles (do not crowd the fish) and cook in two batches if necessary. Pour over the white wine and add the mustard seed, peppercorns, bay leaf and onion. Cover loosely and cook for 12 minutes on HIGH. Set aside and keep warm. Melt the butter in a small, deep bowl for 30 seconds on HIGH. Stir in the flour, milk and strained liquid from the fish. Cook, uncovered, for 2-3 minutes on

HIGH, stirring often until thickened. Add salt, pepper, mustard and herbs. Peel the skin from one side of the mackerel and coat each one with some of the sauce to serve. Serve the remaining sauce separately.

Crab-Stuffed Trout

PREPARATION TIME: 15 minutes

MICROWAVE COOKING TIME: 14 minutes

SERVES: 4 people

4 rainbow trout
4 tbsps butter
Juice of 1 lemon

STUFFING
8oz flaked crabmeat
3 green onions, chopped
2 sticks celery, finely chopped
1 small green pepper, finely chopped
¼ cup black olives, sliced
Fresh breadcrumbs from 4 slices of white bread, crusts removed
2 tbsps chopped parsley
2 tbsps sherry
Salt and pepper

GARNISH
Lemon slices
Chopped chives

Buy the trout fresh or frozen with the bones removed. Mix the stuffing ingredients together and fill the trout. Put the trout into a large casserole and cook, covered, in two batches if necessary. Cook 4 trout together for 12 minutes on HIGH, or 2 trout for 6 minutes on HIGH. Melt the butter for 2 minutes on HIGH and add the lemon juice and pour over the trout before serving. Garnish with lemon slices and chives.

Facing page: Hangchow Fish.

Sole and Asparagus Rolls

PREPARATION TIME: 15 minutes

MICROWAVE COOKING TIME:
7 minutes

SERVES: 4 people

8 fillets of sole
16 asparagus spears
½ cup water
1 tbsp lemon juice

SAUCE
3 egg yolks
2 tbsps lemon juice
½ cup butter
Cayenne pepper
Salt

This page: Sole and Asparagus Rolls. Facing page: Crab-Stuffed Trout.

Cook the asparagus with 2 tbsps water for 2 minutes on HIGH in a covered casserole. Rinse under cold water and drain dry. Divide the asparagus evenly between all the sole fillets and roll the fish around them. Tuck the ends of the fillets under the asparagus evenly between all the sole fillets and roll the fish around them. Tuck the ends of the fillets under the asparagus and place in a casserole.

Pour over the water and 1 tbsp lemon juice. Cover the dish loosely and cook for 2-3 minutes on HIGH. Set aside and keep warm. Melt the butter in a small, deep bowl for 1 minute on HIGH. Beat the egg yolks, lemon juice, salt and Cayenne pepper together. Have a bowl of iced water ready. Pour the yolk mixture into the butter and beat well. Cook for 30 seconds on HIGH and beat well. Repeat the process until the sauce thickens – about 2 minutes. Put the sauce bowl into the iced water to stop the cooking. Pour over the hot fish and asparagus rolls to serve. Sprinkle on paprika if desired.

Sole with Limes and Chili Peppers

PREPARATION TIME: 15 minutes

MICROWAVE COOKING TIME:
6 minutes

SERVES: 4 people

2lbs sole fillets
2 limes
1 green chili pepper, very thinly sliced
1 small bunch chives
2 tbsps butter
Salt and pepper

Melt the butter in a large casserole for 1 minute on HIGH. Put in the fish and cook for 30 seconds each side on HIGH. Remove from the casserole and keep warm. Grate the peel off one of the limes, pare off the white pith and cut the lime into very thin rounds. Squeeze the remaining lime for its juice. Pour the lime juice into the casserole with the butter. Add the chili pepper slices and cook for 30 seconds on HIGH. Add the lime slices, rind and snipped chives. Season and pour over the fish fillets to serve.

Salmon with Tomato Chive Hollandaise

PREPARATION TIME: 15 minutes

MICROWAVE COOKING TIME:
4 minutes

SERVES: 4 people

4 salmon fillets or tail portions
2 tomatoes, peeled, seeded and chopped
2 tbsps snipped chives
3 egg yolks
½ cup butter
1 tsp red wine vinegar
Salt and pepper

Poach the fish fillets in enough water to come half way up the side of the fillets. Cover loosely and cook for 2 minutes on HIGH. Keep warm. Beat the yolks with salt, pepper and chives. Add the vinegar and set aside. Melt the butter for 1 minute on HIGH in a small, deep bowl. Beat the yolks into the butter. Have a bowl of iced water ready. Put the sauce ingredients into the oven and cook for 20 seconds on HIGH. Stir and cook for 20 seconds more. Repeat until the sauce thickens – about 2 minutes. Put the bowl into the iced water to stop the cooking process. Add the tomatoes to the sauce and serve with the salmon fillets.

Sole Bonne Femme

PREPARATION TIME: 20 minutes

MICROWAVE COOKING TIME:
8-11 minutes

SERVES: 4 people

2lbs sole fillets
8oz whole mushrooms, stalks removed
4oz button or pickling onions, peeled
½ cup white wine
1 bay leaf

WHITE SAUCE
2 tbsps butter or margarine
2 tbsps flour
½ cup milk
Salt and pepper

BUTTER SAUCE
2 egg yolks
¼ cup butter
½ tbsp white wine vinegar
Salt and pepper

For the butter sauce, melt ¼ cup butter in a small, deep bowl for 30 seconds on HIGH. Mix the egg yolks, vinegar, salt and pepper together and beat into the butter. Have a bowl of iced water ready. Cook the sauce for 15 seconds on HIGH and beat well. Repeat until the sauce has thickened – about 1 minute. Put immediately into a bowl of iced water to stop the cooking. Set the sauce aside. Tuck the ends of each sole fillet under and place the fish into a large casserole. Add the mushrooms, onions, wine and bay leaf. Cover loosely and cook for 5-6 minutes on HIGH. Arrange the fish, mushrooms and onions in a clean casserole or serving dish and keep warm. In a small bowl melt the remaining butter on HIGH for 30 seconds. Stir in the flour, milk, cooking liquid from the fish, salt and pepper. Cook for 2-3 minutes on HIGH, stirring frequently until thickened. Beat in the butter sauce and pour over the fish to serve.

Cod with Bacon

PREPARATION TIME: 15 minutes

MICROWAVE COOKING TIME:
12 minutes

SERVES: 4 people

4 fillets of cod
¼ cup white wine
8 strips bacon, rind and bones removed
1 green pepper, diced
2 green onions, chopped
1 tbsp flour
½ cup milk
1 bay leaf
Salt and pepper

Put the cod, wine and bay leaf into a large casserole. Cover loosely and cook on HIGH for 3 minutes. Set aside. Heat a browning dish for 3 minutes on HIGH. Chop the bacon roughly, put it into the browning dish

Facing page: Sole Bonne Femme (top) and Salmon with Tomato Chive Hollandaise (bottom).

and cook for 2-3 minutes on HIGH. Stir frequently until the bacon has browned. Add the pepper and onion and cook for 30 seconds on HIGH. Stir in the flour, milk, salt, pepper and liquid from the fish. Cook for 2-3 minutes on HIGH, stirring frequently until the sauce has thickened. Pour over the fish and re-heat for 30 seconds on HIGH. Serve with parsley new potatoes.

Sole with Oranges

PREPARATION TIME: 15 minutes

MICROWAVE COOKING TIME: 5 minutes

SERVES: 4 people

2lbs sole fillets
¾ cup orange juice
1 tbsp lemon juice
2 tsps butter
2 tsps flour
¾ cup heavy cream
1 tbsp chopped basil
Salt and pepper

GARNISH
2 oranges, peeled and cut in segments
Fresh basil leaves, if available

Tuck in the ends of the sole fillets. Put into a casserole with the orange and lemon juice. Cover loosely and cook on HIGH for 2 minutes. Set aside. Melt the butter in a small, deep bowl for 30 seconds on HIGH. Add the flour and fish cooking liquid. Stir in the cream, basil, salt and pepper, and cook, uncovered, for 2 minutes on HIGH. Stir frequently until the sauce thickens. Pour over the fish and serve with the orange segments and basil leaves.

Cod with Crumb Topping

PREPARATION TIME: 10 minutes

MICROWAVE COOKING TIME: 5-7 minutes

SERVES: 4 people

4 cod fillets
Lemon juice
½ cup water

TOPPING
4 tbsps butter or margarine
1½ cups seasoned breadcrumbs
2 tbsp paprika
¼ cup grated Parmesan cheese
2 tbsps sesame seeds
Salt and pepper

GARNISH
Lemon wedges

Heat a browning dish for 3 minutes on HIGH. Melt the butter in the dish and add the breadcrumbs. Stir well and heat for 1 minute on HIGH to lightly brown. Add the remaining

This page: Cod with Crumb Topping (top) and Cod with Bacon (bottom). Facing page: Sole with Limes and Chili Peppers (top) and Sole with Oranges (bottom).

ingredients and heat for 1 minute more on HIGH. Set aside. Put the cod, a squeeze of lemon juice, and water into a casserole. Cover loosely and cook for 3-4 minutes on HIGH. Drain the fillets and top each one with the breadcrumb mixture. Heat through for 30 seconds on HIGH. Serve with lemon wedges.

Lychee Sole

PREPARATION TIME: 20 minutes

MICROWAVE COOKING TIME: 4-5 minutes

SERVES: 4 people

2lbs sole fillets
8oz lychees (canned or fresh), peeled
8oz can pineapple chunks, ½ cup juice reserved
Juice and rind of 2 limes
1-2 tbsps sugar
1 tbsp light soy sauce
2 tsps cornstarch
2 green onions, shredded
Salt and pepper

With a swivel peeler, peel strips off the limes, and cut into thin slivers. Cover well and set aside. Squeeze the lime juice, and mix with the pineapple juice, sugar, soy sauce and constarch in a small, deep bowl. Fold the fish fillets in half and place in a large casserole, thinner ends of the fillets towards the middle of the dish. Pour over enough water to cover ½" of the sides of the fillets. Cover the dish loosely and cook for 2 minutes on HIGH. Set aside and keep warm. •

This page: Lychee Sole. Facing page: Sole Italienne (top) and Halibut and Green Grapes (bottom).

Cook the sauce ingredients for 2-3 minutes on HIGH, stirring often until thickened. Add the cooking liquid from the fish, strained. Stir in the pineapple chunks, lychees, green onions and lime rind. Add a pinch of salt and pepper and pour the sauce over the fish. Serve with fried rice or chow mein noodles.

Halibut and Green Grapes

PREPARATION TIME: 10 minutes

MICROWAVE COOKING TIME: 10-13 minutes

SERVES: 4 people

2lbs halibut steaks
1 small bunch green seedless grapes
½ cup white wine
Lemon juice
¾ cup heavy cream
1 tsp tarragon
Salt and pepper

Put the fish into a casserole and pour on the wine and lemon juice. Cook for 4-5 minutes on HIGH. Remove the fish from the casserole, cover and keep warm. Heat the wine for 2-3 minutes on HIGH to reduce by half. Cut the grapes in half if large, and add to the wine. Add the tarragon, salt and pepper, and cream. Heat through for 1 minute on HIGH. Pour over the fish to serve.

Halibut in Sesame Ginger Sauce

PREPARATION TIME: 20 minutes

MICROWAVE COOKING TIME: 6 minutes

SERVES: 4 people

4 halibut steaks
2 carrots, cut in Julienne strips
1 cup water
3 tbsps ginger wine
¼ cup light brown sugar
¼ cup sesame seeds
2 tbsps chopped fresh ginger root
2 tbsps rice vinegar
2 tsps cornstarch
Dash of sesame seed oil
Salt and pepper

Put the fish into a casserole with the ginger wine and water. Cover and cook for 2 minutes on HIGH. Put the carrots into a small bowl with 1 tbsp water. Cover loosely and cook for 1 minute on HIGH. Leave to stand while preparing the sauce. Combine the sugar, cornstarch,

ginger, sesame seed oil, rice vinegar, sesame seeds and cooking liquid from the fish. Cook for 4 minutes on HIGH, stirring often until thickened. Add the carrot, salt and pepper and pour over the fish to serve.

Sole Italienne

PREPARATION TIME: 15 minutes

MICROWAVE COOKING TIME: 6-8 minutes

SERVES: 4 people

8 sole fillets
4oz Parma ham
½ cup white wine
1 tbsp butter or margarine
1 tbsp flour
¾ cup heavy cream
Pinch sage
Pinch thyme
Pinch chopped parsley
1 bay leaf
Salt and pepper

GARNISH
Fresh sage or bay leaves

Cut the ham into ½" strips. Wrap the ham strips lattice fashion around the fish and tuck the ends underneath. Put into a casserole with the bay leaf and wine. Cook for 3-4 minutes on HIGH. Remove the fish from the dish, cover and keep it warm. Discard the bay leaf. Melt the butter for 30 seconds on HIGH in a small casserole. Stir in the flour and fish cooking liquid, and add the thyme, parsley, sage, salt and pepper. Cook for 2 minutes on HIGH and stir in the cream. Cook for a further 1 minute on HIGH and spoon over the fish. Garnish with sage or bay leaves.

Fillets of Salmon with Peppercorn Sauce

PREPARATION TIME: 15 minutes

MICROWAVE COOKING TIME: 8-12 minutes

SERVES: 4 people

1 side of salmon, about 1½-2lbs
2 tbsps butter or margarine
1 cup heavy cream
⅓ cup dry vermouth
1 tbsp canned green peppercorns, rinsed and drained
Salt and pepper

Slice the salmon horizontally into very thin slices. Heat a browning dish for 3 minutes on HIGH. Drop in the butter and heat for 30 seconds on HIGH. Lay in the salmon slices and cook for 30 seconds each side. Cook the fish in several batches. Remove the cooked fish from the dish, cover it, and keep it warm. Pour the vermouth into the dish and add the peppercorns. Cook on HIGH for 2 minutes or until reduced by half. Add the cream, stir well, and cook for 2-3 minutes on HIGH until bubbling. Season with salt and pepper. Pour over the salmon scallops to serve. Serve with lightly cooked green beans or pea-pods.

Fruits of the Sea

PREPARATION TIME: 15 minutes

MICROWAVE COOKING TIME: 5-9 minutes

SERVES: 4 people

2lbs mixture of:
  raw scallops, cut in half
  raw shrimp, peeled
  1 lobster tail, shelled and cut into 1" chunks
  sole fillets, cut into 2" chunks
  oysters, shelled
  mussels, shelled
1 cup white wine
2 tsps cornstarch
1 tbsp lemon juice
½ cup whole-milk yogurt
2 tbsps chopped chives
8oz edible seaweed, soaked or cooked in 2 tbsps water
Salt and pepper

Facing page: Fruits of the Sea (top) and Fillets of Salmon with Peppercorn Sauce (bottom).

Cook all the seafood in the wine for 2-3 minutes on HIGH. Cook the seaweed with 2 tbsps water for 1-2 minutes on HIGH. Mix the cornstarch and lemon juice. Remove the fish from the casserole and arrange on a serving dish with the seaweed. Combine the cornstarch and lemon juice with the cooking liquid from the seafood. Cook for 2-3 minutes on HIGH, stirring frequently until thickened. Add the yogurt and chives and heat through for 30 seconds on HIGH. Season with salt and pepper and pour over the seafood.

Salmon in Madeira

PREPARATION TIME: 15 minutes

MICROWAVE COOKING TIME: 8 minutes

SERVES: 4 people

4 salmon steaks, about 1" thick
8oz mushrooms, stalks trimmed
5 sprigs fresh rosemary
1 cup Rainwater Madeira
½ cup water
1 tbsp butter or margarine
1 tbsp flour
Small pinch ground cloves
¼ cup heavy cream
Salt and pepper

Put the salmon steaks in a casserole with the Madeira. Strip the leaves off one sprig of rosemary and add to the salmon. Cover the dish loosely and cook for 5 minutes on HIGH. Add the mushrooms half way through the cooking time. Melt the butter in a small casserole for 2 minutes on HIGH until browning slightly. Add the flour and cook for 1 minute on HIGH. Stir in the cooking liquid from the fish and a pinch of cloves. Season with salt and pepper. Arrange the salmon and mushrooms on plates and pour over the Madeira sauce. Drizzle 1 tbsp cream over each salmon steak and garnish each with a sprig of fresh rosemary.

Curried Cod Nuggets

PREPARATION TIME: 15 minutes

MICROWAVE COOKING TIME: 7 minutes

SERVES: 4 people

2lbs cod, cut in 2" chunks
¼ cup lime juice
¾ cup water
2 tbsps butter or margarine
2 tbsps flour
1 large onion, chopped
1 tbsp curry powder
½ cup orange juice
2 oranges, peeled and segmented
2 tomatoes, peeled and seeded
Desiccated coconut

Combine the cod, lime juice and water in a large casserole. Cover loosely and cook on HIGH for 2 minutes. Set aside and keep warm. Melt the butter for 30 seconds on HIGH in a small, deep bowl. Add the

This page: Curried Cod Nuggets. Facing page: Halibut in Sesame Ginger Sauce (top) and Salmon in Madeira (bottom).

onion, cover loosely and cook for 1 minute on HIGH. Stir in the curry powder and cook for 1 minute on HIGH. Add the flour, orange juice and cooking liquid from the fish. Stir well and cook, uncovered, for 2-3 minutes. Stir often until the sauce is thick. Slice the tomatoes into thin strips and add to the sauce with the orange segments. Cook the sauce for 10 seconds on HIGH to heat the orange and tomato through. Pour the sauce over the cod nuggets and sprinkle with desiccated coconut.

Monkfish and Ribbons

PREPARATION TIME: 20 minutes

MICROWAVE COOKING TIME:
5-6 minutes

SERVES: 4 people

2lbs monkfish tails
½ cup white wine
2 carrots, peeled
2 zucchini, ends trimmed
1 large or 2 small leeks, washed and
    trimmed, retaining some green
½ cup heavy cream
2 tbsps chopped parsley
½ tsp ground oregano
1 bay leaf
Salt and pepper

Cut the monkfish tails into ½"
rounds. Put the pieces into a
casserole with the wine and bay leaf.
Cover loosely and cook for 2
minutes on HIGH. Set aside and
keep warm. With a swivel vegetable
peeler, pare thin ribbons of carrot and
zucchini. Cut the leeks in half
lengthwise and then into ½" strips.
Put the vegetables into a small
casserole with 1 tbsp water. Cover
loosely and cook for 1 minute on
HIGH. Set aside. Remove the fish
from the casserole and heat the wine
for 2-3 minutes on HIGH to reduce.
Pour in the cream, and add the
oregano, salt and pepper. Heat
through for 30 seconds on HIGH.
Pour the sauce over the fish and
sprinkle on the chopped parsley.
Surround with the vegetable ribbons
to serve.

Cod Steaks with Mushrooms

PREPARATION TIME: 15 minutes

MICROWAVE COOKING TIME:
5-7 minutes

SERVES: 4 people

4-8 cod steaks, depending on size
½ cup white wine
1 bay leaf
2 shallots, finely chopped
2 tbsps butter
1½ cups sliced mushrooms
1 tbsp flour
½ cup milk
1 tsp Worcestershire sauce
1 tsp chopped parsley
Salt and pepper

Put the cod and wine into a casserole
with the bay leaf and shallot. Cover
loosely and cook for 2 minutes on
HIGH. Leave covered and set aside.
Melt the butter in a small bowl for
30 seconds on HIGH. Add the
mushrooms. Cover loosely and cook
for 1 minute on HIGH to soften
slightly. Stir in the flour, milk and
Worcestershire sauce. Remove the
bay leaf from the fish and add the
fish cooking liquid to the sauce
ingredients. Cook, uncovered, for 2-3
minutes on HIGH, stirring often
until thickened. Add salt, pepper and
parsley. Pour over the cod to serve.

Sole Aurora

PREPARATION TIME: 15 minutes

MICROWAVE COOKING TIME:
6-7 minutes

SERVES: 4 people

2lbs sole fillets
½ cup white wine
1 bay leaf

SAUCE
2 tbsps butter or margarine
2 tbsps flour
1 cup milk
Rind and juice of 1 orange
1 tbsp tomato paste
Salt and pepper

GARNISH
4 tomatoes, peeled, seeded and cut into
    thin strips

Cook the fish with the wine and the
bay leaf for 3 minutes on HIGH in a
loosely covered casserole. Melt the
butter in a small, deep bowl for
30 seconds on HIGH. Add the flour,
milk, tomato paste, fish cooking

**Facing page: Monkfish and
Ribbons.**

liquid, salt and pepper. Cook for 2-3 minutes on HIGH, stirring frequently until thickened. Add the rind and juice of the orange and cook for 30 seconds more on HIGH. Pour the sauce over the fish and top with the tomato strips.

Sea Bass and Fennel

PREPARATION TIME: 15 minutes

MICROWAVE COOKING TIME: 23 minutes

SERVES: 4 people

1 sea bass, weighing 2-2¼ lbs, cleaned and trimmed

2 bulbs Florentine fennel
4 oranges
Juice of 1 lemon
1 tbsp anise liqueur
1½ cups whole-milk yogurt
Salt
Coarsely ground pepper

GARNISH
Samphire
Orange slices

Squeeze the juice from one of the oranges and slice the others. Sprinkle the inside of the bass with salt and put it into a large, shallow casserole. Pour over the orange juice and lemon juice, cover and cook for 20 minutes

This page: Sole Aurora (left) and Cod Steaks with Mushrooms (right). Facing page: Sea Bass and Fennel.

on HIGH. Carefully lift out the fish and keep it warm. Cook the fennel in 2 tbsps water for 2 minutes on HIGH and set aside. Stir the liqueur, pepper and yogurt into the fish cooking liquid and heat through for 30 seconds on HIGH. Do not let the sauce boil. Peel the skin from the fish if desired and pour over the sauce. Garnish with the samphire and orange slices to serve. Prepare with other varieties of large whole fish if desired.

Microwave
MEAT & POULTRY

Microwave MEAT & POULTRY

When you cook in a microwave oven you get far more for your meat money. Microwave roasting means less shrinkage and, contrary to popular belief, meat *will* brown. Leave a thin layer of fat on the roast, or rub butter into a chicken or turkey and the high heat of the microwave oven will turn the fat golden brown. Alternatively, there are many marinades, bastes and coatings to give appetizing color to meat, poultry and game.

Because liquids evaporate much more slowly in a microwave oven, there will be more meat juices left to make good sauces and gravies. If you want, use a browning dish to brown the flour for gravies. Red wine, soy sauce, gravy browning and spices also give good color to brown sauces.

In general, stews and braises should be cooked on MEDIUM, regardless of what variety of meat is used. The highest setting in a microwave oven will toughen the cuts of meat used in stews and braises. When cooking small cuts of meat such as chops or steaks in a sauce, a medium setting is also recommended for a tender result. Stir-frying and pan-frying are both possible with a browning dish and the highest setting. Organ meats cook very quickly, so a high setting suits them as well.

When roasting poultry, cover the legs and wings with foil to prevent them from drying out. Uncover for a portion of the cooking time and the whole bird will be evenly cooked. Depending on your oven, you may find that all roast meats need to be covered with foil on both ends for part of their cooking time. This is especially important for roasts that are uneven in thickness.

Microwave roasts must be left to stand after cooking just like any roast meat. The standing time helps to finish off the cooking, so microwaved roast meat and poultry is usually covered for 5-15 minutes before carving.

Special microwave meat thermometers take the guesswork out of roasting, but times will vary from oven to oven. The following chart will serve as a quick reference, but is meant only as a guideline.

Time and Setting per 1lb		
	HIGH	**MEDIUM**
Beef		
Rare	6-7 minutes	11-13 minutes
Medium	7-8 minutes	13-15 minutes
Well done	8-9 minutes	15-17 minutes
Chicken (whole)	6-8 minutes	9-11 minutes
Duck (whole)	6-8 minutes	9-11 minutes
Leg of Lamb	8-10 minutes	11-13 minutes
Pork	9-11 minutes	13-15 minutes
Veal	8-9 minutes	11-12 minutes
Steaks (1½″ thick)		
Rare	9 minutes	
Medium rare	10 minutes	
Medium	12 minutes	
Well done	14 minutes	

There is also a method of roasting, Hazelnut Lamb is an example, which cuts down on the cooking time and depends on a longer standing time to finish cooking to the desired doneness. Also, meats and poultry can be roasted for part of their cooking time on HIGH and part on MEDIUM.

All the recipes were tested in both a conventional 700 watt microwave oven and a Combination microwave-convection oven with a maximum setting of 600 watts. The Combination oven does a superb job of roasting. It is nearly as fast as the conventional microwave oven, yet browns and crisps like a regular convection oven. These new ovens have a variety of settings, so it is best carefully to follow the instruction booklet that each manufacturer provides. Either way, the time saving is impressive, and the result delicious when a microwave oven is used on meat and poultry.

LAMB DISHES

Lamb Shanks with Leeks and Rosemary

PREPARATION TIME: 15 minutes

MICROWAVE COOKING TIME: 45 minutes

SERVES: 4 people

2 tbsps vegetable oil
2-2¼ lbs lamb shanks
1 clove garlic, roughly chopped
2 sprigs fresh rosemary
1 cup red wine
1 cup beef stock
1 tbsp butter
1 tbsp flour
2-4 leeks, washed and thinly sliced
Salt and pepper

Heat the oil in a browning dish for 5 minutes on HIGH. Put in the lamb shanks and cook for 5 minutes on HIGH. Turn the lamb over and cook for further 5 minutes on HIGH. Add the garlic, rosemary, salt and pepper, wine and stock. Cover and cook on MEDIUM for 25 minutes. Melt the butter in a small bowl for 30 seconds on HIGH. Stir in the flour. Pour on the cooking juices from the lamb and stir well. Pour the sauce over the lamb and scatter over the sliced leeks. Cook a further 5 minutes on HIGH, until the leeks soften and the sauce has thickened. Remove the rosemary before serving.

Spiced Lamb Chops with Peaches

PREPARATION TIME: 15 minutes

MICROWAVE COOKING TIME: 20 minutes

SERVES: 4 people

4 lamb chops, fat slightly trimmed
2 tbsps butter or margarine
1 tbsp ground allspice
1 tbsp ground ginger
1 tbsp brown sugar
Salt and pepper
8oz sliced peaches, juice reserved
3 tbsps soy sauce
3 tbsps brown sugar
2 tbsps cider vinegar
1 tsp cornstarch
2 tsps water

This page: Spiced Lamb Chops with Peaches (top) and Lamb Shanks with Leeks and Rosemary (bottom). Facing page: Orange Glazed Lamb with Beans.

Heat a browning dish for 5 minutes on HIGH. Drop in the butter and heat 30 seconds on HIGH. Mix 1 tbsp brown sugar with the spices, salt and pepper and rub into both sides of the chops. Fry the chops in the butter on HIGH for 2 minutes

each side. Mix the peach juice with the soy sauce, remaining brown sugar, vinegar and additional salt and pepper. Pour over the chops and cover loosely. Lower the setting to MEDIUM and cook 10 minutes, turning the chops once and stirring the liquid frequently. Remove the chops and set aside to keep warm. Mix the cornstarch with the water and stir into the hot liquid. Cook on HIGH for 1 minute, stirring frequently until the sauce is clear. Add the peaches to heat through for 30 seconds on HIGH and serve with the chops.

Lamb in Sour Cream Dill Sauce

PREPARATION TIME: 15 minutes

MICROWAVE COOKING TIME:
31 minutes

SERVES: 4 people

2lbs leg of lamb, cut into 1 inch cubes
1 onion, sliced
1 bay leaf
1 tbsp dried dill or dill seed
1½ cups light stock
½ cup white wine
3 tbsps butter or margarine
3 tbsps flour
2 tbsps chopped fresh dill or 1 tbsp dried dill
½ cup sour cream
Salt and pepper

Make sure all the fat is trimmed from the lamb. Put the lamb cubes, onion, bay leaf, dried dill or dill seed, salt, pepper, stock and wine into a casserole. Cover and cook on MEDIUM for 25 minutes. Set aside to keep warm. Melt the butter 30 seconds on HIGH. Stir in the flour and strain on the stock from the lamb. Stir well and cook for 5 minutes on HIGH, stirring frequently, until thickened. Add the dill, adjust the seasoning and stir in the sour cream. Pour over the lamb and heat through 1 minute on HIGH, without boiling. Serve with rice or pasta.

Orange Glazed Lamb with Beans

PREPARATION TIME: 15 minutes

MICROWAVE COOKING TIME:
24 minutes

SERVES: 4 people

2 racks of lamb

GLAZE
¼ cup dark brown sugar
¼ cup red wine
1 tbsp red wine vinegar
Juice and rind of 1 orange

ACCOMPANIMENT
1lb canned navy beans or flageolets, drained
4 green onions, chopped
¼ cup dry white wine
Pinch thyme
Salt and pepper

Trim some of the fat from the lamb and score the remaining fat. Mix the glaze ingredients together and brush over the lamb. Put the lamb on a roasting rack. The bone ends may be covered with foil to protect them during the cooking. Cook on MEDIUM for 10 minutes. Raise the setting to HIGH and cook for 5 minutes, basting often during the whole of the cooking time. Leave to stand 5 minutes before carving. Cook for 20 minutes on the Combination setting of a microwave convection oven until the fat has browned. Mix the beans, wine, onions, thyme, salt and pepper together and cook 4 minutes on HIGH. Reheat any remaining glaze and pour over the lamb. Serve with the beans.

Peppercorn Lamb

PREPARATION TIME: 13 minutes

MICROWAVE COOKING TIME:
21-22 minutes

SERVES: 4 people

1½ lbs lamb fillet or meat from the leg cut into ¼ inch slices
4 tbsps butter or margarine

2 shallots, finely chopped
1 clove garlic, finely minced
3 tbsps flour
1 tsp ground allspice
1 cup beef stock
1 tbsp canned green peppercorns, rinsed and drained
2 caps pimento cut into thin strips
1 tsp tomato paste
¼ cup heavy cream
Salt and pepper

Heat a browning dish for 5 minutes on HIGH. Melt the butter for 1 minute on HIGH and add the slices of lamb. Cook for 2 minutes on HIGH, in 2 or 3 batches. Remove the meat and set aside. Cook the shallots and flour to brown slightly. Add the garlic, allspice, stock and tomato paste. Season with salt and pepper and cook 2-3 minutes on HIGH, until starting to thicken. Add the lamb, cover and cook 10 minutes on MEDIUM, or until the lamb is tender. Add the peppercorns, pimento and cream and cook for 2 minutes on HIGH. Serve with rice.

Leg of Lamb with Aromatic Spices

PREPARATION TIME: 15 minutes

MICROWAVE COOKING TIME:
31 minutes, plus
5-15 minutes standing time

SERVES: 6-8 people

3lbs leg of lamb, fat completely trimmed off
½ cup stock

MARINADE
1 cup plain yogurt
1 small piece fresh ginger root, grated
1 tsp crushed coriander seeds
¼ tsp cloves
1 tsp curry powder
1 tsp cumin
¼ tsp cardamom seeds, removed from the pods
1 clove garlic, minced
Salt and pepper

Facing page: Lamb in Sour Cream Dill Sauce (top) and Peppercorn Lamb (bottom).

SAUCE
Remaining marinade and stock
1 tbsp chopped fresh coriander
½ cup plain yogurt

Blend all the marinade ingredients together. In the lamb, make incisions with a sharp knife about 2 inches apart. Place the lamb in a shallow casserole. Push some of the marinade into each cut and spread the remaining marinade over the surface of the lamb. Cover and leave overnight in the refrigerator. Pour the stock into the casserole around the lamb. Cover the casserole loosely and cook on HIGH for 12 minutes, basting frequently. Turn the lamb over and cook a further 15 minutes, basting frequently. Leave the lamb to stand for 5 minutes in a covered dish if serving rare. For well-done or medium lamb leave it to stand for 15-20 minutes. Meanwhile heat the remaining marinade and stock for 3 minutes on MEDIUM. Stir in the yogurt and coriander leaves. Add more salt and pepper if necessary and heat through 1 minute on HIGH. Do not allow the sauce to boil. Serve with the carved lamb.

Hazelnut Lamb

PREPARATION TIME: 15 minutes

MICROWAVE COOKING TIME:
25-30 minutes, plus
5-15 minutes standing time

SERVES: 6-8 people

4½ lbs leg of lamb
1 clove garlic, finely minced
1 cup dry breadcrumbs
1 cup ground, roasted hazelnuts
2 tbsps chopped parsley
¼ cup butter
Salt and pepper

Trim the fat off the lamb. Mix together the remaining ingredients except the breadcrumbs. Spread the hazelnut paste over the surface of the lamb and press over the crumbs. Cook 25-30 minutes on MEDIUM. Increase the setting to HIGH for 2 minutes. Cook 40 minutes on a Combination setting of a microwave

convection oven. Leave the lamb to stand, loosely covered, 5 minutes before carving for rare. Leave 10-15 minutes if medium to well-done lamb is desired. Serve with minted new potatoes and peapods.

Moroccan Lamb

PREPARATION TIME: 20 minutes

MICROWAVE COOKING TIME:
35 minutes

SERVES: 4 people

1¾ lbs lamb fillet or meat from the leg cut in 1 inch cubes
1 clove garlic, minced
2 tsps ground cinnamon
¼ tsp ground cloves
¼ tsp ground cumin
2 tsps paprika

This page: Hazelnut Lamb. Facing page: Leg of Lamb with Aromatic Spices.

1 large red pepper
2 cups light beef stock
¾ lb okra, trimmed
1 cup whole blanched almonds
¼ cup currants
1 tbsp honey
1 tbsp lemon juice
Salt and pepper

Combine the lamb, garlic, spices, red pepper, salt and pepper in a large casserole. Add the stock, cover the dish and cook on MEDIUM for 25 minutes. Add the okra, currants and almonds. Cook a further 5 minutes on MEDIUM. Remove the meat and vegetables and almonds to

setting of a microwave convection oven for 15 minutes or until potatoes are cooked and slightly browned. Three minutes before the end of cooking time, arrange the pepper rings overlapping on top of the potatoes. Garnish with fresh bay leaves to serve.

Navarin of Lamb

PREPARATION TIME: 20 minutes

MICROWAVE COOKING TIME:
40 minutes

SERVES: 4 people

4 lamb chops
2 tbsps oil
2 tbsps flour
2 cloves garlic, finely minced
1 tbsp tomato paste
1 cup white wine
2 cups stock
2 sprigs fresh rosemary or 1 tbsp dried
1 sprig fresh thyme or 1 tsp dried
Salt and pepper

GARNISH
2 carrots, cut lengthwise in quarters
4oz green beans, trimmed and cut in
  2 inch pieces
8 small new potatoes, scrubbed but not
  peeled
2 sticks celery, cut in 2 inch strips
12 small mushrooms, left whole
4 small turnips, peeled

Heat a browning dish 5 minutes on HIGH. Pour in the oil and put in the lamb chops. Cook 1 minute on HIGH. Turn the chops over and cook 2 minutes on HIGH on the other side. Remove the chops and stir in the flour, tomato paste, wine, stock and garlic. Cook for 2 minutes on HIGH, stirring twice. Season with salt and pepper and return the chops to the dish or transfer the whole to a casserole. Cover and cook on MEDIUM for 15 minutes. Add the vegetables, except the beans and mushrooms, and cook 15 minutes further on MEDIUM. Add remaining vegetables 5 minutes before the end of cooking. Remove the herbs, if using fresh, and the bay leaf before serving.

a serving dish. Add the honey and lemon juice to the sauce and cook on HIGH for 5 minutes to reduce it slightly. Pour over the lamb and serve with rice.

Lamb Hot-Pot

PREPARATION TIME: 15 minutes

MICROWAVE COOKING TIME:
30 minutes

SERVES: 4 people

2 large onions, peeled and thinly sliced
2 tbsps oil
1lb ground lamb
2 tbsps chopped parsley
Pinch thyme
8oz whole mushrooms
1 cup canned tomatoes
2 tbsps Worcestershire sauce
3 potatoes, peeled and thinly sliced
1 red pepper, cut in rings
1 green pepper, cut in rings
Salt and pepper

This page: Navarin of Lamb. Facing page: Moroccan Lamb (top) and Lamb Hot-Pot (bottom).

GARNISH
Fresh bay leaves

In a large casserole, heat the oil for 30 seconds on HIGH. Put in the onions and cover the casserole loosely. Cook 5 minutes on HIGH to soften the onions. Add the lamb and thyme and cook 10 minutes on MEDIUM, mashing the lamb with a fork to break it up while it cooks. Add the mushrooms, tomatoes, parsley, salt and pepper and Worcestershire sauce. Arrange the slices of potato neatly on top of the lamb mixture and sprinkle with more salt and pepper. Cover the casserole and cook on MEDIUM for 15 minutes or until the potatoes are tender. Cook on a Combination

PORK AND HAM

Glazed Ham and Spiced Peaches

PREPARATION TIME: 20 minutes

MICROWAVE COOKING TIME:
57 minutes, plus
5 minutes standing time

SERVES: 6-8 people

3lb ham, boneless and pre-cooked

GLAZE
2 tbsps Dijon mustard
½ cup dark brown sugar
1 cup dry breadcrumbs
Pinch powdered cloves
Pinch ginger

PEACHES
6 fresh peaches or 12 canned peach halves
½ cup light brown sugar
1 tsp each ground cinnamon, cloves and allspice
½ cup water or canned peach juice
2 tbsps cider vinegar
12 walnut halves

If using fresh peaches, put them into a large bowl and cover with boiling water. Heat on HIGH for 3 minutes or until the water boils. Peel the peaches, cut in half and remove the stones. Mix the remaining ingredients for the peaches together and heat 2 minutes on HIGH, stirring frequently until the sugar dissolves. Add the peaches and cook 2 minutes on MEDIUM. Remove the peaches and cook the syrup a further 5 minutes on HIGH. Pour the syrup over the peaches and set them aside. Cover the ham with plastic wrap, or put into a roasting bag. Cook on

This page: Pork à l'Orange. Facing page: Glazed Ham and Spiced Peaches.

MEDIUM for 15 minutes per lb. Pour the glaze over during the last 10 minutes of cooking. Put a walnut half in the hollow of each peach. Let the ham stand 5 minutes before slicing. Serve either hot or cold with the peaches.

Pork à l'Orange

PREPARATION TIME: 15 minutes

MICROWAVE COOKING TIME:
24-25 minutes

SERVES: 4 people

2 tbsps butter or margarine
1½ lbs pork tenderloin cut in ½ inch slices
3 carrots, cut in ½ inch diagonal slices
3 small or 2 large leeks, washed and trimmed and cut in ½ inch diagonal slices
¼ cup dried currants
¼ tsp ground ginger
1 bay leaf

1 large onion, sliced
1 large green pepper, sliced
4oz mushrooms, sliced
1 tbsp tomato paste
2 tbsps molasses
8oz canned tomatoes
1 bay leaf
Pinch Cayenne pepper
Salt and pepper

Melt the butter in a casserole for 30 seconds on HIGH and put in the pork pieces, garlic, onions and mushrooms. Cook 5 minutes on MEDIUM. Add the remaining ingredients and cook a further 5 minutes on MEDIUM, loosely covered. If the pork is not tender after 10 minutes, cook an additional 3 minutes on MEDIUM. Remove the bay leaf before serving.

Ginger Apricot Stuffed Pork

PREPARATION TIME: 15 minutes

MICROWAVE COOKING TIME: 33-34 minutes, plus 5 minutes standing time

SERVES: 6-8 people

3lbs loin of pork, boned
2 cups light stock
1 bay leaf
1 carrot, sliced

STUFFING
¼ lb dried apricots
2 tbsps green ginger wine
2 tbsps lemon juice
¼ cup water
1 green onion, finely chopped
Salt and pepper

SAUCE
1 cup strained reserved stock from the pork
Apricot soaking liquid
2 tbsps butter or margarine
2 tbsps flour
Dash soy sauce

Mix the stuffing ingredients, except the onion, together in a bowl. Cover well and cook 1 minute on HIGH, then leave to stand to soften the

1 cup orange juice
¼ cup orange liqueur
2 tsps cornstarch
Salt and pepper

Heat a browning dish 5 minutes on HIGH. Drop in the butter and add the pork slices. Cook 2 minutes each side on HIGH. Cook the meat in 2 or 3 batches. Add the leeks, carrots, bay leaf, ginger, salt and pepper. Pour over the orange juice and cover the dish loosely. Cook 15 minutes on MEDIUM or until the pork and vegetables are tender. Add the currants during the last 3 minutes of cooking. Remove the pork and vegetables and keep them warm. Mix the liqueur and cornstarch together and stir into the sauce. Cook, uncovered, 2 to 3 minutes on HIGH, stirring frequently until the sauce thickens and looks clear.

This page: Ginger Apricot Stuffed Pork. Facing page: Pork Creole (top) and Sausages, Apples and Cheese (bottom).

Return the meat and vegetables to the sauce and stir carefully. Serve with rice.

Pork Creole

PREPARATION TIME: 15 minutes

MICROWAVE COOKING TIME: 13 minutes

SERVES: 4 people

1 tbsp butter
1½ lbs lean pork shoulder or tenderloin cut into strips
1 clove garlic, finely minced

apricots. Trim most of the fat from the pork. Turn the meat over and sprinkle the surface with pepper. Drain the apricots and reserve the juice. Spread the apricots evenly over the pork and sprinkle on the onion. Roll up the pork starting on the thickest side. Tie at even intervals with string. Place in a deep casserole with the bay leaf, stock and carrot. Cover well and cook 30 minutes on MEDIUM or until the pork is tender and no longer pink. Strain the stock and reserve it. Cover the pork and leave to stand 5 minutes before slicing. Melt the butter in a deep bowl for 30 seconds on HIGH. Stir in the flour and 1 cup stock and the reserved apricot juice. Cook 2 to 3 minutes on HIGH to thicken. Add salt and pepper to taste and serve with the pork.

Speedy Ham Casserole

PREPARATION TIME: 10 minutes

MICROWAVE COOKING TIME: 6 minutes

SERVES: 4 people

8oz cooked ham, cut in ½ inch strips
1 can concentrated cream of mushroom soup
1 can water chestnuts, drained and sliced
2 sticks celery, finely chopped
8oz frozen, sliced green beans
2 tbsps dry sherry
1 cup light cream
Pinch thyme
Salt and pepper

TOPPING
1 can French-fried onions
or
¼ cup seasoned breadcrumbs mixed with 1 tsp paprika

Mix all the ingredients, except the topping ingredients, together in a serving casserole. Cook 5 minutes on HIGH, stirring occasionally, or until the beans have cooked. Sprinkle on the topping and cook a further 1 minute on HIGH.

Sweet and Sour Ham

PREPARATION TIME: 20 minutes

MICROWAVE COOKING TIME: 2-3 minutes

SERVES: 4 people

1lb cooked ham, cut into ½ inch cubes

SAUCE
¼ cup brown sugar
¼ cup rice vinegar
2 tbsps tomato ketchup
2 tbsps soy sauce
1 can pineapple chunks, drained and juice reserved
2 tbsps cornstarch
1 green pepper, sliced
2 green onions, sliced diagonally
½ cup blanched, whole almonds
3 tomatoes, quartered
Salt and pepper

Combine the sugar, vinegar, ketchup, soy sauce, cornstarch and reserved pineapple juice and chunks. Add pepper, almonds, salt, pepper and ham. Cook 2-3 minutes on HIGH until the sauce clears and thickens. Add the tomatoes and green onions and heat 30 seconds on HIGH. Serve with rice or crisp noodles.

Sausages, Apples and Cheese

PREPARATION TIME: 15 minutes

MICROWAVE COOKING TIME: 10-12 minutes

SERVES: 4 people

1 ring smoked sausage
4 medium cooking apples, cored and thinly sliced
2 tbsp brown sugar
2 tbsp flour
1 shallot, finely chopped
1 tbsp chopped sage
1 cup shredded Cheddar cheese
Pinch salt and pepper

Toss the apples, brown sugar, flour, sage and onion together. Slice the

sausage in ½ inch diagonal slices and arrange on top of the apples. Cover loosely and cook on HIGH 5 to 7 minutes or until the apples are tender. Sprinkle over the cheese and cook 5 minutes on Medium to melt. Serve immediately.

Ham Loaf with Mustard Chive Sauce

PREPARATION TIME: 15 minutes

MICROWAVE COOKING TIME: 27-28 minutes, plus 5 minutes standing time

SERVES: 4 people

¾ lb ground, cooked ham
¾ lb ground pork
½ cup dry breadcrumbs
½ cup milk
2 shallots, finely chopped
1 clove garlic, crushed
Salt and pepper

SAUCE
3 tbsps butter or margarine
3 tbsps flour
2 tbsps Dijon mustard
1 cup milk
½ cup light stock
2 tbsps chopped chives
Salt and pepper

Combine all the ingredients for the ham loaf and press into a glass loaf dish. Cook on HIGH for 5 minutes. Reduce setting to MEDIUM, cover with plastic wrap and cook 20-25 minutes, or until firm. Turn the dish after 10 minutes. Leave in the dish for 5 minutes before turning out to slice. Melt the butter for the sauce 30 seconds on HIGH. Stir in the flour and remaining ingredients, except for the chives. Cook 2-3 minutes on HIGH, stirring often until thick. Add the chives and serve with the ham loaf.

Facing page: Speedy Ham Casserole (top) and Sweet and Sour Ham (bottom).

Cranberry-Orange Ham Slices

PREPARATION TIME: 10 minutes

MICROWAVE COOKING TIME: 7-9 minutes

SERVES: 4 people

4 ham steaks
1 tbsp butter or margarine

SAUCE
Juice and rind of 1 orange
8oz whole cranberry sauce
¼ cup red wine
1 tsp cornstarch
1 bay leaf
Pinch salt and pepper

GARNISH
1 orange, sliced

Heat a browning dish 5 minutes on HIGH. Put in the butter and brown the ham 2 minutes on the first side and 1 minute on the other. Combine sauce ingredients in a small, deep bowl. Cook 1-2 minutes on HIGH, until the cornstarch clears. Remove the bay leaf and pour over the ham to serve. Garnish with the orange slices.

Polynesian Ham Steaks

PREPARATION TIME: 20 minutes

MICROWAVE COOKING TIME: 9-10 minutes

SERVES: 4 people

4 ham steaks
1 tbsp oil
1 small fresh pineapple, sliced
1 papaya, sliced
2 bananas, peeled and sliced
1 fresh coconut, grated
1 cup orange juice
Juice and grated rind of 1 lime
2 tsps cornstarch
2 tbsps brown sugar

Heat a browning dish 5 minutes on HIGH. Add the oil to the dish and lay in the ham steaks. Cook 2 minutes on the first side and 1 minute on the other. Set the ham

aside. Combine the orange juice, lime juice and rind, cornstarch and sugar in a large bowl. Cook 1-2 minutes on HIGH, stirring frequently until thickened. Add the fruit and coconut and heat through 1 minute on HIGH. Pour over the ham steaks to serve.

Swedish Meatballs

PREPARATION TIME: 15 minutes

MICROWAVE COOKING TIME: 13-15 minutes

SERVES: 4 people

This page: Cranberry-Orange Ham Slices (top) and Polynesian Ham Steaks (bottom). Facing page: Ham Loaf with Mustard Chive Sauce.

MEATBALLS
8oz ground pork
8oz ground beef
8oz ground veal
2 shallots, finely chopped
¼ cup dry breadcrumbs
Pinch ground cloves, nutmeg and allspice
¼ cup milk
1 egg, beaten
Salt and pepper

SAUCE

2 tbsps flour
1 cup milk
½ cup light cream
2 tsps fresh dill or 1 tsp dried dill
1 tsp lemon juice
1 tsp grated lemon rind
Salt and pepper

Combine all the meatball ingredients in a large bowl and mix very well. Shape into 1 inch balls and arrange in a large baking dish. Cook, uncovered, for 10 to 12 minutes on HIGH, or until firm and no longer pink. Rearrange the meatballs twice during cooking, bringing the ones from the edges of the dish to the middle. When the meatballs are cooked remove them to a serving dish to keep warm. Stir in the flour and add the milk, cream, dill and salt and pepper. Cook, stirring frequently, 3 to 5 minutes on HIGH. Add the lemon juice and rind and pour over the meatballs to serve.

Pork with Prunes and Apples

PREPARATION TIME: 15 minutes and 1 hour soaking time for prunes

MICROWAVE COOKING TIME: 26 minutes

SERVES: 4 people

4 pork chops
½ cup prunes, stones removed
2 cups tea
2 apples, peeled and sliced
1 tsp lemon juice
Pinch mace
Pinch thyme
2 tbsps butter
2 tbsps flour
½ cup heavy cream

GARNISH
Parsley sprigs

Boil 2 cups water in a covered bowl for 8 minutes on HIGH. Put in 2 tea bags and the prunes. Leave to soak 1 hour. Heat a browning dish 5 minutes on HIGH. Melt the butter and brown the pork for 2 minutes on

each side. Remove the chops and set aside. Add the flour to the dish and stir in well. Strain 1 cup of the prune soaking liquid into the dish and add the lemon juice, mace, thyme, salt and pepper. Add the pork and cover the dish loosely. Cook 10 minutes on MEDIUM. Add the apples and prunes during the last 4 minutes of cooking. Stir in the cream and heat 1 minute on HIGH. Serve garnished with parsley sprigs.

Italian Pork Rolls

PREPARATION TIME: 20 minutes

MICROWAVE COOKING TIME: 24 minutes

SERVES: 4 people

4 pork steaks
2 tbsps vegetable oil

FILLING
¼ cup ricotta cheese
2oz salami, roughly chopped
1 cup fresh breadcrumbs
1 cup pimento-stuffed olives, roughly chopped
½ cup pistachio nuts
2 shallots, finely chopped
1 tbsp chopped basil
1 tbsp chopped parsley
Pinch oregano
Salt and pepper
1 egg, beaten

SALPICON
8oz tomatoes, peeled, seeded and quartered
8oz mushrooms, sliced
1 green pepper, cut in thin strips
1 onion, thinly sliced
¼ cup dry white wine or vermouth
1 tbsp tomato paste
Salt and pepper

Flatten the pork pieces with a meat mallet or rolling pin until very thin. Mix the filling ingredients together and spread evenly over the meat. Roll up, tucking in the sides, and fasten with a wooden pick. Heat a browning dish for 5 minutes on HIGH. Add the oil and place the

pork rolls in a circle. Cover loosely and cook on MEDIUM for 10 minutes. Rearrange the rolls twice to cook evenly. Cook a further 3 minutes on MEDIUM if the pork is still pink. Remove to a serving dish to keep warm. Cook the onion and the mushrooms in the meat juices for 3 minutes on HIGH. Add the wine, paste, peppers, allspice, salt and pepper. Cook further 2 minutes on HIGH. Add the tomatoes and cook 1 minute on MEDIUM to heat through. Remove the wooden picks from the pork and serve it with the salpicon.

Pork with Plums and Port

PREPARATION TIME: 15 minutes

MICROWAVE COOKING TIME: 24-25 minutes

SERVES: 4 people

1½ lbs pork tenderloin cut in ½ inch slices
2 tbsps butter or margarine
2 tbsps flour
1 bay leaf
2 whole cloves
1 cup stock
½ cup port
1lb purple or red plums
Pinch sugar
1 tsp lemon juice

GARNISH
Chopped parsley

Heat a browning dish 5 minutes on HIGH. Melt the butter and put in the pork slices. Cook 2 minutes each side. Cook in 2 to 3 batches. Remove the pork and stir in the flour. Cook 2 minutes on HIGH, stirring frequently to brown the flour lightly and evenly. Stir in the stock and port and add the cloves, bay leaf, salt and pepper. Replace the meat and cover the dish loosely. Cook 10 minutes on MEDIUM. Cut the plums in half and

Facing page: Swedish Meatballs (top) and Pork with Prunes and Apples (bottom).

remove the stones. Cut in quarters if the plums are large. Add to the meat and cook 5 minutes further on MEDIUM. Taste the sauce and add sugar and/or lemon juice to taste. Remove the bay leaf and cloves. Sprinkle on the chopped parsley before serving.

Smoked Pork with Melon

PREPARATION TIME: 15 minutes

MICROWAVE COOKING TIME: 16 minutes

SERVES: 4 people

1 small, ripe melon
3oz peapods
4 smoked pork chops, fat trimmed
1 tbsp butter or margarine
Grated rind and juice or 1 orange
Salt and pepper
Chopped parsley or coriander

Scoop out the flesh of the melon in balls and set it aside. Spoon out any remaining flesh and blend with the orange juice, salt and pepper in a food processor. Add the orange rind. Trim the peapods and cook 1 minute with 1 tbsp water in a covered bowl. Heat a browning dish for 5 minutes

This page: Italian Pork Rolls. Facing page: Pork with Plums and Port (top) and Smoked Pork with Melon (bottom).

on HIGH. Melt the butter and cook the chops 2 minutes each side on HIGH. Pour over the sauce and cook 5 minutes on MEDIUM. Add the reserved melon balls, peapods and parsley or coriander. Heat 1 minute on HIGH before serving.

BEEF, VEAL AND ORGAN MEATS

Spinach and Ricotta Stuffed Veal

PREPARATION TIME: 25 minutes

MICROWAVE COOKING TIME: 34-35 minutes

SERVES: 6 people

2-3lbs loin of veal, boned and trimmed
1 bay leaf
1 slice onion
1 cup stock or water

STUFFING
1lb fresh spinach, washed well
½ cup ricotta cheese
1 egg, beaten
2 tbsps pine nuts, roughly chopped
½ clove garlic, minced
1 tsp chopped basil
Grated nutmeg
Salt and pepper

SAUCE
Pan juices made up to 1½ cups with stock
2 tbsps flour
2 tbsps butter or margarine
2 tbsps dry white wine
Salt and pepper

Cook the spinach with 1 tsp water for 2 minutes on HIGH, in a covered bowl. Drain well and chop roughly. Mix the remaining stuffing ingredients with the spinach and spread on one side of the veal. Roll up from the thicker end of the meat to the thin end. Tie at even intervals with string. Place in a casserole with 1 cup water or stock. Cover loosely and cook for 30 minutes on MEDIUM. Leave to stand 5 minutes before carving. Heat the butter 1 minute on HIGH and add the flour, stock, wine, salt and pepper. Stir to blend well and cook 2-3 minutes on HIGH, until thickened. Serve with the veal and a selection of vegetables.

This page: Spinach and Ricotta Stuffed Veal. Facing page: Veal Involtini (top) and Veal Ragout (bottom).

Liver Lyonnaise with Orange

PREPARATION TIME: 20 minutes

MICROWAVE COOKING TIME: 13-18 minutes

SERVES: 4 people

1lb liver, sliced
3 tbsps flour
2 tbsps butter or margarine
1 onion, sliced
Rind and juice of 1 orange
½ cup stock
Pinch thyme
Salt and pepper

GARNISH
Orange slices
Chopped parsley

Heat a browning dish 5 minutes on HIGH. Melt the butter in the dish for 1 minute on HIGH. Dredge the liver in the flour and add to the butter in the dish. Cook the liver for 1 minute on HIGH. Turn over and cook 1 minute further on HIGH. Remove from the dish. Cook the onions 1 minute on HIGH. Peel 1 orange and cut the peel into very thin strips. Squeeze the juice and add to the liver along with the remaining ingredients. Cook 10-15 minutes on MEDIUM, until the liver is tender. Turn the slices over frequently during cooking. Serve garnished with the orange slices and chopped parsley.

Veal Involtini

PREPARATION TIME: 20 minutes

MICROWAVE COOKING TIME: 21-22 minutes

SERVES: 4 people

8 veal cutlets
8 slices Parma ham
8 slices cheese
2 tbsps chopped sage
Salt and pepper
2 tbsps oil

SAUCE
1 14oz can plum tomatoes
1 clove garlic, crushed
1 small onion, finely chopped
2 tbsps tomato paste
Pinch oregano
Pinch basil
Pinch sugar
1 bay leaf
Salt and pepper

Flatten the veal cutlets. Place on the ham and cheese and sprinkle on the sage, salt and pepper. Roll up, folding in the ends, and secure with wooden picks. Heat a browning dish 5 minutes on HIGH. Pour in the oil and heat 1 minute on HIGH. Add the veal rolls and cook 2 minutes, turning several times. Combine all the sauce ingredients in a deep bowl. Cook 3-4 minutes on HIGH. Remove bay leaf and blend in a food processor until smooth. Pour over the veal and cook, covered, on MEDIUM for 10 minutes. Serve with spinach.

Veal Ragout

PREPARATION TIME: 20 minutes

MICROWAVE COOKING TIME: 37-41 minutes, plus 5 minutes standing time

SERVES: 4 people

1½-2lbs veal shoulder or leg cut in 1 inch cubes
2 onions, sliced
8oz mushrooms, quartered
¼ cup butter or margarine
¼ cup flour
2 tsps thyme
1 bay leaf
1 clove garlic, minced
2 cups beef stock
2 tbsps tomato paste
Salt and pepper

ACCOMPANIMENT
3 cups pasta
1 cup grated cheese

Heat a browning dish 5 minutes on HIGH. Melt the butter 1 minute on HIGH. Brown the meat in 2 batches

Facing page: Liver Lyonnaise with Orange.

2 tsps mustard seeds
2 crushed bay leaves
2 tsps dill
1 tsp crushed allspice berries
1½ cups water
6 carrots, peeled and quartered lengthwise
2 small rutabaga, peeled and cut into
  wedges
6-8 small potatoes, peeled and left whole
1 large head of white cabbage, cut into
  wedges

Put the corned beef, water, herbs and spices into a large, deep casserole. Cover tightly and cook on HIGH for 8 minutes, or until the water boils. Reduce the setting to MEDIUM and cook 30 minutes, covered. Turn over the meat and add the carrots, potatoes and rutabaga. Re-cover the dish and cook a further 30-40 minutes on MEDIUM. Add the cabbage 15 minutes before the end of cooking. Leave to stand for 10 minutes before slicing the meat across the grain. Serve with the vegetables and some of the cooking liquid.

Veal Parmesan with Zucchini

PREPARATION TIME: 20 minutes

MICROWAVE COOKING TIME: 17-22 minutes

SERVES: 4 people

4 veal cutlets
4 zucchini

COATING
2 tbsps seasoned breadcrumbs
3 tbsps grated Parmesan cheese
1 egg, beaten
Salt and pepper

on HIGH for 3 minutes per batch. Cook the onions and mushrooms for 2 minutes on HIGH. Remove the meat and vegetables, and stir in the flour. Cook the flour for 3 minutes to brown slightly. Add the remaining ingredients and return the meat and the vegetables to the dish, or transfer to a casserole, cover and cook on MEDIUM 15 minutes. Put the pasta in water and partially cover with plastic wrap. Cook 6-10 minutes on HIGH, stirring occasionally. Leave to stand 5 minutes and drain and rinse in hot water. Remove the bay leaf from the ragout. Arrange the pasta in a serving dish and spoon the ragout into the middle. Sprinkle on grated cheese and heat 1 minute on HIGH to melt the cheese before serving.

New England Boiled Dinner

PREPARATION TIME: 20 minutes

MICROWAVE COOKING TIME: 1 hour 8 minutes to 1 hour 18 minutes

SERVES: 6-8 people

2-3lbs corned beef brisket
1 tsp coarsely crushed black peppercorns

This page: New England Boiled Dinner. Facing page: Veal Parmesan with Zucchini.

SAUCE

1 14oz can plum tomatoes
1 clove garlic, crushed
1 small onion, finely chopped
2 tbsps tomato paste
Pinch oregano
Pinch basil
Pinch sugar
Pinch grated nutmeg
1 bay leaf
Salt and pepper

TOPPING

1 cup mozzarella cheese
¼ cup grated Parmesan cheese

Slice the zucchini and cook 2 minutes on HIGH, with enough water to cover in a deep bowl. Mix the crumbs, Parmesan cheese, salt and pepper for the coating. Dip the veal in the egg and then in the breadcrumb coating. Put the veal into a shallow dish, cover loosely and cook 8-10 minutes. Do not turn the veal over, but rearrange once during cooking. Combine all the sauce ingredients in a deep bowl. Cook 3-4 minutes on HIGH. Arrange the zucchini slices in a serving dish, place the veal on top of the zucchini and pour over the tomato sauce. Top with the mozzarella and Parmesan cheeses and cook 4-6 minutes on HIGH or Combination setting on a microwave convection oven. Serve immediately.

Beef Enchiladas

PREPARATION TIME: 20 minutes

MICROWAVE COOKING TIME: 12-14 minutes

SERVES: 4 people

8oz package tortillas

SAUCE

1 onion, finely chopped
3 tbsps tomato paste
1lb 10oz can tomatoes
1-2 small chili peppers, seeded and finely chopped
1 tsp ground coriander
1 bay leaf
Salt and pepper

FILLING

2 tbsps oil
8oz ground beef
1 clove garlic, finely minced
2 tsps ground cumin
1 green pepper, roughly chopped
12 black olives, stoned and chopped
Salt and pepper

GARNISH

1 avocado, sliced
1 cup grated Cheddar or Monterey Jack cheese

If the tortillas are dry, brush them with water, cover in paper towels and heat 2 minutes on HIGH before rolling up. Combine all the sauce

This page: Risotto Stuffed Peppers (top) and Beef Enchiladas (bottom). Facing page: Chicken Livers and Walnut Pasta (top) and Kidney and Bacon Kebabs with Red Pepper Sauce (bottom).

ingredients in a deep bowl, cover the bowl loosely and cook 3 minutes on HIGH. Stir the sauce frequently to break up the tomatoes. If desired, blend the sauce until smooth in a food processor. Heat a browning dish for 3 minutes on HIGH. Pour in the oil and add the meat, breaking it up with a fork. Add the garlic and cumin and cook on HIGH for 3 minutes, breaking up the meat frequently. Add the green pepper and cook a further

minute on HIGH. Add the olives, salt and pepper. Roll up the filling in the tortillas and lay them in a shallow casserole, seam side down. Pour over the sauce and cook, uncovered, 1 minute on HIGH to heat through. Top with the avocado slices and cheese and heat 1 minute further on HIGH to melt the cheese.

Pepper Steak

PREPARATION TIME: 20 minutes

MICROWAVE COOKING TIME: 14 minutes

SERVES: 4 people

1 green pepper, sliced
1 red pepper, sliced
1 yellow pepper, sliced
2lbs rump steak, cut in thin strips
2 tbsps oil
1 large onion, finely sliced
1 clove garlic
2 tbsps cornstarch
2 tbsps soy sauce
2 tbsps dry sherry
1½ cups beef stock
1 small piece ginger root, grated
Salt and pepper

Heat a browning dish for 5 minutes on HIGH. Pour in the oil and add the strips of steak. Cook 2 minutes on HIGH. Add the onion, garlic and pepper slices. Mix the cornstarch and the remaining ingredients and pour over the steak. Cook, uncovered, 7 minutes on HIGH or until the meat is cooked but the vegetables are still crisp. Serve with rice or chow mein noodles.

Filet Mignon with Mustard Peppercorn Hollandaise

PREPARATION TIME: 15 minutes

MICROWAVE COOKING TIME:
Steak 9 minutes rare
     10 minutes medium rare
     12 minutes medium
     14 minutes well done
Sauce 2 minutes

SERVES: 4 people

4 filet mignon/fillet steaks cut 1½ inches thick, brushed with oil on both sides

SAUCE
3 egg yolks
1 tbsp white wine vinegar
½ cup butter
1 tbsp Dijon mustard
1 tsp green peppercorns
1 tsp chopped parsley
Salt and pepper

Heat a browning dish 5 minutes on HIGH. Cook the steak 2 minutes on one side and 2½ on the other for rare. For medium rare – 2 minutes on one side and 3½ minutes on the other. For medium – 3 minutes on one side and 4½ minutes on the other. For well done – 3 minutes on one side and 6 minutes on the other. Melt the butter 1 minute on HIGH. Mix the egg yolks, vinegar, salt and pepper in a glass measuring cup. Beat in the butter and cook 15 seconds on HIGH and stir. Continue until the sauce thickens, about 2 minutes. Stir in the mustard, parsley and peppercorns. Serve with the steaks.

Kidney and Bacon Kebabs with Red Pepper Sauce

PREPARATION TIME: 20 minutes

MICROWAVE COOKING TIME:
9 minutes, plus
1 minute standing time

SERVES: 4 people

16 kidneys
8 strips bacon
1 green pepper
¼ cup butter or margarine

SAUCE
2 tbsps dry mustard
2 tbsps Worcestershire sauce
2 tbsps steak sauce
2 large caps pimento
Salt and pepper

Pierce the kidneys 2 or 3 times. Cut the kidneys in half through the

middle and remove the cores with scissors. Wrap the kidneys in bacon and thread onto wooden skewers with the green pepper. Melt the butter for 1 minute on HIGH and brush over the kebabs. Blend the sauce ingredients together with any remaining butter in a food processor until smooth. Cook the sauce 2 minutes on HIGH. Put the kebabs on a roasting rack and cook 5 minutes on HIGH, turning once. Leave to stand 1 minute before serving. Brush with the cooking juices before serving with the sauce. Saffron rice may also be served.

Risotto Stuffed Peppers

PREPARATION TIME: 20 minutes

MICROWAVE COOKING TIME: 20 minutes

SERVES: 4 people

2 large or 4 small red, green or yellow
     peppers
2 tbsps oil
1 small onion, chopped
1 clove garlic, minced
1 cup Italian risotto rice
½ cup mushrooms
1 cup roughly chopped salami
¼ cup chopped black olives
8oz canned tomatoes
¼ tsp basil
¼ tsp oregano
1 cup mozzarella cheese, grated

Paprika
Salt and pepper

In a large casserole, cook the garlic, onion and mushrooms in the oil for 2 minutes on HIGH. Stir in the tomatoes, rice, herbs, salt and pepper. Cover the dish and cook on HIGH for 5 minutes. Stir in the meat and olives and leave to stand 5 minutes for the rice to continue cooking. If the peppers are small, cut 1 inch off the top to form a lid. Remove the core and seeds. If the peppers are large, cut in half lengthwise and

Facing page: Filet Mignon with Mustard Peppercorn Hollandaise (top) and Pepper Steak (bottom).

remove the core and seeds. Fill the peppers and place them in the casserole. Cover with plastic wrap and cook 8 minutes on HIGH, until the peppers are just tender. Top with the cheese and cook 2 minutes on MEDIUM to melt.

Veal Kidneys in Mustard Sauce

PREPARATION TIME: 20 minutes

MICROWAVE COOKING TIME: 12 minutes

SERVES: 4 people

2 veal kidneys
2 shallots, chopped
3 tbsps butter or margarine
3 tbsps flour
2 tbsps Dijon mustard
½ cup stock
½ cup light cream
½ cup dry white wine
1 tbsp capers
1 tbsp chopped chives
Salt and pepper

Remove the core from the kidneys and cut them into small pieces. Heat a browning dish for 5 minutes on HIGH. Melt the butter for 1 minute on HIGH and add the kidneys and the shallots. Cook 2 minutes on HIGH, stirring frequently. Add the flour, wine, stock, salt and pepper and cook a further 3 minutes on HIGH. Add the remaining ingredients and cook 2 minutes on HIGH. Serve immediately.

Sherried Sweetbreads

PREPARATION TIME: 20 minutes

MICROWAVE COOKING TIME: 17 minutes

SERVES: 4 people

1lb lamb or veal sweetbreads, soaked in cold water
½ cup stock
¼ cup dry sherry
4oz mushrooms, sliced
8oz small onions, peeled
¼ cup heavy cream
Grated nutmeg

1 tbsp tomato paste
2 tbsps chopped parsley
Salt and pepper

Drain the sweetbreads and pierce several times. Cover with fresh water and cook 3 minutes on HIGH. Drain and allow to cool slightly. Peel the outer membrane off the sweetbreads. Cut the sweetbreads in half if they are large. Put the sweetbreads into a casserole with the onions, mushrooms, sherry, stock, salt, pepper and nutmeg. Cook 8 minutes on HIGH, or until tender. Remove

This page: Sherried Sweetbreads (top) and Veal Kidneys in Mustard Sauce (bottom). Facing page: Roast Beef with Stuffed Zucchini and Tomatoes (bottom).

the onions, mushrooms and sweetbreads. Cook the liquid until well reduced, about 5 minutes on HIGH. Add the cream and tomato paste and cook 1 minute on HIGH. Mix all the ingredients together in the sauce. Serve with rice or in puff pastry shells.

Chicken Livers and Walnut Pasta

PREPARATION TIME: 15 minutes

MICROWAVE COOKING TIME:
13 minutes

SERVES: 4 people

1lb chicken livers, trimmed and pierced
¼ cup butter or margarine
1·clove garlic
½ cup walnuts, roughly chopped
1 cup stock
4 spring onions
2 tbsps chopped parsley
1 red pepper, chopped
2 tbsps sherry
Salt and pepper
8oz pasta, cooked

Heat a browning dish for 5 minutes on HIGH. Melt the butter for 1 minute on HIGH and add the liver. Cook for 2 minutes on HIGH and add the garlic, salt and pepper and stock. Cook 3 minutes on HIGH. Remove the livers from the stock and pour the stock into a food processor. Add the walnuts and blend until smooth. Chop the green onions and add to the sauce with the parsley, red peppers, and sherry. Pour over the livers and heat 2 minutes on HIGH. Pour over pasta to serve.

Roast Beef with Stuffed Zucchini and Tomatoes

PREPARATION TIME: 20 minutes

MICROWAVE COOKING TIME:
Beef 14-21 minutes – rare
      16-24 minutes – medium
      18-27 minutes – well done
plus 10 minutes standing time
COMBINATION MICROWAVE CONVECTION TIME:
Beef 10-12 minutes – rare
      11-13 minutes – medium
      12-14 minutes – well done
Vegetables 13 minutes

SERVES: 6-8 people

2-3lbs boneless beef roast
6-8 tomatoes
6-8 zucchini
4 tbsps chopped parsley
6oz mushrooms, roughly chopped
4 tbsps chopped chives
½ cup breadcrumbs
1 cup grated cheese
Salt and pepper

Put the beef, fat side up, into a large casserole, cover loosely and cook for 14-21 minutes for rare, 16-24 minutes for medium, 18-27 minutes for well done on HIGH. Turn the beef over halfway through the cooking time. When cooked for the chosen amount of time cover with foil and leave to stand for 10 minutes before carving. The beef may also be cooked in a combination microwave and convection oven. Trim the ends of the zucchini and cook, in enough water to cover, for 5 minutes on HIGH. Cut in half lengthwise and scoop out the flesh, leaving the shell intact. Chop the flesh roughly and mix with the chives, salt and pepper. Fill the shells and sprinkle on the grated cheese. Cut the tops from the round end of the tomatoes, scoop out the seeds and strain the juice. Mix the mushrooms, tomato juice, parsley, breadcrumbs, salt and pepper. Fill the tomatoes and replace the tops. Cook the zucchini 5 minutes on HIGH and the tomatoes 3 minutes on HIGH, or until the vegetables are tender. Serve with the beef.

Beef Bourguignonne

PREPARATION TIME: 20 minutes

MICROWAVE COOKING TIME:
53 minutes, plus
10 minutes standing time

SERVES: 4 people

2 thick-cut slices bacon cut in ½ inch strips
1½ lbs-2lbs chuck steak cut in 1 inch cubes
1 clove garlic, minced
8oz small onions
4 tbsps flour
1 cup Burgundy
1 cup beef stock
1 tsp tomato paste
8oz mushrooms, left whole
1 bay leaf
1 tsp thyme or majoram
Salt and pepper

Heat a browning dish for 5 minutes on HIGH. Add the bacon and cook 3 minutes on HIGH, stirring frequently until brown. Remove the bacon and add the meat. Cook 3 minutes on HIGH to brown slightly. Remove the meat and add the onions. Cook 2 minutes on HIGH. Stir in the flour, stock, wine and tomato paste. Add the bay leaf, salt and pepper. Return the bacon and meat to the casserole and add the mushrooms. Cover and cook 40 minutes on MEDIUM, or until the meat is tender. Stir occasionally. Leave to stand for 10 minutes before serving. Serve with parsley potatoes.

Steak and Mushroom Pudding

PREPARATION TIME: 25 minutes

MICROWAVE COOKING TIME:
51-52 minutes, plus
10 minutes standing time

SERVES: 4 people

PASTRY
2 cups flour
2 tsps baking powder
4oz shredded suet or ¼ cup butter or margarine
1 tsp salt
½ cup water

FILLING
8oz whole mushrooms
1lb chuck steak
2 tbsps butter or margarine
2 tbsps flour
1 small onion, finely chopped
1 cup beef stock
2 tsps chopped parsley
1 tsp thyme
Salt and pepper

Facing page: Steak and Mushroom Pudding (top) and Beef Bourguignonne (bottom).

Melt the butter in a deep bowl for 30 seconds on HIGH. Stir in the flour and the stock and cook for 1-2 minutes on HIGH. Add the remaining ingredients for the filling and cover the bowl loosely. Cook for 35 minutes on MEDIUM. Meanwhile, make the pastry. Sift the flour and baking powder and salt into a mixing bowl. Cut in the butter or stir in the suet. Mix to a soft dough with the water. Roll out ⅔ of the dough and line a 4 cup glass bowl, spoon in the filling and dampen the edges of the pastry. Roll out the remaining pastry for the cover. Place it over the top of the filling, pressing down the edges to seal well. Make 2-3 cuts in the top to let out the steam. Cover loosely with plastic wrap and cook on LOW for 15 minutes, turning the bowl around several times. Leave to stand for 10 minutes before turning out.

Veal Escalopes with Vegetables

PREPARATION TIME: 20 minutes

MICROWAVE COOKING TIME: 20 minutes

SERVES: 4 people

4 veal cutlets
2 tbsps oil
2oz peapods
2 carrots, peeled and thinly sliced
2oz mushrooms, sliced
2 leeks, washed and thinly sliced
1 cup low-fat soft cheese
½ cup dry white wine
1 tbsp lemon juice
1 tbsp chopped dill
Grated nutmeg
Salt and pepper

Heat a browning dish 3 minutes on HIGH. Add the oil and heat 1 minute on HIGH. Cook the veal for 8 minutes on HIGH. Add the mushrooms halfway through the cooking time. Combine the carrots and the leeks with the wine in a shallow dish and cook for 5 minutes on HIGH. Add the peapods and cook a further 1 minute on HIGH.

Drain the vegetables and reserve the liquid. Mix the cheese, vegetable cooking liquid, lemon juice, dill, nutmeg, salt and pepper in a deep bowl. Heat for 1 minute on HIGH, but do not allow the sauce to boil. Combine with the drained vegetables. Pour over the veal and heat through 1 minute on HIGH before serving.

Veal with Saffron Sauce

PREPARATION TIME: 20 minutes

MICROWAVE COOKING TIME: 26-27 minutes

SERVES: 4 people

4 veal chops
3 tbsps butter or margarine
2 tbsps flour
2 shallots, finely chopped
1 red pepper, thinly sliced
½ cup white wine
½ cup light stock
½ cup light cream
Good pinch saffron
Salt and pepper

Heat a browning dish for 5 minutes on HIGH. Melt the butter for 1 minute on HIGH and put in the chops. Cook for 2 minutes on HIGH per side. Remove the chops from the dish and add the shallots. Cook for 1 minute on HIGH. Stir in the flour, wine, stock, salt, pepper and saffron.

Cook 2-3 minutes on HIGH until thickened. Return the chops to the dish and add the sliced red pepper. Cover the dish or transfer to a covered casserole. Cook on MEDIUM for 15 minutes, or until the chops are tender. Remove the chops from the dish and stir in the cream. Pour the sauce over the chops to serve.

Veal Chops with Lemon and Thyme

PREPARATION TIME: 20 minutes

MICROWAVE COOKING TIME: 26-27 minutes

SERVES: 4 people

4 veal chops
¼ cup butter or margarine
¼ cup flour
1 clove garlic, minced
½ cup white wine
½ cup light stock
2 tbsps lemon juice
Salt and pepper

GARNISH
Sprigs of fresh thyme
Lemon slices

Heat a browning dish 5 minutes on HIGH. Melt the butter for 1 minute on HIGH. Put in the chops and cook 2 minutes on HIGH per side.

Facing page: Veal Chops with Lemon and Thyme (top) and Veal with Saffron Sauce (bottom). This page: Veal Escalopes with Vegetables.

Remove the chops from the dish and add the flour. Cook 1 minute to brown slightly. Stir in the wine, stock and lemon juice. Cook 2-3 minutes on HIGH until thickened. Season with salt and pepper and add a sprig of fresh thyme. Return the chops to the dish or transfer to a covered casserole. Cook on MEDIUM 15 minutes. Garnish with lemon slices and more fresh thyme.

Microwave
MEAT & POULTRY

POULTRY DISHES

Orange Glazed Duck

PREPARATION TIME: 15 minutes

MICROWAVE COOKING TIME:
40 minutes

SERVES: 3-4 people

4½-5lbs duck
1 slice orange
1 slice onion
1 bay leaf
Salt

GLAZE
¼ cup bitter orange marmalade
4 tbsps soy sauce
1 cup chicken stock
2 tsps cornstarch
Salt and pepper

GARNISH
Orange slices and watercress

Prick the duck all over the skin with a fork, brush some of the soy sauce over both sides of the duck and sprinkle both sides lightly with salt. Place the duck breast side down in a roasting rack. Cook 10 minutes on HIGH and drain well. Return the duck to the oven, reduce the power to MEDIUM and continue cooking a further 15 minutes. Combine remaining soy sauce with the orange marmalade. Turn the duck breast side up and brush with the glaze. Continue cooking for 15 minutes on MEDIUM, draining away the fat often and brushing with the glaze. Remove the duck from the roasting rack and leave to stand, loosely covered with foil, for 5 minutes before carving. Alternatively, cook 20-25 minutes on Combination in a microwave convection oven. Drain all the fat from the roasting tin, but leave the pan juices. Combine the chicken stock, cornstarch, salt, pepper and remaining glaze with the pan juices and pour into a small, deep bowl. Cook 2-3 minutes on

This page: **Orange Glazed Duck.**
Facing page: **Turkey with Broccoli (top)** and **Turkey Tetrazzini (bottom).**

Stuffed Turkey Leg

PREPARATION TIME: 20 minutes

MICROWAVE COOKING TIME:
33-34 minutes

SERVES: 4 people

1 large turkey leg, bone removed

STUFFING
2 slices white bread made into crumbs
4oz cooked ham, finely ground
½ cup shelled pistachio nuts
1 apple, cored and chopped
2 sticks celery, finely chopped
1 shallot, finely chopped
Pinch thyme
1 egg, beaten
Salt and pepper

SAUCE
1 tbsp dripping from turkey
2 tbsps flour
Pan juices
1 cup chicken stock
2 tbsps dry sherry
Salt and pepper

GARNISH
1 bunch watercress

Combine all the stuffing ingredients and push into the cavity of the turkey leg, but do not overstuff. Close any openings with wooden picks. Prick the turkey skin lightly all over and put the turkey leg on a roasting rack. Cover loosely with wax paper and cook for 15 minutes on MEDIUM. Turn the turkey leg over and continue cooking on MEDIUM a further 15 minutes. Alternatively, cook 20 minutes on Combination in a microwave convection oven. When the turkey is tender and no longer pink, remove from the roasting rack and keep warm. Remove all but 1 tbsp of the fat from the roasting dish. Stir in the flour and add the chicken stock, sherry, salt and pepper. Transfer to a deep bowl if desired and

HIGH until thickened. Remove the onion, orange slice and bay leaf from the cavity of the duck and put in a bouquet of watercress. Surround the duck with orange slices and serve the sauce separately.

Lemon Pepper Chicken

PREPARATION TIME: 20 minutes

MICROWAVE COOKING TIME:
10 minutes

SERVES: 4 people

4 chicken breasts
Juice of 1 lemon
1 tbsp coarsely ground black pepper
Paprika
Salt

GARNISH
Lemon slices
Watercress

Heat 2 metal skewers in a gas flame or on an electric burner. Skin the chicken breasts. Make a criss-cross pattern on the chicken flesh with the hot skewers. Place the chicken in a casserole and sprinkle over the paprika, pepper, lemon juice and salt. Cover the dish tightly and cook 10 minutes on MEDIUM. Pour the juices back over the chicken to serve. Garnish with the lemon slices and watercress.

This page: Stuffed Turkey Leg. Facing page: Lemon Pepper Chicken (top) and Lime and Chili Chicken (bottom).

cook 3-4 minutes on HIGH, stirring frequently until thickened. Slice the stuffed turkey leg and pour over some of the sauce. Garnish with watercress and serve the remaining sauce separately.

Chinese Wings

PREPARATION TIME: 15 minutes

MICROWAVE COOKING TIME: 17 minutes

SERVES: 4 people

3lbs chicken wings
1 cup hoisin sauce (Chinese barbecue sauce)
3 tbsps sesame seeds
2 tbsps vegetable oil
1 tbsp sesame seed oil
8oz peapods
8oz bean sprouts
Small piece grated fresh ginger root
Salt and pepper

Brush the chicken wings with the hoisin sauce and cook for 10 minutes on HIGH on a roasting rack. Baste the chicken wings often with the sauce while cooking. When the wings are cooked and well coated with sauce, sprinkle with sesame seeds and set aside. Heat the oil in a browning dish for 5 minutes on HIGH. Add the peapods, bean sprouts, ginger, salt and pepper. Cook for 2 minutes on HIGH and add the sesame seed oil after cooking. Serve the Chinese wings with the stir-fried vegetables.

Lime and Chili Chicken

PREPARATION TIME: 20 minutes

MICROWAVE COOKING TIME: 12 minutes

SERVES: 4 people

4 chicken breasts, boned
2 limes
1 green chili pepper
½ cup heavy cream
Salt and pepper
Pinch sugar

Heat 2 metal skewers in a gas flame or on an electric burner. Skin the chicken breasts and make a pattern on the chicken flesh with the hot skewers. Squeeze 1 lime for juice. Peel and slice the other lime thinly. Remove the seeds from the chili pepper and slice it very thinly. Put the chicken into a casserole. Sprinkle over a pinch of sugar, the sliced chili pepper, salt, pepper and lime juice. Cover and cook 10 minutes on MEDIUM. Remove the chicken and keep warm. Stir the cream into the juices in the casserole. Cook 2 minutes on HIGH, stirring frequently. Pour over the chicken and garnish with the sliced lime.

Tandoori Poussins

PREPARATION TIME: 20 minutes, plus 1 hour to marinate

MICROWAVE COOKING TIME: 15 minutes

SERVES: 4 people

4 Cornish game hens

MARINADE
½ cup chopped onion
1 small piece fresh ginger, grated
2 tsps ground coriander
2 tsps ground cumin
2 tsps paprika
1 tsp turmeric
1 tsp chili powder
1 cup plain yogurt
Juice of 1 lime
2 chopped green chili peppers
2 tbsps chopped chives
Salt and pepper

ACCOMPANIMENT
1 head of lettuce, broken into leaves
4 tomatoes, cut in wedges
1 lemon, cut in wedges

Combine all the marinade ingredients together. Skin the hens and cut them in half. Prick the flesh and rub in the marinade. Leave for 1 hour. Cook on HIGH or a Combination setting for 15 minutes, basting frequently with the marinade. Leave to stand, loosely covered, for 5 minutes before serving. Heat any

remaining marinade on MEDIUM for 1 minute, but do not allow to boil. Pour over the hens and serve on a bed of lettuce with lemon and tomato wedges.

Turkey with Broccoli

PREPARATION TIME: 20 minutes

MICROWAVE COOKING TIME: 13-14 minutes

SERVES: 4 people

4 turkey cutlets
12 broccoli spears
½ cup chicken stock
1 bay leaf
Salt and pepper

SAUCE
3 tbsps butter or margarine
3 tbsps flour
1½ cups milk
½ cup Colby cheese
Pinch Cayenne pepper
Salt and pepper
Paprika

Trim the broccoli, and divide evenly among the turkey cutlets. Roll the turkey around the broccoli and lay the rolls in a casserole, seam side down. Pour over the chicken stock, sprinkle on salt and pepper and add the bay leaf. Cover and cook 10 minutes on MEDIUM. Leave to stand while preparing the sauce. Melt the butter for 30 seconds in a deep bowl. Stir in the flour and the milk. Add the salt, pepper, mustard, Cayenne pepper and cook until thickened, about 3-4 minutes on HIGH. Add the cheese and stir to melt. Transfer the turkey and broccoli rolls to a serving dish and pour some of the sauce over each one. Sprinkle on paprika and serve the rest of the sauce separately.

Facing page: Chinese Wings (top) and Tandoori Poussins (bottom).

during cooking, baste with oil and cover loosely with wax paper. Reserve 1 tbsp fat from the roasting pan and skim off the rest and discard. Reserve the pan juices. Mix the reserved fat with the flour and stir into the pan juices. Add the stock, wine, salt and pepper and cook 2-3 minutes until thickened. Stir in the chopped herbs and serve with the carved chicken.

Duck with Peaches

PREPARATION TIME: 20 minutes

MICROWAVE COOKING TIME: 9 minutes

SERVES: 4 people

2 whole duck breasts
¼ cup butter
Salt and pepper

SAUCE
2 cans sliced peaches, drained and juice reserved
½ cup red wine
2 tsps cornstarch
1 tbsp lime or lemon juice
1 bay leaf
Pinch cinnamon
Pinch nutmeg
1 tbsp whole allspice berries
½ cup whole blanched almonds

Heat a browning dish for 5 minutes on HIGH. Melt the butter and put in the duck breasts. Brown the duck breasts 2 minutes on the skin side and 4 minutes on the other side. Remove from the dish and leave to stand while preparing the sauce. Mix the cornstarch with the peach juice, red wine, lemon juice and the spices and bay leaf in a deep bowl. Cook on HIGH for 2-3 minutes until thickened. Remove the bay leaf and add the peaches. Slice the duck breast into thin slices. Pour the peach sauce over the duck breasts to serve.

This page: Herb Roasted Chicken. Facing page: Turkey Macadamia (top) and Duck with Peaches (bottom).

Herb Roasted Chicken

PREPARATION TIME: 25 minutes

MICROWAVE COOKING TIME: 26-33 minutes, plus 5-10 minutes standing time

SERVES: 4-6 people

3lbs roasting chicken
1 tsp each fresh thyme, basil, parsley, marjoram, chervil or tarragon
2 tbsps oil
Juice of 1 lemon
Salt and pepper

GRAVY
3 tbsps flour
Cooking juices from the chicken
1½ cups chicken stock
2 tbsps white wine
2 tbsps chopped mixed herbs as above
Salt and pepper

Chop the herbs finely. Loosen the skin of the chicken and stuff the herbs underneath. Prick the skin lightly and brush with the oil. Sprinkle over the lemon juice and pepper. Put onto a roasting rack breast-side down, and cook 30 minutes on MEDIUM, 25 minutes on HIGH and 30 minutes on a Combination setting. Turn the chicken halfway through cooking. Leave the chicken standing 5-10 minutes before carving. If the chicken appears to be drying out at any time

Spicy Tomato Chicken

PREPARATION TIME: 15 minutes

MICROWAVE COOKING TIME:
17 minutes, plus
5 minutes standing time

SERVES: 4 people

4 chicken breasts, skinned and boned
¼ cup chicken stock or water
1lb canned tomatoes
2 tbsps Worcestershire sauce
1 clove garlic, crushed
2 tbsps tomato paste
2 tbsps cider vinegar
2 tbsps light brown sugar or honey
1 small onion, finely chopped
1 bay leaf
Pinch allspice
Salt and pepper

GARNISH
4 tomatoes, skinned, seeded and cut into
  thin strips

Place the chicken in 1 layer in a large
casserole with the stock or water.
Cover tightly and cook on
MEDIUM for 10 minutes. Leave to
stand, covered, for at least 5 minutes
while preparing the sauce. Combine
all the sauce ingredients with the
cooking liquid from the chicken in a
deep bowl. Cook, uncovered, for
7 minutes on HIGH, until the sauce
reduces and thickens. Remove the
bay leaf and blend the sauce in a food
processor until smooth. Arrange the
chicken breasts on a serving plate
and coat with the sauce. Add the
tomato strips and reheat for
30 seconds on HIGH before serving.

Chicken with Watercress Sauce

PREPARATION TIME: 15 minutes

MICROWAVE COOKING TIME:
12 minutes, plus
5 minutes standing time

SERVES: 4 people

4 large chicken breasts, skinned and
  boned
2 tbsps water
¼ cup lemon juice

SAUCE
1 cup low fat soft cheese
½ cup light cream or milk
1 large bunch watercress, well washed
  and drained
Salt and pepper

GARNISH
Lemon slices
Watercress

Place the chicken in one layer in a
large casserole. Pour over the water
and the lemon juice. Cover tightly
and cook 10 minutes on MEDIUM.
Leave to stand, covered, at least
5 minutes while preparing the sauce.
Combine the cheese and the cream
or milk with the chicken cooking
liquid and salt and pepper. Cook
1 minute on HIGH. Discard any
tough stalks from the watercress and
chop roughly. Add to the sauce and
cook 1 minute on HIGH. Blend the
sauce in a food processor until
smooth and a delicate green color.
Coat over the chicken to serve.
Garnish with lemon slices and
watercress.

**This page: Country Captain's
Chicken. Facing page: Chicken
with Watercress Sauce (top) and
Spicy Tomato Chicken (bottom).**

Country Captain's Chicken

PREPARATION TIME: 20 minutes

MICROWAVE COOKING TIME:
36 minutes

SERVES: 4 people

3lbs chicken pieces
4 tbsps butter
2 tbsps curry powder
1 clove garlic, minced
1 large onion, sliced
½ cup blanched whole almonds
½ cup golden raisins
2 apples, peeled and diced
1 16oz can tomatoes
2 tbsps tomato paste
1 bay leaf
2 tbsps chopped coriander (optional)
Pinch sugar
Salt and pepper

GARNISH
Desiccated coconut

Heat a browning dish for 5 minutes on HIGH. Melt the butter and add the chicken pieces. Cook 15 minutes on both sides or cook in 2 batches for 7½ minutes each batch if necessary. Remove the chicken and add the onion, garlic and curry powder. Cook 1 minute on HIGH. Replace the chicken, skin side down, and add the raisins, apples and almonds. Mix the tomatoes, tomato paste, lime juice, coriander, bay leaf, sugar, salt and pepper together and pour over the chicken. Cook 15 minutes on HIGH, or until the chicken is tender and no longer pink. Turn the chicken over halfway through cooking. Remove the bay leaf and serve with rice and garnish with desiccated coconut.

Piquant Duck

PREPARATION TIME: 25 minutes

MICROWAVE COOKING TIME: 27 minutes

SERVES: 4 people

8 duck portions
¼ cup butter
4 large cloves garlic, minced

SAUCE
¼ cup vinegar
1 cup dry white wine
3 tbsps Dijon mustard
2 tbsps tomato paste
2 tbsps chives
1 red pepper, very thinly sliced
½ cup heavy cream

Salt and pepper

Heat a browning dish for 5 minutes on HIGH, melt the butter and add the duck pieces skin side down. Brown the duck for 5 minutes per side. Add the garlic and cover the dish tightly. Cook until the duck is tender, about 15 minutes on HIGH. Pour off all the fat and leave the duck covered while preparing the sauce. Combine all the sauce ingredients except the red pepper and the cream

in a deep bowl. Add the garlic and any juices from the duck. Cook for 10 minutes on HIGH until well reduced. Add the cream and the red pepper and cook a further 2 minutes on HIGH. Trim the duck pieces neatly and pour over the sauce to serve.

Turkey Macadamia

PREPARATION TIME: 20 minutes

MICROWAVE COOKING TIME: 18 minutes

SERVES: 4 people

4 turkey breast cutlets
1 (8oz) can pineapple chunks, juice reserved
4 green onions, sliced
4 tomatoes, peeled, seeded and quartered
1 cup macadamia nuts

SAUCE
2 tbsps soy sauce
1 cup stock
2 tbsps vinegar
2 tbsps brown sugar
3 tsps cornstarch
Reserved pineapple juice

Place the turkey breasts in a casserole dish and pour over the pineapple juice. Cover the dish tightly and cook 10-15 minutes on MEDIUM. Leave to stand while preparing the sauce. Drain the pineapple juice from the turkey and combine it in a deep bowl with the remaining sauce ingredients. Add the pineapple pieces and the macadamia nuts. Cook, uncovered, for 2-3 minutes on HIGH, stirring frequently until thickened. Immediately add the tomatoes and the onions to the hot sauce and pour over the turkey to serve.

Turkey Tetrazzini

PREPARATION TIME: 20 minutes

MICROWAVE COOKING TIME: 6-8 minutes

SERVES: 4-6 people

¼ cup butter or margarine
2oz flour

4oz mushrooms, sliced
1 clove garlic, crushed
2 sticks celery, sliced
1 cup chicken stock
1 cup milk
½ cup double cream
2 tbsps dry white wine or sherry
12 black olives, pitted and roughly chopped
8oz cooked turkey, cut in cubes
8oz spaghetti
Salt and pepper
¼ cup each seasoned breadcrumbs and Parmesan cheese

Cook spaghetti in enough water to cover for 12 minutes on HIGH. Stir frequently. Drain and set aside. Melt the butter 30 seconds on HIGH, and add mushrooms, garlic and celery. Cook 1 minute on HIGH. Stir in the flour and add milk, stock and wine or sherry. Cook, uncovered, until thickened, about 5 minutes on HIGH. Add the cream and the olives. Combine with the turkey and spaghetti and pour into a casserole. Sprinkle cheese and crumbs on top and cook 8-10 minutes on HIGH. Serve immediately.

Duck with Cherries

PREPARATION TIME: 20 minutes

MICROWAVE COOKING TIME: 9 minutes

SERVES: 4 people

2 whole duck breasts
¼ cup butter or margarine
Salt and pepper

SAUCE
2 cans dark, pitted cherries, drained and juice reserved
½ cup red wine
2 tbsps red wine vinegar
Grated rind and juice of 1 orange
2 tsps cornstarch
1 bay leaf
1 sprig thyme
Pinch salt

Facing page: Duck with Cherries (top) and Piquant Duck (bottom).

Heat a browning dish 5 minutes on HIGH. Add the butter and put in the duck breasts. Brown the duck breasts 2 minutes on the skin side and 4 minutes on the other side. Remove the duck from the dish and keep warm. Mix the reserved cherry juice with the wine, vinegar, orange rind and juice, cornstarch, bay leaf and thyme in a small bowl. Cook for 3 minutes on HIGH until thickened, stirring frequently. Add a pinch of salt and remove the bay leaf and thyme. Add the cherries to the sauce and slice the duck breasts into thin slices. Pour over the cherry sauce to serve.

Pecan Poussins

PREPARATION TIME: 25 minutes

MICROWAVE COOKING TIME:
35 minutes

SERVES: 4 people

4 Cornish game hens
¼ cup Worcestershire sauce

STUFFING
6 slices white bread made into crumbs
8oz cooked ham
4 green onions, chopped
1 tsp thyme
1 egg, beaten
Salt and pepper

SAUCE
1½ cups brown stock
⅔ cup light brown sugar
⅓ cup cider vinegar
1 cup chopped pecans

GARNISH
Watercress

Process the ham and bread in a food processor until finely chopped. Add the egg, salt, pepper and thyme and process once or twice to mix thoroughly. Stir in the onion by hand. Stuff the hens and tie the legs together with string. Brush each hen with Worcestershire sauce. Cook 15-20 minutes on HIGH or 20 minutes on a Combination setting. Leave to stand 5 minutes

before serving. Mix the sauce ingredients together and cook on HIGH, uncovered, for 10-15 minutes. The sauce should be reduced and of syrupy consistency. Pour over the hens to serve and garnish with watercress.

Chicken Paprika

PREPARATION TIME: 20 minutes

MICROWAVE COOKING TIME:
32 minutes, plus
5 minutes standing time

SERVES: 4-6 people

3lbs chicken pieces
2 tbsps butter
2 onions, sliced
2 tbsps paprika
1 clove garlic, finely minced
2 tbsps tomato paste
1lb can tomatoes
4oz mushrooms
1 green pepper, thinly sliced
1 bay leaf
Salt and pepper

This page: **Chicken Paprika.**
Facing page: **Pecan Poussins.**

GARNISH
Sour cream

Melt the butter for 30 seconds on HIGH in a large casserole. Add the paprika, onions and garlic. Cook, uncovered, 2 minutes on HIGH. Lay the chicken pieces into the casserole skin-side down with the thickest portions to the outside of the dish. Combine the tomato paste with the tomatoes, bay leaf, salt and pepper. Pour the tomato sauce over the chicken and cover the casserole tightly. Cook for 15 minutes on HIGH. Turn over the chicken pieces and scatter the mushrooms and the pepper slices on top. Cook a further 15 minutes, or until the chicken is tender and no longer pink. Leave to stand, covered, for 5 minutes. Top with sour cream before serving with pasta or potatoes.

GAME DISHES

Quail with Artichokes and Vegetable Julienne

PREPARATION TIME: 25 minutes

MICROWAVE COOKING TIME: 19-21 minutes

SERVES: 4 people

8 quail
¼ cup butter or margarine
2 large artichokes, cooked
2 carrots, peeled
2 potatoes, peeled
2 leeks, washed

SAUCE
1 tbsp flour
½ cup white wine
1 cup heavy cream
2 tbsps Dijon mustard
Salt and pepper

GARNISH
Reserved artichoke leaves

Peel the leaves from the artichokes and remove the chokes. Set the leaves aside and cut the artichoke bottoms into thin slices. Cut the carrots, potatoes and leeks into julienne strips. Heat a browning dish for 5 minutes on HIGH. Melt the butter and add the carrots and potatoes. Cook on HIGH for 2 minutes. Add the leeks and artichoke bottoms and cook for a further 1 minute on HIGH. Remove the vegetables and set them aside. Add the quail to the butter in a dish and cook for 4-6 minutes on HIGH, turning frequently to brown lightly. Remove the quail from the dish and add the flour, white wine and Dijon mustard. Return the quail to the dish, cover tightly and cook for

5 minutes on HIGH. Set the quail aside to keep warm. Add the cream and salt and pepper to the dish and stir well. Cook for 1 minute on HIGH to thicken slightly. Add the vegetables to the sauce and cook a further 1 minute on HIGH to heat through. Pour the sauce over the

This page: Quail with Raspberries. Facing page: Quail with Apples and Calvados (top) and Quail with Artichokes and Vegetable Julienne (bottom).

quail to serve and surround with the artichoke leaves.

Juniper Venison

PREPARATION TIME: 25 minutes

MICROWAVE COOKING TIME:
55 minutes, plus
10 minutes standing time

SERVES: 4 people

2lbs venison, cut in 1 inch cubes
¼ cup butter or margarine
¼ cup flour
2 cups beef stock
¼ cup red wine
1 shallot, finely chopped
1 sprig rosemary
1 tbsp juniper berries
1 bay leaf
Salt and pepper

ACCOMPANIMENT
1lb potatoes, peeled and cut into small
  pieces
1 tbsp butter or margarine
1 egg, beaten
Salt and pepper
Rowanberry jelly, redcurrant jelly or whole
  cranberry sauce

Cook the potatoes in enough water to cover for 15 minutes on HIGH. Leave to stand for 5 minutes before draining and mashing. Season the potatoes with salt and pepper and add the butter. Beat in half the egg and pipe the mixture out into small baskets on a plate or a microwave baking sheet. Cook for 1 minute on HIGH and then brush with the remaining beaten egg and sprinkle with paprika. Cook a further 2 minutes on HIGH and set aside. Heat a browning dish for 5 minutes on HIGH. Melt the butter and brown the meat and the shallot for 4-6 minutes on HIGH. Remove the meat and shallot and stir in the flour, stock, red wine, salt, pepper, juniper berries, rosemary and bay leaf. Return the meat to the dish or transfer to a casserole. Cover and cook for 30 minutes on MEDIUM, stirring frequently. Remove the bay leaf and the sprig of rosemary before serving. Reheat the potato baskets for 30 seconds on HIGH and fill each with a spoonful of the jelly or cranberry sauce. Serve the potato

baskets with the venison. Garnish with fresh rosemary if desired.

Marmalade Venison

PREPARATION TIME: 15 minutes

MICROWAVE COOKING TIME:
40 minutes, plus
10 minutes standing time

SERVES: 4 people

2lbs venison, cut in 1 inch cubes
8oz small onions, peeled and left whole
¼ cup butter or margarine

**This page: Juniper Venison (top)
and Marmalade Venison (bottom).
Facing page: Pheasant Alsacienne.**

¼ cup flour
2 cups beef stock
¼ cup orange marmalade

GARNISH
Orange slices
Chopped parsley

Heat a browning dish for 5 minutes on HIGH. Melt the butter and add the venison. Cook 4-6 minutes on

HIGH, stirring frequently. Remove the meat and add the onions. Cook 1-2 minutes on HIGH to brown slightly. Remove the onions and add the flour, stock and marmalade. Return the meat and the onions to the casserole, cover and cook 30 minutes on MEDIUM. Leave to stand 10 minutes before serving. Garnish with orange slices and sprinkle with chopped parsley before serving.

Garlic Roast Pigeon

PREPARATION TIME: 20 minutes

MICROWAVE COOKING TIME:
15 minutes, plus
5 minutes standing time

SERVES: 4 people

4 pigeons
4 tbsps butter or margarine
12 cloves garlic, peeled
¼ cup white wine
1 cup chicken stock
1 bay leaf
1 sprig thyme
Salt and pepper

ACCOMPANIMENT
4 heads Belgian endive
1 cup water and white wine mixed
Pinch sugar
Salt and pepper

Spread the butter on the pigeons and place them breast side up on a roasting rack with the cloves of garlic. Cook on HIGH or a Combination setting for 10 minutes. Leave the pigeons to stand for 5 minutes before serving. They may be served slightly pink. Meanwhile, mash the cloves of garlic and mix with the stock, wine, bay leaf and salt and pepper. Cook, uncovered, for 3 minutes to reduce the liquid. Purée the sauce until smooth. Cut the endive in half lengthwise and remove the cores. Put into a casserole dish with the wine and water mixed, sugar, salt and pepper. Cover loosely and cook for 2 minutes on HIGH. Drain and serve around the pigeons. Pour

the sauce over the pigeons and the endive to serve.

Pigeon Kebabs with Walnut Grape Pilaf

PREPARATION TIME: 20 minutes

MICROWAVE COOKING TIME:
14 minutes

SERVES: 4 people

3-4 pigeons, depending on size
8 strips of bacon
2 tbsps butter or margarine, melted

WALNUT GRAPE PILAF
1½ cups brown rice
2 cups stock and wine mixed
2 tsps thyme
1 cup walnuts, chopped
1 small bunch purple or red grapes
Salt and pepper

Combine the rice with the stock and wine, salt, pepper and thyme in a large casserole. Cover loosely and cook for 10 minutes on HIGH. Cover completely and leave to stand 10 minutes for the rice to absorb the liquid. Add the chopped walnuts, cut the grapes in half and remove the seeds and add to the pilaf. Remove the breast meat from the pigeons and cut each breast half into 3 pieces. Thread onto skewers with the bacon. Brush each kebab with the melted butter or margarine and place on a roasting rack. Cook the kebabs 2 minutes per side. Set them aside, loosely covered, for 5 minutes before serving. Brush the kebabs with the cooking juices and serve on top of the pilaf.

Quail with Apples and Calvados

PREPARATION TIME: 20 minutes

MICROWAVE COOKING TIME:
17-19 minutes

SERVES: 4 people

8 quail
2 large apples, peeled and thinly sliced
¼ cup butter or margarine

SAUCE
1 tbsp flour
½ cup white wine or cider
1 cup heavy cream
¼ cup Calvados or brandy
2 tbsps chopped parsley
Salt and pepper

Heat a browning dish for 5 minutes on HIGH. Melt the butter and brown the quail for 4-6 minutes, turning often to brown evenly. Remove the quail and set aside. Add the sliced apples to the browning dish and cook for 2 minutes, turning over often to brown on both sides. If the apples are not browning sprinkle lightly with sugar. Remove the apples and set them aside. Stir the flour into the juices in the dish and add the white wine and the Calvados. Return the quail to the dish or transfer to a casserole. Cover the dish tightly and cook for 5 minutes on HIGH. Remove the quail and keep warm. Add the cream and the parsley to the dish with salt and pepper. Cook for 1 minute on HIGH. Add the apples to the sauce and pour over the quail to serve.

Pheasant Alsacienne

PREPARATION TIME: 20 minutes

MICROWAVE COOKING TIME:
28-30 minutes

SERVES: 4 people

2 pheasants, dressed
2 onion slices
2 sprigs thyme
2 tbsps oil

ACCOMPANIMENT
3 tbsps butter
3 tbsps flour
1 head white cabbage, shredded

Facing page: Pigeon Kebabs with Walnut Grape Pilaf (top) and Garlic Roast Pigeon (bottom).

2 apples, peeled and grated
2 tbsps caraway seeds
8oz smoked sausage, sliced
1 cup white wine
1 bay leaf
Salt and pepper

Prick the pheasants lightly all over the skin and brush with oil. Place the pheasants breast side down on a roasting rack, one at a time if necessary. Cook for 10 minutes on MEDIUM. Turn over and cook for a further 10 minutes on MEDIUM. Cook for 15 minutes on the Combination setting of a microwave convection oven, turning once. Cover and leave to stand while preparing the cabbage. Melt the butter in a large casserole for 30 seconds on HIGH. Add the flour and the wine and combine with the remaining ingredients. Cook for 8-10 minutes on HIGH, stirring frequently. Serve with the pheasants.

Wild Duck with Limes and Onions

PREPARATION TIME: 20 minutes

MICROWAVE COOKING TIME:
25 minutes

SERVES: 4 people

2 wild ducks
2 slices onion
2 bay leaves
¼ cup butter or margarine

SAUCE
3 tbsps flour
Cooking juices from the duck
1 cup stock
2 onions, finely sliced
Grated rind and juice of 1 lime
Pinch of sugar
Salt and pepper

GARNISH
Lime wedges

Prick the skin of the duck all over and rub with half of the butter. Put an onion slice and a bay leaf inside each duck. Put onto a roasting rack breast side down and cook for 5 minutes on MEDIUM. Turn the

ducks over and cook for 10 minutes further on MEDIUM. Cook on the Combination setting of a microwave convection oven for 16 minutes. Turn over after 8 minutes. Cover loosely and leave to stand for 5 minutes. Combine the pan juices with the remaining butter in a small bowl, and cook 30 seconds on HIGH to melt. Add the sliced onions, cover the dish loosely, and cook for 2 minutes on HIGH. Stir in the flour, stock, lime juice and grated rind. Add a pinch sugar, salt and pepper and cook a further 5 minutes on HIGH, or until thickened. Pour over the ducks to serve and surround with lime wedges.

Wild Duck with Blackcurrants and Port

PREPARATION TIME: 15 minutes

MICROWAVE COOKING TIME:
20-25 minutes

SERVES: 4 people

2 wild ducks
2 onion slices
2 sprigs thyme
2 tbsps butter or margarine
1lb can blackcurrants (if unavailable substitute other red berries or dark cherries)
1 tbsp red wine vinegar
½ cup port
1 tbsp cornstarch
Pinch of salt and pepper

Prick the duck skin all over and rub each duck with the butter. Put a slice of onion and a sprig of thyme inside each duck and place them breast side down on a roasting rack. Cook on MEDIUM for 5 minutes. Turn over the ducks and cook a further 10 minutes on MEDIUM. Cook for 16 minutes on the Combination setting of a microwave convection oven. Turn halfway through the cooking time. Cover loosely and set aside for 5 minutes. Combine the blackcurrants with the port, vinegar, cornstarch, pan juices from the duck, salt and pepper in a deep bowl. Cook, uncovered, for 5 minutes on HIGH or until thickened, stirring

frequently. Remove the onion and the thyme from the ducks and pour over the blackcurrant sauce to serve.

Quail with Raspberries

PREPARATION TIME: 15 minutes

MICROWAVE COOKING TIME:
9-11 minutes

SERVES: 4 people

8 quail
8oz frozen raspberries
1 cup red wine
1 tbsp red wine vinegar or raspberry vinegar
1 tbsp sugar
1 sprig rosemary
1 tbsp cornstarch

GARNISH
Whole raspberries and watercress

Prick the quail lightly all over with a fork and rub with a bit of butter. Put the quail breast side down on a roasting rack in a circle with the thicker part of the quail pointing to the outside of the dish. Cook for 2 minutes on HIGH. Turn the quail over and cook for a further 3 minutes on HIGH. Cook for 6 minutes on the Combination setting of a microwave convection oven without turning. Cover loosely and set aside while preparing the sauce. Reserve 16 raspberries for garnish and combine the raspberries with the remaining sauce ingredients in a deep bowl. Cook for 4-6 minutes on HIGH, stirring frequently to break up the raspberries. When thickened, purée in a food processor until smooth. Strain to remove the raspberry seeds. Cut the quail in half and coat with the raspberry sauce. Garnish with the reserved whole raspberries and watercress to serve.

Dijon Rabbit with Capers

PREPARATION TIME: 15 minutes

MICROWAVE COOKING TIME:
34 minutes

SERVES: 4 people

8 rabbit quarters
3 tbsps butter or margarine
3 tbsps flour
1 cup stock
½ cup white wine
½ cup double cream
2 tbsps Dijon mustard
2 tbsps capers
1 tbsp chopped chives
Salt and pepper

Heat a browning dish for 5 minutes on HIGH. Melt the butter and brown the rabbit for 2 minutes on each side. Remove the rabbit and add the flour, stock, wine, salt, pepper and mustard. Return the rabbit to the dish or transfer to a casserole. Cook, covered, for 25 minutes on MEDIUM. Remove the rabbit from the dish and add the capers, chives and cream. Cook a further 2 minutes on HIGH and pour over the rabbit to serve. Serve with green beans.

Pepper Rabbit and Mushrooms

PREPARATION TIME: 15 minutes

MICROWAVE COOKING TIME: 34 minutes

SERVES: 4 people

---

8 rabbit quarters
3 tbsps butter or margarine
3 tbsps flour
2 shallots, finely chopped
1 cup stock
½ cup white wine
½ lb mushrooms, sliced
½ cup heavy cream

Left: Pepper Rabbit and Mushrooms (top) and Dijon Rabbit with Capers (bottom). Right: Wild Duck with Limes and Onions (top) and Wild Duck with Blackcurrants and Port (bottom).

1 tsp coarsely ground black pepper
1 tbsp chopped parsley
Salt

Heat a browning dish for 5 minutes on HIGH. Melt the butter and brown the rabbit pieces and the shallots for 1 minute per side on HIGH. Add the stock, wine, pepper and salt. Cook, covered, for 25 minutes on MEDIUM. Add the mushrooms and cook a further 2 minutes on HIGH. Remove the rabbit from the casserole and stir in the cream and parsley. Pour the sauce over the rabbit to serve.

Microwave
COOKING FOR 1&2

Microwave
COOKING FOR 1&2

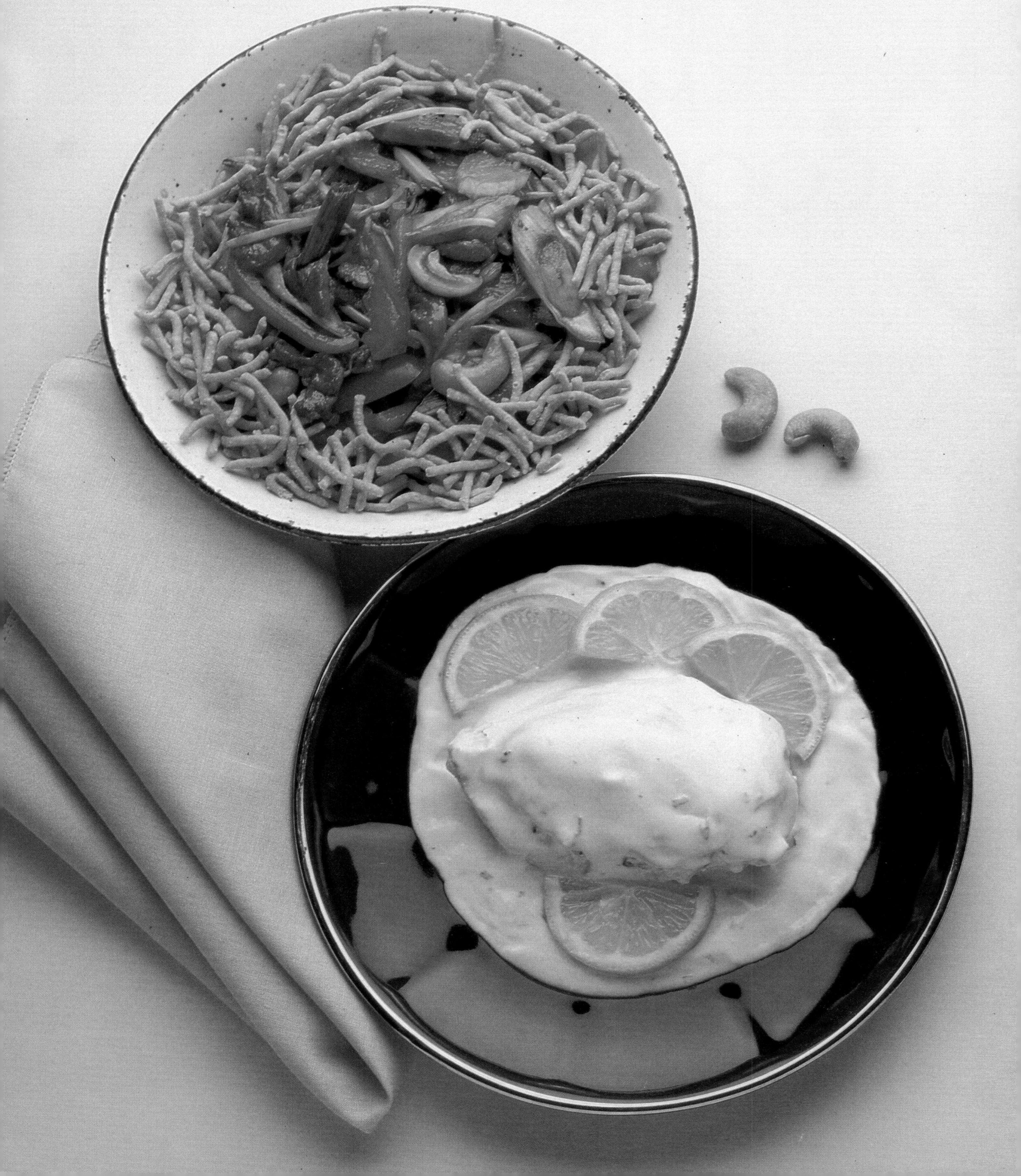

Do meals for singles or couples have to be uninspiring? Do people on their own have to rely on pre-prepared food for speed and convenience? Not when there is a microwave around. Small portions cook beautifully in practically the time it takes to open the package and read the cooking instructions. With a microwave oven there is no need to sacrifice variety for convenience.

Small packages of fresh vegetables and meat are readily available in supermarkets and specialty food stores. Even turkey and duck are available in manageable sizes for the small household. Cooking a dinner party for one special guest can be cheaper than dinner out. It can also be an occasion for experimenting with more elaborate preparations than you might want to attempt for large numbers.

However, leftovers come in handy, so don't shy away from cooking a whole turkey or a large piece of meat. Leftovers can be frozen and used as a basis for completely different meals later on. Small portions, well covered, will defrost in 2-3 minutes on a LOW or DEFROST setting. Soups can be kept refrigerated for up to two days and reheated on MEDIUM in about 2-5 minutes. Vegetable and flour-thickened soups can also be frozen, and then defrosted and reheated in about 10 minutes on a LOW or DEFROST setting, with frequent stirring. Meat, poultry and game stews and braises can be reheated as well, usually on MEDIUM for about 4-6 minutes. If frozen, they can be defrosted and reheated in about 12-15 minutes on LOW or DEFROST. Individual portions should be frozen in bags or containers that are suitable for reheating in microwave ovens or in individual serving dishes of the freezer-to-table variety.

All the recipes in this book were tested in an oven with a maximum power of 700 watts. Certain recipes were cooked in a combination microwave-convection oven, which combines the speed of microwave cooking with browning ability. However, any dish that requires browning can be placed under a preheated broiler for a minute or two before serving. Also, toppings such as breadcrumbs, crushed cereals or cheeses can give an eye-pleasing finish to your very own brand of 'convenience' food.

SOUPS AND APPETIZERS

Confetti Spread and Sesame Crackers

PREPARATION TIME: 15 minutes

MICROWAVE COOKING TIME: 10-12 minutes

SERVES: 2 people

SPREAD
1 cup cream cheese
2 strips bacon, diced
1 tbsp chopped chives
Red pepper flakes
4 chopped black olives
Crushed garlic
¼ cup chopped green and red peppers, mixed
2 tbsps frozen corn
Salt and pepper

CRACKERS
¼ cup all-purpose flour
¼ cup whole-wheat flour
1½ tbsps butter
2 tsps sesame seeds
1-2 tbsps cold water
1 egg, beaten with a pinch of salt
Salt and pepper

Put the flours, salt and pepper into the bowl of a food processor. Cut the butter into small pieces and add to the flour. Process until the mixture looks like fine breadcrumbs. Add 1 tbsp sesame seeds and add the water with the machine running until the mixture forms a dough. Roll out thinly on a floured board and brush with the egg. Sprinkle on the remaining sesame seeds and cut into 1″ squares. Arrange into a circle on a large plate and cook on HIGH for 3-6 minutes until crisp. Cool on a wire rack. Makes 12 crackers.
Heat a browning dish for 3 minutes

and cook the diced bacon on HIGH for 1-2 minutes or until crisp. Drain on paper towels and allow to cool. Put the chopped peppers and corn into a small bowl and cover with water. Cover the bowl with pierced plastic wrap and cook on HIGH for 2 minutes. Rinse with cold water and leave to drain dry. Put the cream

This page: Confetti Spread with Sesame Crackers. Facing page: Oriental Kebabs.

cheese into a small bowl and heat for 30-40 seconds on MEDIUM to soften. Add the bacon, peppers and the remaining ingredients, and mix

well. Serve with the sesame seed crackers. Unused peppers can be frozen.

Marinated Shrimp and Sour Cream Sauce

PREPARATION TIME: 15 minutes

MICROWAVE COOKING TIME: 5 minutes

SERVES: 2 people

½ lb fresh large shrimp, shelled and cleaned

MARINADE
½ cup white wine
2 tbsps white wine vinegar
1 bay leaf
2 black peppercorns
1 whole allspice berry
2 whole cloves
½ tsp dill seeds
½ small onion, sliced
Salt

SAUCE
½ cup sour cream
2-3 tbsps strained reserved marinade
½ tsp chopped dill, fresh or dried
½ tsp grated horseradish
Salt and pepper

GARNISH
Lettuce leaves
Sprigs of fresh dill

Combine all the marinade ingredients in a 1 pint casserole and cover. Cook for 2-3 minutes on HIGH until boiling. Stir in the shrimp, cover, and cook on MEDIUM for 2 minutes. Allow to cool in the marinade. If using fresh dill, reserve 2 small sprigs for garnish and chop ½ tsp. Drain the marinade and mix with the sour cream, dill, horseradish, and salt and pepper. Arrange lettuce on serving plates, and place on the shrimp. Top with some of the sauce and the reserved dill. Serve remaining sauce separately.

Scallop Parcels with Curry Sauce

PREPARATION TIME: 15 minutes

MICROWAVE COOKING TIME: 3-4 minutes

SERVES: 2 people

6 large or 8 small scallops
1 small sweet red pepper
2 large mushrooms
2 tbsps white wine
1 tsp black pepper
¼ tsp salt
¼ tsp ground ginger
Garlic powder
1 tbsp oil
Whole fresh chives

SAUCE
1 tbsp curry powder
½ cup plain yogurt
Juice of ½ a lime
½ tsp mango chutney
Salt and pepper

Mix the wine, salt, pepper, oil, ginger, and a pinch of garlic powder together well. Put in the scallops and turn them to coat evenly. Cut the pepper into pieces the size of the scallops. Cut the mushrooms into ¼″ slices. Layer the pepper, mushrooms and scallops, and tie each parcel with 2 whole chives. Put the parcels on their sides onto a microwave roasting rack and cook on HIGH for 30 seconds. Turn every 30 seconds, ending with the parcels scallop-sides up. Cook for a total of 2-3 minutes, brushing frequently with the ginger basting liquid. Serve hot or cold, with the curry sauce.
Put the curry powder for the sauce onto a small plate and cook for 1 minute on HIGH. Allow to cool, and combine with the other ingredients. Serve with the scallops.

Oriental Kebabs

PREPARATION TIME: 20 minutes

MICROWAVE COOKING TIME: 5-6 minutes

SERVES: 2 people

3oz ground pork or beef
1 tbsp breadcrumbs
1 tsp chopped onion
1 small can pineapple chunks
6 cherry tomatoes

BASTING MIXTURE
¼ cup honey
¼ cup soy sauce
¼ cup rice wine
1 tbsp sesame seed oil
1 tsp ground ginger
Pepper

SWEET AND SOUR SAUCE
Remaining basting mixture
1 tbsp ketchup
1 tsp cornstarch
Reserved pineapple juice
1 tbsp cider vinegar
½ tsp garlic powder

Mix together the basting ingredients. Mix the meat, breadcrumbs, chopped onion and 1 tbsp of the basting mixture. Shape into 8 meatballs. Drain the can of pineapple and reserve the juice. Thread the meatballs onto wooden skewers, alternating with the pineapple chunks and tomatoes. Place the kebabs on a roasting rack and brush with the baste. Cook on HIGH for 3 minutes, turning and basting each minute. Combine the ingredients for the sauce, and cook on HIGH for 2-3 minutes until thickened. Stir every 30 seconds. Serve with the kebabs. For one person only, use half the amount of all the ingredients. Cook the kebabs for 2 minutes, and the sauce for 1-2 minutes.

Tomato and Basil Soup

PREPARATION TIME: 15 minutes

MICROWAVE COOKING TIME: 5 minutes

SERVES: 2 people

Facing page: Scallop Parcels with Curry Sauce (top) and Marinated Shrimp and Sour Cream Sauce (bottom).

vegetables lengthwise into thin strips. Add the carrot noodles to the consommé, cover with pierced plastic wrap, and cook on HIGH for 3 minutes. Add the zucchini and cook for an additional 1 minute on HIGH. Stir in the sherry before serving.

Cheesy Spinach Soup

PREPARATION TIME: 15 minutes

MICROWAVE COOKING TIME: 5 minutes

SERVES: 1 person

½ cup frozen spinach
½ cup shredded Colby cheese
2 tbsps hot water
1 tbsp butter
1 tbsp flour
½ a chicken bouillon cube
1 tbsp chopped onion
1 cup milk
Pinch of thyme
Pinch of nutmeg
Salt and pepper

2 cups tomato sauce
1 cup hot water
½ a beef bouillon cube, or 1 tsp instant beef bouillon granules
2 tbsps cream
2 tbsps red wine
¼ tsp cornstarch
Pinch sugar
2 tbsps fresh basil leaves
2 tbsps parsley
½ clove garlic
2 tbsps olive oil
Salt and pepper

Mix the tomato sauce, water, beef bouillon, sugar, and salt and pepper together in a 1 quart casserole. Cover and cook for 2 minutes on HIGH. Mix the cornstarch and wine together and stir into the soup. Heat for 2 minutes on HIGH, stirring every 30 seconds. Put the basil leaves, parsley and garlic into a blender and purée. Add the oil in a thin, steady stream with the machine running. Re-heat the soup for 1 minute on HIGH, and stir in the cream just before serving. Add the basil mixture, and stir through the

soup.
To serve one person only, use half of all the ingredients, and cook the soup for a total of 2 minutes.

Consommé with Vegetable Noodles

PREPARATION TIME: 15 minutes

MICROWAVE COOKING TIME: 5 minutes

SERVES: 2 people

10½ oz can condensed beef or chicken consommé
1½ cups water
1 bay leaf
1 tbsp sherry
1 small zucchini
1 small carrot, peeled

Combine the consommé and the water. Add the bay leaf and heat through for 1 minute on HIGH. Cut ends off the zucchini and carrot and, using a swivel peeler, pare the

Put the spinach, onion and water into a small bowl and cover with pierced plastic wrap. Cook for 1 minute on HIGH and set aside. Put the butter into another bowl and cook for 30 seconds on HIGH or until melted. Add the flour, bouillon cube, nutmeg, thyme, milk, and salt and pepper. Cook on MEDIUM for 4 minutes or until thickened. Stir frequently. Add the spinach and its cooking liquid to the soup, and purée in a food processor until smooth. Stir in the cheese, reserving 1 tbsp. Re-heat on MEDIUM for 1 minute. Sprinkle the reserved cheese on top to serve.
To serve 2 people, double the ingredients and cook the soup for 5-6 minutes on MEDIUM.

This page: Consommé with Vegetable Noodles. Facing page: Cheesy Spinach Soup (top) and Tomato and Basil Soup (bottom).

Microwave
COOKING FOR 1 & 2

SNACKS

Italian Ham Sandwiches

PREPARATION TIME: 10 minutes

MICROWAVE COOKING TIME:
4 minutes

SERVES: 2 people

¼ lb Parma, or other Italian ham
2oz sliced mozzarella cheese
4 mild Italian peppers
1 tbsp butter or margarine
Pinch garlic powder
Pinch of oregano
2 French rolls

Mix the butter, garlic and oregano.
Split the rolls and spread the butter
thinly on each of the cut sides. Layer
the ham, peppers and cheese on the
bottom half of the roll. Place the top
on and press down. Place the
sandwiches on a paper towel in the
oven. Cook on MEDIUM for 4-5
minutes or until the cheese melts.
Serve immediately.

Sloppy Joes

PREPARATION TIME: 15 minutes

MICROWAVE COOKING TIME:
14 minutes

SERVES: 2 people

½ lb ground beef or pork
1 small onion, finely chopped
¼ cup chopped green pepper
1 cup tomato sauce
2 tsps Worcestershire sauce

**This page: Italian Ham
Sandwiches (top) and Cheese and
Mushroom Croissants (bottom).
Facing page: Sausage and
Sauerkraut Sandwiches (top) and
Sloppy Joes (bottom).**

½ tsp dry mustard
1½ tsps cider vinegar
1 tsp brown sugar
Salt and pepper
2 Kaiser rolls or hamburger buns

Mix the meat and onion in a casserole and cook, uncovered, for 7 minutes on HIGH. Mash the meat with a fork several times while cooking, to break it up into small pieces. Strain off any fat. Add the remaining ingredients and stir well. Cover and cook for a further 5 minutes on HIGH, stirring occasionally. Wrap the rolls in paper towels and heat for 1-2 minutes on MEDIUM. Split and fill with the Sloppy Joe filling. Mixture freezes well.

Tacos

PREPARATION TIME: 15 minutes
MICROWAVE COOKING TIME: 6 minutes
SERVES: 2 people

4 taco shells
¼ lb ground beef
¼ cup chopped onion
1 tbsp raisins
1 tbsp pine nuts
1 tbsp corn
1 tsp chili powder
¼ cup tomato sauce
Salt and pepper

TOPPINGS
½ cup grated cheese
½ cup sour cream
½ cup chopped tomatoes
1 cup shredded lettuce
1 chopped avocado

Put the beef and onion into a 1 quart casserole. Break the meat up well with a fork. Cover and cook for 2 minutes on HIGH, stirring occasionally to break into small pieces. Drain any fat from the meat and add salt and pepper, chili powder, corn, nuts, raisins and tomato sauce. Cover and cook on MEDIUM for 4 minutes. Spoon into the taco shells and serve with the various toppings.

Sausage and Sauerkraut Sandwiches

PREPARATION TIME: 10 minutes
MICROWAVE COOKING TIME: 1½ minutes
SERVES: 2 people

4 slices rye bread, light or dark
¼ lb smoked sausage (kielbasa or bratwurst), thinly sliced
4 slices Muenster or Tilsit cheese
½ cup drained sauerkraut
2 tbsps butter or margarine

DRESSING
1 tbsp spicy brown mustard
2 tbsps mayonnaise
1½ tsps chopped dill pickle

Melt the butter for 30 seconds on HIGH in a small bowl. Mix dressing and spread on both sides of the bread slices. Layer on the sauerkraut, sausage and cheese. Heat a browning dish for 5 minutes on HIGH. Brush 1 side of the bread with melted butter and place the sandwich in the dish. Cook for 15 seconds, or until golden brown. Turn over and brush the other side with butter and cook that side for 20-30 seconds or until the bread is browned and the cheese melted. Serve hot.

Cheese and Mushroom Croissants

PREPARATION TIME: 15 minutes
MICROWAVE COOKING TIME: 3 minutes
SERVES: 1 person

1 croissant or crescent roll
1 tsp butter
½ tsp flour
2 mushrooms, sliced
¼ cup Gruyère cheese
¼ cup milk
1 tbsp white wine
½ tsp Dijon mustard
Nutmeg
Salt and pepper

Split the top of the croissant, taking care not to cut through to the bottom or the ends. Melt ½ tsp butter in a small bowl for 15 seconds on HIGH. Add the mushrooms and cook for 30 seconds on HIGH and set aside. Melt the remaining butter in a 1 pint measure. Stir in the flour and add the milk and wine gradually. Add a pinch of nutmeg, mustard and salt and pepper. Cook on HIGH for 1 minute or until thick. Stir in the cheese and spoon into the croissant. Top with the mushrooms and heat through for 1 minute on MEDIUM. Serve immediately.

Pizza Muffins

PREPARATION TIME: 10 minutes
MICROWAVE COOKING TIME: 2 minutes
SERVES: 1 person

1 English muffin, split
2 tbsps tomato paste
2 tbsps water
1 green onion, sliced
¼ tsp oregano
Pinch garlic powder
¼ cup pepperoni or Italian salami, chopped, or 4 anchovies
2-3 Italian olives, stoned and halved
1 tsp capers
⅓ cup grated mozzarella cheese
1 tbsp Parmesan cheese
Salt and pepper

Mix the tomato paste with the water, salt and pepper, onion, oregano and garlic powder, and spread on the muffin halves. Arrange the sausage or a cross of anchovies on top. Add the olives and capers and sprinkle on the mozzarella cheese. Sprinkle on the Parmesan cheese last and put the pizzas on a paper towel, then cook for 1½-2 minutes on HIGH. Turn the pizzas once or twice during cooking. For 2 people, double the ingredients and cook for 4-4½ minutes on HIGH.

Facing page: Tacos.

Vegetable Pockets

PREPARATION TIME: 10 minutes

MICROWAVE COOKING TIME:
4-5 minutes

SERVES: 2 people

1 piece whole-wheat pitta bread
1 tbsp olive oil
1 tsp lemon juice
1 tomato, roughly chopped
1 red onion, thinly sliced or 2 green onions, sliced
1 green pepper, thinly sliced
1 cup fresh spinach leaves
½ tsp chives
1 tbsp fresh basil leaves, if available
1 small zucchini, thinly sliced
6 black olives, stoned
¼ cup crumbled feta cheese
Salt and pepper

Cut the pitta bread in half and open out the pockets. Mix the lemon juice and oil together with the salt and pepper. Toss the cheese, tomato, vegetables, herbs and olives together in the dressing. Fill the pockets with the vegetables and heat for 4-5 minutes on MEDIUM. Serve immediately.

Tuna Melt

PREPARATION TIME: 10 minutes

MICROWAVE COOKING TIME:
2 minutes

SERVES: 1 person

1 English muffin, split
1 small can white tuna
2 tbsps cottage cheese
2 tbsps mayonnaise
1 stick celery, chopped
1 tsp chopped parsley
2 tsps chopped chives
½ tsp lemon juice
Alfalfa sprouts
¼ cup grated Colby cheese
Salt and pepper

Mix together the tuna, cottage cheese, mayonnaise, celery, parsley, chives, and salt and pepper. Taste and add lemon juice if desired. Put alfalfa sprouts on the muffin halves and spoon on the tuna mixture. Top with

the cheese and heat for 1 minute on MEDIUM. Increase the heat to HIGH and heat for 1 minute further, turning once or twice during cooking. Serve immediately.

Pocketful of Shrimp

PREPARATION TIME: 10 minutes

MICROWAVE COOKING TIME:
2-4 minutes

SERVES: 2 people

1 piece pitta bread, cut in half
½ cup bean sprouts
½ cup cooked shrimp, peeled and de-veined
1 tbsp chili sauce
2 tbsps mayonnaise
½ tsp horseradish

This page: Pizza Muffins (top) and Tuna Melt (bottom). Facing page: Pocketful of Shrimp (top) and Vegetable Pockets (bottom).

1 stick celery, chopped
1 ripe avocado, peeled and thickly sliced
1 tbsp lemon juice
Salt and pepper

Cut the pitta bread in half and open a pocket in each half. Toss the avocado slices in lemon juice and place them in the sides of the pockets. Fill each pocket with bean sprouts. Mix the shrimp, chili sauce, mayonnaise, horseradish, salt, pepper and chopped celery together. Put on top of the bean sprouts and heat through for 2-4 minutes on MEDIUM. Serve immediately.

EGG AND CHEESE

Piperade

PREPARATION TIME: 10 minutes

MICROWAVE COOKING TIME:
6 minutes, plus 1 minute standing time

SERVES: 1 person

1 tbsp finely chopped onion
½ tbsp butter
½ cap pimento, finely chopped
1 tomato
Pinch garlic powder
2 eggs
Pinch oregano
Salt and pepper

Put 2 cups water into a bowl and cover with pierced plastic wrap. Heat for 3 minutes on HIGH or until boiling. Put in the tomato and leave for 30 seconds. Peel and seed the tomato, and chop roughly. Put the butter into a medium-sized bowl with the garlic powder and onion. Cook on HIGH for 3 minutes. Add the pimento, tomato and oregano. Cook on HIGH for 1 minute. Beat the eggs, salt and pepper together, and add to the bowl. Cook on HIGH for about 2 minutes, stirring every 30 seconds, or until the eggs are softly scrambled. Leave to stand for 1 minute before serving. Serve on buttered toast or English muffins, or with French bread.

Sunrise Scramble

PREPARATION TIME: 15 minutes

MICROWAVE COOKING TIME:
5 minutes, plus 1 minute standing time

SERVES: 1 person

2 tbsps ham, finely chopped
2 eggs
1 tbsp butter
1 tbsp grated cheese
¼ cup mushrooms, sliced
1 tomato
1 tbsp chopped parsley
Salt and pepper

Put the butter into a small bowl, add the mushrooms, and cook for 2 minutes on HIGH or until soft. Drain away any excess liquid. Add the ham, and cook for 1 minute on HIGH. Cut the tomato in quarters, but leave attached at the base. Heat for 1 minute on HIGH, and keep warm. Beat the eggs and add the cheese, parsley, and salt and pepper. Add the eggs to the bowl with the ham and mushrooms, and cook for 2 minutes on HIGH, stirring every 30 seconds until softly scrambled. Leave to stand for 1 minute. Fill the tomato with the egg mixture and serve.

Spinach and Cheese Layered Quiche

PREPARATION TIME: 20 minutes

MICROWAVE COOKING TIME:
11-14 minutes, plus 6 minutes standing time

SERVES: 2 people

PASTRY
⅓ cup all-purpose flour
⅓ cup whole-wheat flour
¼ cup margarine
2 tbsps shortening
¼ cup ice cold water
Pinch of salt

FILLING
½ cup shredded Gruyère or Swiss cheese
3 eggs
¼ cup half and half
¼ cup chopped frozen spinach, well drained
Nutmeg
Cayenne pepper or Tabasco
Salt and pepper

Put the flours, salt, margarine and shortening into the bowl of a food processor and work until the mixture resembles fine breadcrumbs. With the machine running, add the water gradually until the dough holds together. It may not be necessary to add all the water. Roll out the pastry on a floured board to ⅛" thick, and put into a 7" pie plate. Trim the edge and flute. Refrigerate for 10 minutes. Mix the eggs, cheese, half and half and salt and pepper together well. Divide the mixture in half: add the spinach and pinch of nutmeg to one half, and a pinch of Cayenne pepper or a dash of Tabasco to the other. Prick the base of the pastry with a fork and cook on HIGH for 2-3 minutes or until it starts to crisp. Pour in the cheese mixture and cook for 4 minutes on MEDIUM, or until softly set. Leave to stand for 1 minute. Pour on the spinach mixture and cook for a further 7-10 minutes or until the center is softly set. Leave to stand for 6 minutes before serving.

Facing page: Sunrise Scramble (top) and Piperade (bottom).

Niçoise Eggs

PREPARATION TIME: 10 minutes

MICROWAVE COOKING TIME:
9 minutes

SERVES: 2 person

2 eggs
4 tomatoes, peeled, seeded and chopped
1 tsp butter
2 mushrooms, chopped
2 tbsps white wine
1 tbsp capers
4 black olives, stoned and sliced
2 anchovies, chopped
1 tbsp tarragon
Pinch of paprika
Salt and pepper
¼ cup Gruyère or Swiss cheese, grated

Put the butter into a small casserole

This page: Italian Fondue (left) and Niçoise Eggs (right). Facing page: Tuna and Tomato Quiche (top) and Spinach and Cheese Layered Quiche (bottom).

and melt for 30 seconds on HIGH. Add the chopped mushrooms, tarragon and half the wine, and cook for 2 minutes on HIGH. Add the remaining ingredients except the cheese, eggs and paprika, and cook for 1-2 minutes on HIGH. Divide the tomato mixture into 2 custard cups and make a well in the center. Put an egg into the center of the mixture in each cup. Pierce the yolk with a sharp knife. Pour over the remaining wine. Cook for 3 minutes on HIGH or until the white is set and yolk is still

soft. Sprinkle on the cheese and paprika and cook for 1 minute on LOW to melt the cheese.

Italian Fondue

PREPARATION TIME: 10 minutes

MICROWAVE COOKING TIME:
5 minutes

SERVES: 1 person

1 cup shredded mozzarella cheese
½ cup shredded mild Cheddar cheese
1 tsp cornstarch
⅓ cup red wine
1 tbsp tomato paste
1 tsp dry vermouth
½ clove garlic, crushed

½ tsp basil
½ tsp oregano
1 French roll, cut into cubes, or broccoli
  flowerets, carrot sticks and celery sticks

Toss the cheese and cornstarch to mix. Put the wine into a deep bowl and cook on MEDIUM for 1-2 minutes, or until it begins to bubble – do not allow it to boil. Add the remaining ingredients except the bread (or vegetables), and stir well to blend completely. Cook for a further 2-3 minutes on MEDIUM, or until the cheese melts. Stir every few seconds. If the mixture begins to boil, reduce the setting to LOW. Serve with the bread cubes or vegetables. Re-heat on LOW if necessary. Serve as an appetizer or as an entrée with a tossed salad.
To serve 2 people, double the ingredients. Cook the wine for 2-3 minutes on MEDIUM, and the cheese and other ingredients for 3-4 minutes on MEDIUM.

Tuna and Tomato Quiche

PREPARATION TIME: 20 minutes

MICROWAVE COOKING TIME:
18 minutes, plus 6 minutes standing time

SERVES: 2 people

PASTRY
⅔ cup all-purpose flour
¼ cup margarine
2 tbsps shortening
1 tbsp paprika
Pinch of salt
¼ cup ice cold water

FILLING
1 can (about 6oz) white tuna, drained
  and flaked
3 eggs
2 tomatoes, peeled
½ cup shredded Cheddar cheese
¼ cup half and half
1 tbsp chopped green onion
Salt and pepper

TOPPING
1 tbsp dry, seasoned breadcrumbs
2 tbsps grated Parmesan cheese

Put the flour, salt, paprika, margarine and shortening into the bowl of a food processor and work until the mixture resembles fine breadcrumbs. With the machine running, add the water gradually until the dough holds together. It may not be necessary to add all the water. Roll out the pastry on a floured board to ⅛" thick and put into a 7" pie plate. Trim the edge and flute. Refrigerate for 10 minutes. Beat the eggs with the salt, pepper and half and half. Add the cheese, onion and tuna. Cut the tomatoes into quarters and take out the seeds. Prick the base of the pastry and cook on HIGH for 2-3 minutes, or until starting to crisp. Pour the filling into the pastry shell and decorate the top with the tomatoes. Cook on MEDIUM for 10-15 minutes. Mix

the topping ingredients and sprinkle over the top of the quiche 5 minutes before the end of baking. Left-over quiche can be refrigerated for up to 2 days. Eat cold or re-heat on MEDIUM for 2 minutes.

Ham, Broccoli and Pineapple au Gratin

PREPARATION TIME: 15 minutes

MICROWAVE COOKING TIME:
10-12 minutes

SERVES: 2 people

4 slices cooked ham
8 broccoli spears

broccoli for 3 minutes on HIGH. Once assembled, cook for 2-3 minutes on MEDIUM. Left-over cheese sauce can be frozen, or kept in the refrigerator for 2 days. Bring to room temperature, re-heat on MEDIUM for 1-2 minutes to serve the sauce.

Asparagus and Tomato Omelette

PREPARATION TIME: 15 minutes

MICROWAVE COOKING TIME: 15 minutes

SERVES: 2 people

4 eggs, separated
½ cup chopped asparagus, fresh or frozen
2 tbsps water
2 tomatoes, peeled, seeded and chopped
⅓ cup Gruyère cheese, grated
⅓ cup milk
1 tbsp butter or margarine
1 tsp flour
Salt and pepper

Put the asparagus and water into a 1 pint casserole. Cover and cook for 5-6 minutes on HIGH. Beat the egg yolks, milk, flour, and salt and pepper together. Beat the egg whites until stiff but not dry and fold into the yolks. Melt the butter in a 9″ pie plate for 30 seconds on HIGH. Pour the omelette mixture onto the plate and cook on MEDIUM for 7 minutes or until set. Lift the edges of the omelette to allow the uncooked mixture to spread evenly. Sprinkle with the cheese, and spread on the asparagus and chopped tomato. Fold over and cook for 1 minute on LOW to melt the cheese. Serve immediately.

¼ cup sliced mushrooms
1 tbsp butter
4 pineapple rings, drained
2 tbsps water
Pinch of salt
1 tsp dark brown sugar

SAUCE
1 tbsp flour
1 tbsp butter
¼ tsp dry mustard
½ cup milk
2 tbsps shredded Cheddar cheese
Salt and pepper

TOPPING
¼ cup dry seasoned breadcrumbs

Put 1 tbsp butter in a small bowl and cook for 30 seconds on HIGH. Add the mushrooms and cook for 1 minute on HIGH and set aside. Put the broccoli spears into a casserole with the water and a pinch of salt.

Cover and cook for 4 minutes on HIGH. Leave covered while preparing the sauce. In a 2 cup measure, melt 1 tbsp butter for 30 seconds on HIGH. Stir in the flour, mustard, salt and pepper. Add the milk gradually and cook on HIGH for 1-2 minutes, stirring frequently until thick. Stir in the cheese. Put 2 broccoli spears on each ham slice, stalks towards the middle, and top each with the mushrooms. Roll up and put seam-side down in a baking dish. Arrange pineapple rings on each side and sprinkle with the dark brown sugar. Coat the cheese sauce over the broccoli and ham rolls and top with the crumbs. Cook on MEDIUM for 3-4 minutes or until hot. Serve immediately.

To serve 1 person, make full quantity sauce and cut all other ingredients to half quantity. Cook the mushrooms for 30 seconds on HIGH and the

This page: Ham, Broccoli, and Pineapple au Gratin. Facing page: Asparagus and Tomato Omelette.

Egg Foo Yung

PREPARATION TIME: 15 minutes

MICROWAVE COOKING TIME:
10 minutes

SERVES: 2 people

CRAB PATTIES
½ cup frozen crabmeat, defrosted
1 tbsp chopped green pepper
1 tbsp chopped green onion
¼ cup chopped mushrooms
1 small clove garlic, crushed
½ cup bean sprouts

2 eggs, beaten
¼ tsp ground ginger
Salt and pepper

SAUCE
½ cup chicken bouillon
1 tsp sherry
1 tbsp soy sauce
1 tsp oyster sauce (optional)
½ tsp brown sugar
2 tsps cornstarch

Beat the eggs in a medium-sized bowl
and stir in the remaining ingredients
for the patties. Cook on HIGH for

2 minutes, stirring frequently, until
softly set. Heat a browning dish on
HIGH for 5 minutes. Pour the
mixture into the hot dish in ½ cup
amounts, and cook for about 30
seconds per side on HIGH. Cover
and keep warm. Combine the sauce
ingredients in a 2 cup measure and
cook for 1-2 minutes, stirring
frequently until clear and thickened.
Pour over the patties and serve
immediately.

Microwave COOKING FOR 1 & 2

RICE, PASTA AND GRAINS

Bulgur and Spicy Lamb

PREPARATION TIME: 20 minutes

MICROWAVE COOKING TIME:
26 minutes

SERVES: 2 people

1 cup bulgur wheat
1 cup water
1 small onion, finely chopped
¼ lb ground lamb
¼ tsp oil
1 cup canned plum tomatoes
1 tsp cumin
¼ tsp cinnamon
1 tsp chopped mint
2 tbsps raisins
2 tbsps almonds, chopped
¼ cup yogurt
1 egg
Salt and pepper
1 bay leaf

Put the bulgur and water into a 2 quart casserole with a pinch of salt. Cover and cook on HIGH for 5 minutes, and leave covered while preparing the rest of the ingredients. Heat a browning dish for 5 minutes on HIGH. Put in the oil, add the onion and lamb, breaking the latter up into small pieces with a fork. Add the cumin, cinnamon, and salt and pepper. Return the dish to the oven and cook for 5 minutes on HIGH, stirring frequently. Add the tomatoes, mint, bay leaf, and salt and pepper. Cover and cook for 5 minutes on HIGH. Add the raisins and almonds, and leave to stand. Drain the bulgur wheat well, pressing to remove excess moisture. Mix with the egg and yogurt. Add salt and pepper and put half the bulgur in the bottom of a baking dish. Spread with the lamb filling and cover with another layer of bulgur. Cook uncovered for 5-6 minutes on MEDIUM. Leave to stand, to firm up, for 5 minutes before serving. Serve with a cucumber and yogurt salad.

Facing page: Egg Foo Yung. This page: Polenta with Pepper and Leek Salad (top) and Bulgur and Spicy Lamb (bottom).

To serve 1 person, prepare the full quantity casserole and divide into two. One of the casseroles may be frozen.

Sausage Risotto

PREPARATION TIME: 15 minutes

MICROWAVE COOKING TIME:
29 minutes

SERVES: 2 people

½ cup Italian rice, uncooked
¼ cup broken, uncooked spaghetti
1 Italian sausage, mild or hot
1 tbsp oil
1 small onion, finely sliced
½ clove garlic, crushed
½ cup quartered mushrooms
2 tomatoes, peeled and seeded
1½ tsps chopped parsley
½ tsp basil
1 cup beef bouillon
¼ cup Parmesan cheese
Salt and pepper

Remove sausage meat from casing. Heat a browning dish for 5 minutes on HIGH. Add the oil and sausage. Cook for 4 minutes on HIGH, breaking up the sausage meat with the fork. Add the onion, garlic and mushrooms, and cook for 2 minutes more on HIGH, stirring frequently. Put the contents of the browning dish into a 1 quart casserole and add the rice, spaghetti, basil, salt and pepper, and beef bouillon. Cover and cook for 15 minutes on HIGH. Stir in the parsley and chopped tomatoes, and leave to stand 3 minutes before serving. Sprinkle with Parmesan cheese.

Tri-colored Tagliatelle and Vegetables

PREPARATION TIME: 10 minutes

MICROWAVE COOKING TIME:
12 minutes, plus 2 minutes standing time

SERVES: 1 person

2oz tagliatelle or fettucini (mixture of red, green and plain)
½ a small sweet red pepper, cut into ¼" strips
½ a small onion, thinly sliced
½ cup broccoli flowerets
2 tbsps butter
1 small clove garlic, crushed
1½ tsps dried rosemary (or 1 sprig fresh)
Grated Parmesan cheese
Salt and pepper

Put the pasta into a large bowl and cover with water. Cook for 6 minutes on HIGH. Leave to stand for 2 minutes. Rinse in hot water and leave to drain. If using fresh pasta, cut the cooking time in half. Put 1 tbsp butter into a medium-sized bowl and add the broccoli, onion and

This page: Sausage Risotto. Facing page: Tri-colored Tagliatelle and Vegetables.

red pepper strips. Cover with pierced plastic wrap and cook for 1-2 minutes on HIGH. Toss with the pasta and keep warm. Melt the remaining butter with the crushed garlic and rosemary for 30 seconds on HIGH in a small bowl or custard cup. Strain the butter onto the pasta and vegetables and discard the rosemary and garlic. Season with salt and pepper. Heat the pasta through on MEDIUM for 2 minutes. Toss with Parmesan cheese and serve.

For 2 people, double all the ingredients. Cook the pasta for 10 minutes on HIGH if using dried, and 5 minutes on HIGH if using fresh. Cook the broccoli, onion and red pepper for 2-3 minutes on HIGH.

Polenta with Pepper and Leek Salad

PREPARATION TIME: 15 minutes

MICROWAVE COOKING TIME: 12 minutes, plus 5 minutes standing time

SERVES: 2 people

½ cup yellow cornmeal
1½ cups water
1 tbsp finely chopped onion
¼ cup shredded mozzarella cheese
¼ cup Parmesan cheese
Salt and pepper

SALAD
1 red pepper
1 large or 2 small leeks

DRESSING
1 tbsp vinegar
2 tbsps oil
½ tsp dry mustard
¼ tsp sugar
¼ tsp fennel seeds, crushed
¼ tsp marjoram

Mix the cornmeal, salt and pepper, onion and water in a large bowl. Cook for 6 minutes on HIGH. Add the mozzarella, cover and leave to stand for 5 minutes. Spread into a square pan and sprinkle the top with the Parmesan cheese. Refrigerate, and when ready to use, cut into squares and heat for 1 minute on HIGH before serving. Slice the pepper into ¼" strips. Trim off the dark green tops of the leeks and slice the white part into quarters. Mix the dressing ingredients together and put the vegetables into a 1 pint casserole. Pour over the dressing and mix together well. Cover and cook for 5 minutes on MEDIUM. Serve warm with the polenta.

Barley Ring with Turkey Filling

PREPARATION TIME: 20 minutes

MICROWAVE COOKING TIME: 31 minutes, plus 5 minutes standing time

SERVES: 2 people

1 cup pearl barley
3 cups water
1 egg, beaten
½ cup whole cranberries
½ tsp sugar
Grated rind and juice of half an orange
½ cup chopped walnuts
2 tbsps butter or margarine
1 shallot
¾ cup mushrooms, sliced
½ lb uncooked boned turkey, cut into 1" pieces
1 tbsp flour
½ cup chicken bouillon
2 tbsps parsley
½ cup cream
Salt and pepper

Put the barley into a large bowl with the water and a pinch of salt. Cover with pierced plastic wrap and cook for 20 minutes on HIGH, stirring once. Leave to stand, covered, for at least 5 minutes. Combine the cranberries, sugar and orange juice in a small bowl. Cook uncovered for 1-2 minutes on HIGH. Drain the barley well, and fold in the parsley, cranberries, walnuts, orange rind and beaten egg. Press into a 2 cup microwave ring-mold. Put the butter into a 2 cup casserole and cook for 30 seconds on HIGH to melt. Add the turkey, shallot and mushrooms. Cover and cook for 2 minutes on HIGH, stirring every 30 seconds. Sprinkle on the flour and stir in well. Add the stock and cream and blend well. Season, cover and cook for an additional 3 minutes on HIGH, stirring every 30 seconds until thickened. Keep warm. Re-heat the barley ring covered with pierced plastic wrap for 3 minutes on HIGH. Turn it out and fill the center with the turkey.
To serve one person, cut all the ingredients to half quantity, and omit

the egg. Serve the barley as a pilaff topped with the turkey filling.

Indian Pilaff

PREPARATION TIME: 15 minutes

MICROWAVE COOKING TIME: 30 minutes

SERVES: 2 people

½ cup long-grain rice (basmati, if available)
¼ cup almonds, toasted
1 small onion, sliced
1 tbsp oil
2 tbsps peas
2 okra, sliced
2 tbsps coconut
2 tbsps golden raisins
1 cup chicken bouillon
1 tbsp lemon juice
1 tbsp curry powder
1 tbsp chopped parsley
½ tsp dried red pepper flakes
Salt and pepper

Heat a browning dish for 5 minutes on HIGH. Sprinkle on the almonds and return the dish to the oven. Cook on HIGH for 3 minutes, stirring the almonds every 30 seconds until golden brown. Remove the almonds from the dish and allow to cool. Add the oil to the browning dish and stir in the sliced onion. Return to the oven and cook for 2 minutes on HIGH or until golden brown. Add the curry powder and cook for 1 minute on HIGH. Put the onion into a casserole and add the rice, pepper flakes, coconut, chicken bouillon and lemon juice. Cover and cook on HIGH for 3 minutes until boiling. Reduce the setting to MEDIUM, add the raisins and cook for 12 minutes. Add the peas, okra and parsley 2 minutes before the end of the cooking time. Sprinkle with toasted almonds before serving. (One serving may be kept in the refrigerator for 2 days. Re-heat for 2-3 minutes on MEDIUM.)

Facing page: Barley Ring with Turkey Filling.

Fried Rice

PREPARATION TIME: 15 minutes

MICROWAVE COOKING TIME:
12 minutes

SERVES: 2 people

½ cup quick-cooking rice
¾ cup water
3 dried Chinese mushrooms
2 green onions, sliced
¼ cup shrimp, peeled and de-veined
Small piece ginger root
Small can sliced bamboo shoots or lotus
   root
1 egg
1½ tsps soy sauce
½ tsp sesame oil
1 tbsp vegetable oil
Salt and pepper

Put the mushrooms into a bowl with
enough water to cover. Cover with
pierced plastic wrap and cook for
3 minutes on HIGH. Leave to stand
until softened. Put the rice, water and
a pinch of salt in a 1 quart casserole.
Cover and cook on HIGH for
2½ minutes. Leave to stand while
preparing the other ingredients.
Drain and slice the mushrooms. Slice
the ginger into thin slivers. Beat the
egg with the soy sauce. Heat a
browning dish for 5 minutes on
HIGH, pour in the vegetable oil and
quickly add the mushrooms, bamboo
shoots, ginger, and half the onion.
Stir and return to the oven, and cook
for 1 minute on HIGH. Mix the rice
with the egg, soy sauce and sesame
oil, and stir into the mixture in the
browning dish. Cook, uncovered, for
3 minutes on HIGH, stirring every
30 seconds until the egg sets. Add
the shrimp after 2 minutes. Serve
garnished with the remaining green
onion.

Clam Shells in Saffron Sauce

PREPARATION TIME: 15 minutes

MICROWAVE COOKING TIME:
16 minutes, plus 5 minutes
standing time

SERVES: 2 people

1½ cups whole-wheat
1 cup canned whole clams, liquid
   reserved
2 tbsps chopped parsley
1-2 tomatoes, peeled, seeded and cut into
   ¼″ strips
1 shallot, finely chopped
1 tbsp saffron
1 tbsp butter
½ tbsp flour
½ cup heavy cream
Reserved clam juice, made up to ½ cup
   with water if necessary

2 tbsps white wine
Salt and pepper

Put the pasta shells into a large bowl
with enough hot water to cover.
Cook for 8 minutes on HIGH and
leave to stand for 5 minutes. Rinse
under hot water and leave in cold
water. Melt the butter in a small bowl
on HIGH for 30 seconds. Stir in the
flour and add the clam juice gradually. Add the wine, shallot and
saffron and cook, covered with

SAUCE

1½ cups canned plum tomatoes
1 tbsp oil
½ cup sliced mushrooms
½ clove garlic, crushed
¼ tsp basil
Pinch ground allspice
1 tsp tomato paste
1 bay leaf
Salt and pepper

FILLING

½ cup frozen chopped spinach, defrosted
¼ cup pepperoni sausage, skinned and
   chopped
1 cup ricotta cheese
¼ cup grated Parmesan cheese (plus extra
   for serving if desired)
Nutmeg
Salt and pepper

Put the cannelloni or large shell pasta into a large, shallow casserole, and pour over enough hot water to cover. Cook for 8 minutes on HIGH. Leave to stand for 5 minutes. Rinse in hot water and leave standing in cold water. Put the oil into a 1 quart casserole and heat for 30 seconds on HIGH. Add the mushrooms and garlic and cook for 1 minute on HIGH. Add the remaining sauce ingredients, cover, and cook for 5 minutes on HIGH. Stir well and mash the tomatoes to break them up. Meanwhile drain the pasta well. Mix the filling ingredients together and fill the pasta. Put the pasta into a small casserole dish and pour over the tomato sauce. Cook on HIGH for 5 minutes to heat through. Serve with additional Parmesan cheese. To serve one person, halve the quantity of each ingredient. Cook the sauce for 3 minutes total in a smaller casserole or bowl. Alternatively, prepare this recipe in full and freeze one half for later use.

pierced plastic wrap, for 3 minutes on HIGH until thickened. Stir every 30 seconds. Stir in the cream and cook for 1 minute on HIGH. Mix in the clams, parsley, and salt and pepper. Cover and cook for 2 minutes on HIGH to heat through. Add the tomato strips and cook for 1 minute on MEDIUM. Pour over the pasta and serve immediately. To serve 1 person, cut the quantity of all the ingredients by half. Cook the sauce for half of the recommended time.

Cannelloni Stuffed with Spinach, Cheese and Pepperoni

PREPARATION TIME: 15 minutes

MICROWAVE COOKING TIME: 19 minutes, plus 5 minutes standing time

SERVES: 2 people

6-8 (depending on size) cannelloni or large shell pasta

Facing page: Indian Pilaff (top) and Fried Rice (bottom). This page: Clam Shells in Saffron Sauce (top) and Cannelloni Stuffed with Spinach, Cheese and Pepperoni (bottom).

Microwave
COOKING FOR 1 & 2

FISH AND SEAFOOD

Stuffed Trout

PREPARATION TIME: 15 minutes

MICROWAVE COOKING TIME:
5 minutes

SERVES: 1 person

1 whole rainbow trout, cleaned
1 shallot, finely chopped
½ cup frozen chopped spinach, thawed
Pinch of nutmeg
¼ cup flaked crabmeat
1 tbsp chopped hazelnuts
1 cap pimento, chopped
2 tbsps heavy cream
1 tbsp lemon juice
Paprika
Salt and pepper

Put the spinach, nutmeg and shallot
into a small bowl. Cover with
pierced plastic wrap and cook for
1 minute on HIGH to soften the
shallot. Stir in the crab, nuts, paprika,
salt, pepper, pimento and cream.
Trim the tail and fins of the trout,
and spoon the stuffing into the
cavity. Sprinkle with lemon juice and
cook in a shallow baking dish
covered with pierced plastic wrap for
4 minutes on HIGH. Peel the skin off
the body of the trout, but leave on
the head and tail. Garnish with
lemon if desired.

Salmon Steaks Bernaise

PREPARATION TIME: 10 minutes

MICROWAVE COOKING TIME:
4-5 minutes

SERVES: 1 person

1 salmon steak

1 tbsp lemon juice
Salt and pepper

SAUCE
2 egg yolks
1 tsp tarragon or white wine vinegar
1 tsp lemon juice
1 tsp chopped tarragon
1 tsp chopped parsley
Cayenne pepper
¼ cup butter, melted

**This page: Portuguese Seafood
Stew. Facing page: Salmon Steaks
Bernaise (top) and Stuffed Trout
(bottom).**

Have a bowl of ice water ready.
Combine the egg yolks, vinegar,
lemon juice and herbs in a 1 pint glass
measure. In a small bowl, melt the
butter for 1 minute on HIGH until
very hot. Whisk it into the egg yolks.
Cook on HIGH for 15 seconds and

whisk again. Repeat the process until the sauce is thick: this usually takes about 2 minutes. Put immediately into the bowl of ice water to stop the cooking. Add the Cayenne pepper, and salt if necessary. If the sauce begins to curdle, put the measure immediately into ice water and beat vigorously. Put the fish into a small baking dish with salt and pepper and lemon juice. Cover with pierced plastic wrap and cook on MEDIUM for 2-3 minutes. Leave to stand, covered, while making the sauce.

Flounder with Avocado

PREPARATION TIME: 15 minutes

MICROWAVE COOKING TIME: 8 minutes

SERVES: 2 people

½ lb flounder fillets, skinned
1 small ripe avocado
2 tbsps cream cheese
1 tsp chives
Juice of 1 lime (or of half a lemon)
1 tbsp white wine
1 tsp butter
½ tsp flour
½ cup heavy cream
Salt and pepper

GARNISH
Reserved chives
Reserved avocado slices

Reserve 2-4 thin slices of avocado and brush with the lemon or lime juice. Mash the rest of the avocado with the cream cheese, chives, salt and pepper, and 1 tsp lime or lemon juice. Spread the filling over the fish and fold each fillet in half. Put the fillets in a shallow casserole and pour over the wine and remaining juice. Cover with pierced plastic wrap and cook for 6 minutes on MEDIUM. Keep warm. In a small bowl, melt the butter for 30 seconds on HIGH and stir in the flour. Strain on the cooking liquid from the fish and add the cream. Cook, uncovered, for 2 minutes on HIGH until thickened. Remove the fish to serve on plates and pour some of the sauce over

each fillet. Garnish with the reserved avocado slices and chives.

Lemon and Almond Sole

PREPARATION TIME: 10 minutes

MICROWAVE COOKING TIME: 11 minutes

SERVES: 2 people

2 whole sole fillets
1 lemon
2 tbsps butter
½ cup almonds
¼ cup cornflake crumbs
2-4 parsley sprigs
Salt and pepper

Cut 4 thin slices from the lemon and squeeze the rest for juice. Cut 2 circles of unwaxed paper and grease with 1 tbsp butter. Lay on the fillets of fish and sprinkle over the lemon juice, salt and pepper. Seal up the parcels by twisting the open edges of the paper together. Cook for 5 minutes on MEDIUM. Heat a browning dish on HIGH for 4 minutes and add the remaining butter. Stir in the almonds and cook for 2 minutes, stirring frequently until brown. Stir in the cornflake crumbs. Open the parcels to serve and spoon on the almond topping. Garnish with reserved lemon slices and parsley.

Portuguese Seafood Stew

PREPARATION TIME: 15 minutes

MICROWAVE COOKING TIME: 11 minutes

SERVES: 2 people

3 tomatoes, chopped
½ a green pepper, chopped
½ cup canned clams, in shells if possible, and liquid
1 cod fillet (about ¼ lb), cut into 2" pieces
1 red snapper fillet (about ¼ lb), cut into 2" pieces
4 large raw shrimp, peeled and de-veined, or ½ cup small shrimp

½ a clove garlic, chopped
¼ cup chopped onion
2 tbsps olive oil
1 tsp tomato paste
1 tbsp chopped parsley
6 chopped black olives
½ cup white wine
1 potato, cut into 1" pieces
Salt and pepper

Put the cod and snapper into a casserole. Put the olive oil into another casserole with the onion and garlic and heat for 1 minute on HIGH. Add the potatoes, liquid from the clams, and the wine. Cover and cook for 6 minutes on HIGH. Stir in the tomato paste, add the fish and peppers, and cook for 2 minutes on HIGH. Add the shrimp and cook a further minute on HIGH. Add the tomatoes, clams and olives and cook for another minute on HIGH. Season, and garnish with chopped parsley.

Macadamia Fillets

PREPARATION TIME: 10 minutes

MICROWAVE COOKING TIME: 5 minutes

SERVES: 2 people

2 sole or flounder fillets
1 small can pineapple chunks
¼ of a green pepper, cut into ¼" strips
1 green onion, shredded
⅓ cup Macadamia nuts, roughly chopped

SAUCE
Reserved pineapple juice
1 tbsp honey
2 tsps soy sauce
1 tbsp vinegar
¼ tsp dry mustard
1 tsp cornstarch

Facing page: Flounder with Avocado (top) and Lemon and Almond Sole (bottom).

Drain the pineapple and set aside the chunks. Mix the juice and the other sauce ingredients together in a bowl. Add the green pepper and cook uncovered for 1-2 minutes on HIGH or until thickened, stirring every 30 seconds. Add the pineapple chunks, nuts and onions, and set aside. Put the fish into a shallow casserole, thinner portion towards the center of the dish. Cover with pierced plastic wrap, and cook for 2 minutes on HIGH. Allow to stand for 30 seconds. Remove carefully to serving dishes. Coat with the Macadamia sauce. Serve with fried rice or stir-fried vegetables.

This page: Shrimp and Broccoli au Gratin. Facing page: Macadamia Fillets.

Shrimp and Broccoli au Gratin

PREPARATION TIME: 10 minutes

MICROWAVE COOKING TIME: 6 minutes

SERVES: 2 people

1 cup broccoli flowerets
½ lb large cooked shrimp, peeled and de-veined
2 tbsps Parmesan cheese
1 tbsp dry breadcrumbs
1 tsp paprika

SAUCE
2 tbsps Cheddar cheese
1 tbsp butter
1 tbsp flour
½ cup milk
Pinch of dry mustard
Pinch of Cayenne pepper
Salt and pepper

Melt 1 tbsp butter in a small bowl for

Melt the butter in a 1 pint casserole for 30 seconds on HIGH and add the shallot. Cook for 1 minute on HIGH, add the flour, white wine and saffron, and stir well to mix. Add the scallops (cut in half if large) and cook for 1-2 minutes on HIGH. Stir in the cream, parsley and pepper, and cook for a further 2 minutes on HIGH. Serve on parsley rice.

Lobster in Sherry Cream

PREPARATION TIME: 20 minutes

MICROWAVE COOKING TIME: 4 minutes

SERVES: 2 people

1 whole large lobster, boiled; or 1 large
   lobster tail
½ cup sliced mushrooms
½ tsp celery salt
½ cup heavy cream
2 tbsps sherry
½ tsp butter
½ tsp flour
½ cup Gruyère cheese
Paprika
Pepper

Crack the lobster claws and remove the meat. Remove the meat from the tail, and combine. Reserve the empty tail shell to cook in if desired. Melt the butter for 15 seconds on HIGH, and add the mushrooms. Cook for 1 minute on HIGH and add the flour, sherry, cream, celery salt, and pepper. Cook for 2 more minutes on HIGH until thick, stirring frequently. Add the lobster and spoon into the shell, or a baking dish. Sprinkle on the cheese and plenty of paprika. Cook for 2 minutes on HIGH. Serve immediately.

30 seconds on HIGH. Stir in the flour, mustard and Cayenne pepper. Add the milk gradually until smooth. Cook for 1-2 minutes on HIGH, stirring every 30 seconds. Add salt and pepper and stir in the Cheddar cheese. Cover and set aside. Put the broccoli in a small bowl with 2 tbsps water. Cover with pierced plastic wrap and cook for 3 minutes on HIGH until almost tender. In individual dishes or 1 large baking dish, scatter over the broccoli and shrimp. Coat over the sauce, and sprinkle on the Parmesan cheese, crumbs and paprika. Heat through for 1-2 minutes on HIGH before serving.

Scallops in Saffron Cream

PREPARATION TIME: 10 minutes

MICROWAVE COOKING TIME: 8 minutes

SERVES: 2 people

2 cups uncooked scallops (or 1 cup, if very
   large)
1 shallot, finely chopped
1 small red pepper cut into ¼″ strips
1 tsp parsley
1 tsp saffron
½ cup white wine
1½ tbsps butter
1½ tbsps flour
½ cup heavy cream

This page: Scallops in Saffron Cream (top) and Lobster in Sherry Cream (bottom). Facing page: Orange Glazed Lamb Chops with Glazed Vegetables.

MEAT, POULTRY AND GAME

Orange Glazed Lamb Chops with Glazed Vegetables

PREPARATION TIME: 20 minutes

MICROWAVE COOKING TIME: 14 minutes

SERVES: 2 people

2 lamb shoulder chops
½ cup orange juice
2 tsps dark corn syrup
½ tsp red wine vinegar or cider vinegar
½ tsp cornstarch
1 tbsp water
1 tbsp oil
1 carrot, cut into thick barrel shapes
1 turnip, quartered
½ cup small onions
1 small potato, quartered
1 tbsp butter
Salt and pepper

GARNISH
Orange slices

Heat a browning dish for 5 minutes on HIGH. Put in the oil and chops and cook for 2 minutes on HIGH, turning once, until lightly browned on both sides. Transfer the chops to a casserole dish. Melt the butter and add the vegetables. Cook for 5 minutes on HIGH, stirring frequently to brown evenly. Add to the casserole dish with the chops. De-glaze the browning dish with the orange juice and vinegar, scraping any sediment off the base of the dish. Stir in the corn syrup, salt and pepper, and pour over the chops and vegetables. Cover with pierced plastic wrap and cook on MEDIUM for 6 minutes, or until chops are cooked as much as desired. The chops may be served slightly pink. Remove the chops and vegetables from the casserole and dissolve the cornstarch in the water. Stir into the liquid in the casserole and cook, uncovered, for 1 minute on HIGH or until boiling and clear. Pour over the chops and vegetables and garnish with orange slices.

To serve 1 person, reduce the quantity of each ingredient by half, but cook for the same length of time.

warm vegetable salad instead of the red cabbage garnish.

To serve 1 person, prepare the complete recipe and use half. The other half will freeze well.

Spicy Steak Kebabs

PREPARATION TIME: 10 minutes, plus 1 hour to marinate meat

MICROWAVE COOKING TIME: 6 minutes

SERVES: 2 people

½ lb sirloin steak, cut into 1½" cubes
1 leek, white part only
4 large mushrooms
4 cherry tomatoes
½ green pepper, sliced into 1" squares

MARINADE
2 tbsps oil
1 tbsp lemon juice
½ clove garlic, crushed
¼ tsp ground cumin
¼ tsp ground coriander
¼ tsp gravy browning
Pinch Cayenne pepper
Salt and pepper

Mix the marinade ingredients together and put in the steak cubes, turning to coat evenly. Leave for 1 hour. Thread the meat and vegetables onto wooden skewers. Do not pack the ingredients too tightly together. Put on a roasting rack and cook on MEDIUM for about 6 minutes, turning and basting frequently until cooked as much as desired. Put remaining marinade into a smaller dish and cook for 2-3 minutes on HIGH until syrupy. Serve on a bed of rice. Pour the sauce over the cooked kebabs.

To serve one person, prepare only half of each ingredient, but cook for the same length of time.

Pheasant in Gin

PREPARATION TIME: 15 minutes

MICROWAVE COOKING TIME: 22 minutes

SERVES: 2 people

1 small pheasant, dressed (about 1½-1¾ lbs)
1 apple, peeled and chopped
¼ cup gin
1 tsp juniper berries
½ tsp rosemary
2 tbsps chicken bouillon
1 tbsp butter
1½ tsps flour
1½ cups shredded red cabbage

Heat a browning dish for 5 minutes on HIGH. Put in the butter and, when foaming, add the pheasant. Cook for 3 minutes to lightly brown all sides of the pheasant, turning four times while cooking. Transfer to a medium-sized deep casserole and set aside. Add flour to the dish and scrape up any sediment. Cook for 1 minute to lightly brown the flour. De-glaze the pan with chicken bouillon and add the casserole with the remaining ingredients except the cabbage. Cover and cook for 10 minutes or until the pheasant is tender. It may be served slightly pink. During the last 3 minutes, add the red cabbage. Can be served with the

**This page: Spicy Steak Kebabs.
Facing page: Pheasant in Gin.**

Stuffed Chicken Breasts in Lemon Tarragon Cream

PREPARATION TIME: 15 minutes

MICROWAVE COOKING TIME:
18 minutes

SERVES: 2 people

2 boned chicken breast halves, skinned
1 tsp butter
½ cup finely chopped mushrooms
3oz package cream cheese
2 tbsps white wine
1 tbsp lemon juice
Salt and pepper

SAUCE
1 tbsp butter
½ tbsp flour
Juice of ½ lemon
½ cup chicken stock
¼ cup heavy cream
½ tsp chopped tarragon, fresh or dried
Salt and pepper

GARNISH
Lemon slices

Cut a pocket along the thicker side of each chicken breast half. Melt 1 tbsp butter for 30 seconds on HIGH in a small bowl. Add the white wine, salt and pepper, and mushrooms. Cook, uncovered, for 2 minutes on HIGH to soften the mushrooms. Cook for an additional 1 minute to evaporate liquid if excessive. Mix with the cream cheese and fill the pockets of the chicken. Put the breasts into a small casserole and sprinkle over the lemon juice and about 1 tbsp water. Cover and cook for about 12 minutes on MEDIUM or until white and firm. Keep warm. In a small bowl melt 1 tbsp butter for 30 seconds on HIGH. Stir in the flour and add the stock and lemon juice gradually. Pour in any cooking liquid from the chicken and add the cream and tarragon. Cook for 1-2 minutes on HIGH, stirring every 30 seconds until thickened. Add salt and pepper. Spoon over the chicken breasts to serve and garnish with lemon slices. Serve with French peas or zucchini rolls.
To serve one person, reduce the quantity of each ingredient by half.

Cook the mushroom filling for the same length of time, and the filled chicken breasts for 10 minutes on MEDIUM. Cook the sauce for about 1 minute on HIGH.

Chicken, Ham and Cheese Rolls with Mustard Sauce

PREPARATION TIME: 15 minutes

MICROWAVE COOKING TIME:
9 minutes

SERVES: 1 person

1 chicken breast half, skinned and boned
1 thin slice cooked ham
1 thin slice Swiss cheese
1 tsp chopped capers
1 tsp butter
2½ tbsps cornflake crumbs
¼ tsp paprika
Salt and pepper

SAUCE
1 tbsp butter or margarine
1 tbsp flour
½ cup milk
3 tbsps dry white wine
1 tsp Dijon mustard
1 tsp salad mustard
Salt and pepper

Place the chicken breast between 2 pieces of waxed paper and flatten with a meat mallet to about ⅛". Lay the cheese on top of the slice of ham. Sprinkle on the capers, and roll up, folding in the sides, and fasten with wooden picks. Melt 1 tsp butter for 30 seconds on HIGH. Combine the cornflake crumbs with the paprika and salt and pepper on a sheet of waxed paper. Brush the chicken with the melted butter and then roll in the crumbs to coat. Push the crumb coating into the surface of the chicken. Put the chicken seam side down into a small casserole dish and cook, uncovered, on MEDIUM for 2 minutes. Turn over, cook for a further 1 minute on MEDIUM, and keep warm while preparing the sauce. Melt ½ tbsp butter for 30 seconds on

HIGH in a small bowl. Stir in the flour and add the milk and wine gradually. Stir in the mustards and salt and pepper. Cook, uncovered, for 1-2 minutes on HIGH, stirring every 30 seconds until thickened. Keep warm. Re-heat the chicken on HIGH for 2 minutes and serve with the sauce.
To serve 2 people, double all the ingredients. Cook the chicken for 4 minutes on MEDIUM and the sauce for 2-3 minutes on HIGH. Re-heat the chicken on HIGH for 2 minutes.

Rabbit with Olives

PREPARATION TIME: 15 minutes

MICROWAVE COOKING TIME:
23-28 minutes

SERVES: 2 people

2 rabbit pieces (hind- or fore-quarters)
2 tbsps butter
2 tsps flour
1 shallot, chopped
¼ cup dry vermouth
¼ cup beef bouillon
½ cup whole mushrooms
¼ tsp oregano
¼ tsp thyme
1 tbsp wholegrain mustard
12 stoned green olives, left whole
¼ cup heavy cream
Salt and pepper

Soak the rabbit overnight to whiten the meat, in enough water to cover, with a squeeze of lemon juice and a pinch of salt. Heat a browning dish for 5 minutes on HIGH. Melt the butter and cook the rabbit pieces for 2 minutes on HIGH, turning over after 1 minute to brown both sides. Remove from the dish to a 1 pint casserole. Add the mushrooms and shallot to the browning dish with the flour. Cook for 1 minute on HIGH to brown lightly. De-glaze the pan with the bouillon and pour the contents over the rabbit. Add the vermouth,

Facing page: Chicken, Ham and Cheese Rolls with Mustard Sauce (top) and Stuffed Chicken Breasts in Lemon Tarragon Cream (bottom).

herbs, mustard, and salt and pepper. Cover and cook on MEDIUM for 15-20 minutes, or until the rabbit is tender. After 10 minutes, add the olives and cream. Serve with rice or noodles.

To serve one person, half the complete recipe will freeze well.

Devilled Cornish Hen with Golden Rice Stuffing

PREPARATION TIME: 20 minutes

MICROWAVE COOKING TIME: 16 minutes

SERVES: 1 person

1 Cornish game hen about 1½ lbs
¼ cup quick-cooking rice
⅓ cup hot water
1 shallot, finely chopped
½ cap pimento, diced
1 tbsp chopped pecans
Pinch saffron
2 tbsps bottled steak sauce
1 tbsp butter
½ tsp paprika
½ tsp dry mustard
½ tsp chili powder
1 tsp sugar
Pinch Cayenne pepper
¼ cup chicken bouillon
Salt and pepper

GARNISH
Small bunch watercress or parsley

Put the rice, saffron, shallot and hot water into a 1 pint casserole, cover, and cook on HIGH for 2 minutes or until the rice is tender and has absorbed all the color from the saffron. Add the pimento and pecans, and allow to cool slightly. Stuff the hen with rice. Mix together the spices, salt and pepper, and sugar. Melt 1 tbsp butter for 30 seconds on HIGH and brush it over the hen. Rub the spices over all surfaces of the hen. Close the cavity with wooden picks and place the hen, breast-side down, on a roasting rack. Combine remaining melted butter with the steak sauce and any remaining spices. Cook the hen for 5 minutes on HIGH and baste with the steak sauce mixture. Turn breast-side up, cook for 5 minutes on HIGH, and baste. Cook for 2 minutes more, or until the juices run clear. Leave to stand for 5 minutes before serving. Add the chicken bouillon to the remaining sauce mixture, re-heat for 1-2 minutes on HIGH and pour over the hen to serve. Garnish with watercress or parsley.

To serve 2 people, double all quantities. Add 5 minutes to the cooking time for the hens.

This page: Rabbit with Olives (top) and Venison Bourguignonne (bottom). Facing page: Devilled Cornish Hen with Golden Rice Stuffing.

Venison Bourguignonne

PREPARATION TIME: 15 minutes

MICROWAVE COOKING TIME: 36 minutes, plus 15 minutes standing time

SERVES: 2 people

½ lb venison from the leg
1 thick-cut slice bacon, cut into ¼" pieces
½ cup small onions
¼ cup mushrooms, quartered
½ clove garlic, crushed
1 tbsp butter
1 tbsp flour
⅓ cup red wine
¾ cup beef bouillon
1 tsp tomato paste
1 bay leaf
¼ tsp thyme
Salt and pepper

Melt the butter for 30 seconds on HIGH in a large casserole. Add the onion, bacon, mushrooms and garlic, and cook for 1 minute on HIGH until slightly brown. Remove from the casserole and set aside. Add the venison and cook for 2-3 minutes on HIGH, stirring occasionally to brown slightly. Sprinkle on the flour, and cook for a further minute on HIGH. Stir in the wine, bouillon and tomato paste. Add the thyme and bay leaf and cover the casserole. Cook, stirring occasionally, for 15 minutes on MEDIUM. Add the remaining ingredients, re-cover the casserole, and cook for another 15 minutes on MEDIUM. Leave to stand for 15 minutes before serving. Serve with boiled potatoes or noodles. To serve one person, cook the full recipe, use half and the other half will freeze well.

Fiery Duck

PREPARATION TIME: 15-20 minutes, plus 30-60 minutes to marinate duck

MICROWAVE COOKING TIME:
8 minutes, plus 1 minute standing time

SERVES: 2 people

½ a duck breast, boned and skinned – about ½ lb. If duck parts are unavailable, cut a whole duck into quarters and freeze the leg portions.
½ a small red pepper, sliced into ¼" strips
2 sticks celery, thinly sliced
1 cup bean sprouts
2 green onions, sliced
½ cup roasted cashew nuts
½-1 tsp Szechuan pepper, or crushed dried chili peppers

½ tsp cornstarch
¼ cup chicken bouillon

MARINADE
2 tsps rice or cider vinegar
2 tsps soy sauce
2 tsps sherry
2 tsps sesame seed oil
Pinch ground ginger
½ clove crushed garlic
Salt and pepper

Remove the skin and bone from the breast portions and cut the duck into thin strips. Combine the marinade ingredients in a medium-sized bowl and stir in the duck pieces. Cover the bowl and chill for 30-60 minutes. Drain the duck, reserving the marinade, and mix the cornstarch, bouillon and Szechuan or chili pepper with the marinade. Put the duck into a large casserole and pour over sauce. Stir to mix, cover the dish and cook for 10 minutes on MEDIUM, stirring occasionally. Add the red pepper and celery to the casserole and cook for a further 2 minutes on HIGH. Stir in the cashews, onions and bean sprouts. Serve with fried rice or crisp noodles. Best prepared for 2 people.

Turkey Korma (Mild Curry)

PREPARATION TIME: 15 minutes

MICROWAVE COOKING TIME:
10 minutes

SERVES: 1 person

1 turkey leg
2 tbsps chopped onion
1 tsp oil
1½ tsps butter or margarine
½ tbsp curry powder
1 tsp paprika
1 tsp ground coriander
1½ tbsps flour
½ cup chicken bouillon
1 tbsp golden raisins
1 tbsp roasted cashew nuts or shelled pistachio nuts
2 tsps unsweetened coconut
¼ cup plain yogurt
Salt and pepper

Skin and bone the turkey leg and cut the meat into 1" pieces. Use half and freeze the other half for use later. Heat the oil in a large casserole for 30 seconds on HIGH. Add the butter and, when melted, add the onion, turkey and spices. Cook for 3 minutes on HIGH to cook the spices. Add the flour and bouillon and stir to mix well. Cover the casserole and cook for 5 minutes on HIGH, stirring frequently until the turkey is tender. Add the raisins, coconut, nuts, salt, pepper and yogurt. Leave to stand, covered, for 1 minute. Serve with rice and chutney.
To serve 2 people, use the whole turkey leg and double all other ingredients. Cook the casserole for 8 minutes on HIGH.

Ham Steaks with Mango Sauce

PREPARATION TIME: 10 minutes

MICROWAVE COOKING TIME:
13 minutes

SERVES: 2 people

2 fully cooked ham slices (about ¼ lb each)
1 tbsp butter

SAUCE
1 ripe mango, peeled and thinly sliced
½ tsp ground ginger
Juice of half a lime
½ tsp soy sauce
Pinch Cayenne pepper
¼ tsp cornstarch
⅓ cup orange juice

Cut the ham slices around the outside at 2" intervals, ¼" in from the edge, to stop them from curling. Reserve 4 thin slices of mango and purée the rest in a food processor with the remaining sauce ingredients. Heat a browning dish on HIGH for 5 minutes. Put in the butter and the

Facing page: Fiery Duck (top) and Turkey Korma (Mild Curry) (bottom).

ham steaks and cook for 1 minute on HIGH. Turn the ham steaks once to brown both sides. Remove the ham from the dish to a casserole and pour over the puréed sauce ingredients. Cook, uncovered, for about 5 minutes on MEDIUM, or until the sauce has thickened. If necessary, remove the ham and keep warm while cooking the sauce for a further 2 minutes on HIGH. Garnish with the reserved mango slices. Serve with sesame stir-fry.

To serve one person, use 1 ham slice and ½ tbsp butter. Use full quantity sauce ingredients and cook for the same length of time as for 2 people.

Beef Roulades

PREPARATION TIME: 20 minutes

MICROWAVE COOKING TIME: 19 minutes

SERVES: 2 people

*4 pieces rump steak, cut thin and
　flattened
1 dill pickle, cut into quarters lengthwise
2 green onions, trimmed and cut in half
　lengthwise
1 tbsp oil*

SAUCE
*½ cup mushrooms, quartered
1½ tsp butter or margarine
2 tsps flour
¼ tsp thyme
1 bay leaf
⅔ cup beef bouillon
1 tbsp red wine
Salt and pepper
Gravy browning (if necessary)*

GARNISH
Buttered spinach pasta

Roll each of the beef slices around a quarter of the dill pickle and half a green onion. Sprinkle with pepper and fasten with wooden picks. Heat a browning dish on HIGH for 5 minutes. Put in the oil and add the roulades. Cook for 8 minutes, turning frequently. Remove from the dish and set aside in a casserole dish. Add the butter to the dish and allow to melt. Add the mushrooms and

cook for 1 minute on HIGH. Stir in the flour and cook for 2 minutes to brown lightly. Add the bouillon, wine, thyme and bay leaf, scraping any sediment off the surface of the browning dish. Add gravy browning for extra color if necessary. Season, and pour over the roulades. Cover the dish and cook for 12 minutes on MEDIUM. Test the meat with a knife and if not tender, cook for a further 3 minutes on HIGH. Serve with the pasta or French peas.

To serve one person, prepare only half the quantity of each ingredient and cook the roulades in the sauce for about 10 minutes on MEDIUM.

Alternatively, the full quantity recipe freezes well.

Mexican Pork Casserole

PREPARATION TIME: 15 minutes

MICROWAVE COOKING TIME: 28 minutes

SERVES: 2 people

*½ lb boneless pork loin, cut into 1″ cubes
½ cup canned garbanzo beans/chickpeas
½ cup canned kidney beans
¼ cup chopped sweet red pepper*

for 2 minutes on MEDIUM. Serve with tortilla chips if desired.
To serve 1 person, prepare full quantity casserole, and freeze half.

Veal Chops in Peppercorn Cream Sauce

PREPARATION TIME: 15 minutes

MICROWAVE COOKING TIME: 25 minutes

SERVES: 2 people

2 loin veal chops
1 tbsp butter or margarine
½ cup heavy cream
¼ cup chicken bouillon
2 tbsps brandy
1 tbsp green peppercorns, dried (or packed in brine, drained and rinsed)
½ cap pimento, diced
2 black olives, stoned and sliced thinly
Salt and pepper

Remove some of the fat from the outside of the chops. Heat a browning dish on HIGH for 5 minutes. Put in the butter or margarine and the chops. Cook for 3 minutes on HIGH, turning once, until both sides are lightly browned. Remove the chops to a casserole. Deglaze the dish with the bouillon and add the brandy, salt and pepper. Pour the sauce over the chops, cover with pierced plastic wrap, and cook on MEDIUM for 15 minutes or until the chops are tender. Add the peppercorns, pimento and olives during the last 3 minutes of cooking time. If the chops are not tender after 15 minutes, cook for an additional 2 minutes on MEDIUM. Add the cream and cook 1 minute on HIGH. Serve with zucchini rolls, leeks Provençale, or French peas.
To serve 1 person, cut the quantities of each ingredient by half and cook for the same length of time.

¼ cup chopped green pepper
½ small chili pepper, finely chopped
¼ cup chopped onion
1 tbsp flour
2 tsps oil
¾ cup beef bouillon
1 tbsp instant coffee
½ clove garlic, crushed
¼ tsp ground cumin
¼ tsp ground coriander

GARNISH
Tortilla chips

Heat a browning dish for 5 minutes on HIGH. Put in the oil and add the pork cubes. Cook for 2 minutes on

Facing page: Veal Chops in Peppercorn Cream Sauce (top) and Ham Steaks with Mango Sauce (bottom). This page: Mexican Pork Casserole (top) and Beef Roulades (bottom).

HIGH, stirring frequently, until slightly browned. Add the cumin, coriander, garlic, onion and flour, and cook for 1-2 minutes on HIGH. Dissolve the instant coffee in the bouillon and add to the casserole, stirring well. Add the peppers, cover, and cook on MEDIUM for 17 minutes, or until the pork loses its pink color. Add the beans and heat

Microwave COOKING FOR 1 & 2

VEGETABLES

Corn on the Cob with Flavored Butters

PREPARATION TIME: 10 minutes

MICROWAVE COOKING TIME: 8 minutes

SERVES: 2 people

2 ears of corn
3 tbsps butter with a choice of:
½ tsp wholegrain mustard, or
½ tsp tomato paste and ¼ tsp basil, or
½ tsp garlic powder and ¼ tsp parsley, or
½ tsp chili powder

Clean the husks and silk from the ears of corn and wrap each in plastic wrap, or put into a roasting bag and seal tightly. Cook for about 8 minutes, turning once. Mix the butter with one or more of the flavoring choices and serve with the hot corn.

Leeks Provençale

PREPARATION TIME: 10 minutes

MICROWAVE COOKING TIME: 8 minutes

SERVES: 2 people

3 leeks, washed, trimmed and cut into 2" pieces
1 small clove garlic, finely chopped
2 tomatoes, chopped
1 tbsp oil
2 tbsps white wine
½ tsp thyme
1 tbsp chopped parsley
Salt and pepper

Put the oil into a 1 quart casserole, and add the leeks and garlic, tossing to coat. Cook, uncovered, for 3 minutes on HIGH, stirring occasionally. Add the herbs, white wine, salt and pepper, and cover and

This page: Corn on the Cob with Flavored Butters. Facing page: French Peas (top) and Leeks Provençale (bottom).

cook for a further 5 minutes on HIGH. Add the tomatoes and cook for 1 minute on HIGH. Serve immediately.

To serve one person, use 1 large or 2 small leeks and half of each of the other ingredients. Cook the leeks for 2 minutes on HIGH and after adding the other ingredients, cook for a further 3-4 minutes on HIGH. Add the tomatoes and cook for 1 minute on HIGH.

Eggplant Niramish

PREPARATION TIME: 20 minutes

MICROWAVE COOKING TIME: 17 minutes

SERVES: 2 people

1 eggplant
2 tbsps butter
1 clove garlic, finely chopped
1 small onion, chopped
1 small potato, diced
1 small carrot, diced
¼ cup peas
1 cup canned tomatoes, chopped and juice reserved
1 tsp flour
¼ cup raisins
¼ cup pine nuts or chopped almonds
1 tbsp chopped coriander leaves or parsley
¼ tsp ground coriander
¼ tsp ground cumin
¼ tsp turmeric
¼ tsp fenugreek
¼ tsp ground ginger
Cayenne pepper
Paprika
Salt and pepper

GARNISH
¼ cup plain yogurt
Parsley or coriander leaves

Cut the eggplant in half lengthwise and score the flesh lightly. Sprinkle with salt and leave to stand for 20 minutes. The salt will draw out any bitterness. Rinse the eggplant well and pat dry. Melt the butter for 30 seconds on HIGH in a large casserole. Add the spices and cook for 2 minutes on HIGH. Add the onion, garlic, carrots and potatoes. Cover and cook for 3 minutes on

HIGH. Stir in the flour and add the tomato juice and pulp and chopped coriander or parsley. Cover the bowl and cook on HIGH for a further 5 minutes or until vegetables are just tender. Add the raisins, nuts and peas. Put the eggplant in another casserole, cover, and cook for 5 minutes on HIGH. Scoop out the flesh and reserve the skins. Mix the eggplant with the vegetable filling and fill the skins. Sprinkle with paprika and cook for 3 minutes on HIGH. Serve immediately. Top with a spoonful of yogurt and garnish with sprigs of parsley or coriander.

To serve 1 person, prepare the full quantity, serve one half and freeze the other.

French Peas

PREPARATION TIME: 10 minutes

MICROWAVE COOKING TIME: 6-10 minutes

SERVES: 2 people

1½ cups peas, fresh or frozen
4 leaves Romaine lettuce
½ cup parsley or chervil sprigs
½ cup small onions, peeled
1 tsp sugar
1 tbsp butter
1 tbsp flour
2 sticks celery, diced
½ cup chicken bouillon
Salt and pepper

If using fresh peas, shell them and combine with the celery, onions, half the bouillon, salt and pepper, and sugar in a 1 quart casserole. Cover and cook for 7 minutes on HIGH until almost tender. Add the lettuce and parsley (or chervil) and cook for a further 2 minutes on HIGH. Set aside. (If using frozen peas, combine the lettuce and parsley at the beginning and cook for a total of 5 minutes.) Melt the butter in a small bowl for 30 seconds on HIGH. Add the flour and remaining stock, and cook, uncovered, for 1 minute on HIGH. Stir into the peas, and serve. Best cooked for 2 people.

Stuffed Potatoes

PREPARATION TIME: 15 minutes

MICROWAVE COOKING TIME: 18 minutes, plus 5 minutes standing time

SERVES: 1 person

1 large baking potato
2 tsps chopped chives
2 tbsps milk
2 strips bacon
2 tbsps sour cream
1 tbsp crumbled blue cheese
1 tbsp shredded Cheddar cheese
1 tbsp dry seasoned breadcrumbs
Paprika
Salt and pepper

Heat a browning dish for 5 minutes on HIGH. Put in the bacon and cook for 2-3 minutes on HIGH, or until crisp. Crumble the bacon and set it aside. Pierce the potato skin several times with a fork. Put the potato on a plate and cook on HIGH for 5 minutes, or until soft. Turn over after 2 minutes. Cover it tightly in foil and leave it to stand for 5 minutes. Cut the potato in half lengthwise and scoop out the flesh, reserving the shells. Heat the milk for 30 seconds on HIGH, add to the potato with the sour cream and beat well. Add the chives, salt and pepper, bacon and blue cheese, and spoon into the potato shells. Sprinkle on the Cheddar cheese, crumbs and paprika. Cook on MEDIUM for 3 minutes and increase the setting to HIGH for 1 minute. Serve immediately.

For two people, use the full quantity recipe for a side dish, or double the quantity of each ingredient. Cook the potatoes for 7 minutes on HIGH, and the filled potato shells for 4 minutes on MEDIUM and 1 minute on HIGH.

Facing page: Eggplant Niramish (top) and Stuffed Potatoes (bottom).

INDEX

CLB 1548
© 1986 Illustrations and text: Colour Library Books Ltd.,
    Guildford, Surrey, England.
Text filmsetting by Focus Photoset Ltd., London, England.
All rights reserved.
Printed and bound in Barcelona, Spain by Cronión, S.A.
1986 edition published by Crescent Books, distributed by Crown Publishers, Inc.
ISBN 0 517 60999 1
h g f e d c b a